Cool, Calm & Collected

CAROLYN KIZER

Cool, Calm & Collected

Poems 1960–2000

COPPER CANYON PRESS

Copper Canyon Press is in residence under the auspices of the Centrum Foundation at Fort Worden State Park in Port Townsend, Washington. Centrum sponsors artist residencies, education workshops for Washington State students and teachers, blues, jazz, and fiddle tunes festivals, classical music performances, and The Port Townsend Writers' Conference.

LIBRARY OF CONGRESS CATALOGING-IN-PUBLICATION DATA

Kizer, Carolyn.

Cool, calm & collected: poems 1960–2000 / by Carolyn Kizer.

p. cm.

ISBN 1-55659-146-2 (alk. paper)

I. Title: Cool, calm, and collected. II. Title.

PS3521.I9 C66 2000

811'.54— DC21

00-010243

CIP

3 5 7 9 8 6 4 2

COPPER CANYON PRESS

Post Office Box 271
Port Townsend, Washington 98368
www.coppercanyonpress.org

ACKNOWLEDGMENTS

Many of these poems have appeared in different publications which are
acknowledged in my previous books:

The Ungrateful Garden,
Indiana University Press, Bloomington, Indiana, 1961.

Knock upon Silence,
Doubleday & Company, Inc., Garden City, New York, 1965.

Midnight Was My Cry: New and Selected Poems,
Doubleday & Company, Inc., Garden City, New York, 1971.

Mermaids in the Basement: Poems for Women,
Copper Canyon Press, Port Townsend, Washington, 1984.

Yin, BOA Editions, Ltd., Brockport, New York, 1984.

The Nearness of You,
Copper Canyon Press, Port Townsend, Washington, 1986.

*Carrying Over: Poems from the Chinese, Urdu, Macedonian,
Yiddish, and French African,* Copper Canyon Press,
Port Townsend, Washington, 1988.

Harping On: Poems 1985–1995,
Copper Canyon Press, Port Townsend, Washington, 1996.

Several of the new poems appear in the pages of the following publications:

"Second Time Around" appeared in *The Best American Poetry
1998* (edited by John Hollander and David Lehman) and in
Michigan Quarterly Review; "The Erotic Philosophers" appeared
in *The Best American Poetry 1999* (edited by Robert Bly and David
Lehman) and *The Yale Review;* and "The Oration" appeared in
The Best American Poetry 2000 (edited by Rita Dove and David
Lehman) and in *The Threepenny Review.* "Shalimar Gardens"
appeared in *New Letters;* "Days of 1986" in *Ploughshares;*
"Eleutheria" in *Shenandoah;* "Union of Women" in *The
Progressive;* "The Silent Man" in *Michigan Quarterly Review;*
and finally, "The Ashes" in *Texas Review.*

"One," "Two," and "Three" appeared as parts of "Pro Femina" in
Knock Upon Silence (1965). The fourth part ("Fanny") appeared in
Yin (1984) as a poem by itself, as did the fifth part ("The Erotic
Philosphers") which appeared in *The Best American Poetry 2000*
and was published in the chapbook *Pro Femina* (BkMk Press, 1999).

Be cool inside the mule
G. STEIN

Stagger onward rejoicing
W.H. AUDEN

Contents

THE SIXTIES

Chinese Imitations

A Month in Summer

Pro Femina

THE SEVENTIES

THE EIGHTIES

THE NINETIES

NEW POEMS

CARRYING OVER

Macedonian

French African

German

Romanian

Modern Chinese

Cool, Calm & Collected

THE FIFTIES

The Ungrateful Garden

Midas watched the golden crust
That formed over his streaming sores,
Hugged his agues, loved his lust,
But damned to hell the out-of-doors

Where blazing motes of sun impaled
The serried roses, metal-bright.
"Those famous flowers," Midas wailed,
"Have scorched my retina with light."

This gift, he'd thought, would gild his joys,
Silt up the waters of his grief;
His lawns a wilderness of noise,
The heavy clang of leaf on leaf.

Within, the golden cup is good
To heft, to sip the yellow mead.
Outside, in summer's rage, the rude
Gold thorn has made his fingers bleed.

"I strolled my halls in golden shift,
As ruddy as a lion's meat.
Then I rushed out to share my gift,
And golden stubble cut my feet."

Dazzled with wounds, he limped away
To climb into his golden bed.
Roses, roses can betray.
"Nature is evil," Midas said.

The Intruder

My mother — preferring the strange to the tame:
Dove-note, bone marrow, deer dung,
Frog's belly distended with finny young,
Leaf-mold wilderness, harebell, toadstool,
Odd, small snakes roving through the leaves,
Metallic beetles rambling over stones: all
Wild and natural! — flashed out her instinctive love, and quick, she
Picked up the fluttering, bleeding bat the cat laid at her feet,
And held the little horror to the mirror, where
He gazed on himself, and shrieked like an old screen door far off.

Depended from her pinched thumb, each wing
Came clattering down like a small black shutter.
Still tranquil, she began, "It's rather sweet..."
The soft mouse body, the hard feral glint
In the caught eyes. Then we saw,
And recoiled: lice, pallid, yellow,
Nested within the wing-pits, cozily sucked and snoozed.
The thing dropped from her hands, and with its thud,
Swiftly, the cat, with a clean careful mouth
Closed on the soiled webs, growling, took them out to the
                                                          back stoop.

But still, dark blood, a sticky puddle on the floor
Remained, of all my mother's tender, wounding passion
For a whole wild, lost, betrayed, and secret life
Among its dens and burrows, its clean stones,
Whose denizens can turn upon the world
With spitting tongue, an odor, talon, claw,
To sting or soil benevolence, alien

As our clumsy traps, our random scatter of shot.
She swept to the kitchen. Turning on the tap,
She washed and washed the pity from her hands.

The Worms

This was childhood:
Walking through the worms
After a rain,
Trying not to wound
Anything alive;
Most especially
Not to maim the self
By any kind of death.

Move among the worms,
Pearly and purple,
Curling and opal,
Tickled by the sidewalk,
Heaped over the lines
Of childhood's first map:
Step on a line
Break your mother's spine
Step on a crack
Break your mother's back.

Take care of Mother,
Beware of Father,
Protect foot and finger,
My heart and my heel.
Tiptoe on the spaces,
Don't tread on sex!

Life in small forms —
Hop-toads, lobelia,
Moreover, worms,
The recently born —
Whelms us in childhood:
We grow as we move
Close to the ground,
Eyes in our toes.

Crumbling, cool,
And many-dimensioned,
The morsels of soil
Cling to a worm
When he comes to rain
Fresh from the ground:
Bruised as a blueberry,
Bare as a rose,
Vulnerable as veins,
Naked as a nose.

The earthworm smell
Of each commencement,
The sense that the new
Owns all that it is.
When the torrents end,
God gloats at the world.

By the Riverside

Do not call from memory — all numbers have changed.

FROM THE COVER OF THE
TELEPHONE DIRECTORY

Once I lived at a Riverside
1-3-7-5, by a real stream, Hangman's Creek,
Named from an old pine down the hill,
On which three Indians died. As a child,
I modeled the Crucifixion on that tree
Because I'd heard two Indians were thieves
Strung up by soldiers from Fort Wright in early days,
But no one remembered who the third one was.

Once, in winter, I saw an old Indian wade,
Breaking the thin ice with his thighs.
His squaw crouched modestly in the water,
But he stood up tall, buck-naked. "Cold!" he said,
Proud of his iron flesh, the color of rust,
And his bold manhood, roused by the shock of ice.
He grinned as he spoke, struck his hard chest a blow
Once, with his fist... So I call, from memory,
That tall old Indian, standing in the water.

And I am not put off by an operator
Saying, "Sor-ree, the lion is busy..."
Then, I would tremble, seeing a real lion
Trammeled in endless, golden coils of wire,
Pawing a switchboard in some mysterious
Central office, where animals ran the world,
As I knew they did. To the brave belonged the power.
Christ was a brave, beneath that gauzy clout.

I whispered to the corners of my room, where lions
Crowded at night, blotting the walls with shadows,
As the wind tore at a gutter beneath the eaves,
Moaned with the power of quiet animals
And the old pine, down the hill,
                              where Indians hung:
Telling my prayers, not on a palefaced Sunday
Nor to a red God, who could walk on water
When winter hardened, and the ice grew stronger.

Now I call up godhead and manhood, both,
As they emerged for a child by the Riverside.
But they are all dead Indians now. They answer
Only to me. The numbers have not changed.

A Widow in Wintertime

Last night a baby gargled in the throes
Of a fatal spasm. My children are all grown
Past infant strangles; so, reassured, I knew
Some other baby perished in the snow.
But no. The cat was making love again.

Later, I went down and let her in.
She hung her tail, flagging from her sins.
Though she'd eaten, I forked out another dinner,
Being myself hungry all ways, and thin
From metaphysic famines she knows nothing of,

The feckless beast! Even so, resemblances
Were on my mind: female and feline, though
She preens herself from satisfaction, and does
Not mind lying even in snow. She is
Lofty and bedraggled, without the need to choose.

As an ex-animal, I look fondly on
Her excesses and simplicities, and would not return
To them; taking no marks for what I have become,
Merely that my nine lives peal in my ears again
And again, ring in these austerities,

These arbitrary disciplines of mine,
Most of them trivial: like covering
The children on my way to bed, and trying

To live well enough alone, and not to dream
Of grappling in the snow, claws plunged in fur,

Or waken in a caterwaul of dying.

One to Nothing

The bibulous eagle behind me at the ball game:
"Shucks a'mighty!" coming through the rye
And 7-Up, "I didn't mean to kick you, lady.
When you go to the Eagles' convention, you just *go!*"
Then he needles the batter from Sacramento:
"Too much ego!" he yells. "The old ego curse,
That'll hex him. The old ego never fails.
See?" he says to his phlegmatic friend,
"The bastard fanned!" And "Schucks a'mighty!"
Says again, an American from an English novel,
Named Horace or Homer, a strange colonial bird,
A raw provincial with his outmoded slang.

"Say!" he cries to his friend, "just now I opened
One eye, saw the catcher, then the batter
In a little circle. And everything went brown.
What happened?" "*Nothing!*" says his friend.
He leans beside me, proffers the open pint.
My ego spurns him. "Fly away!" I say
To the badge on his breast. Eagle flaps down,
Confides in the man on first: "Just once a year
I have fun — see? — at the Eagles' convention.
Later I meet the other dignitaries
At the hotel. Forgive me. I'm from a small town,"
He sighs, puts his head in the lap of his friend,

Listens to the portable radio, as the announcer
Makes sense of a blurry ball game
When batters turn brown, curl at the edges,
Fan and fan, like girls in early English novels,

And you can't tell the players, even with a program.
The count is two and one. We hear the *crack!*
Bat skids across the grass. The runner's on!
But eagle sleeps; he dreams away the ball game.
The dozen wasted hits, the double-plays
are lost on him, as we lose, by one run.
Having his inning curled in a little circle,
He emerges, sucks his bottle; his badge mislaid

In the last of the ninth. We surge to the exits
While this bird claws among the peanut shells
In search of his ego. Carry him, friend,
To the dignitaries, to the eagle's aerie,
Where his mate will hone her talons on his breast.
As D.H. Lawrence wished, he has cracked the shell
Of his ego, but devoured it like a nut
Washed down with rye. And he finds oblivion
Like the lost hero of a Modern English Novel.
What happens? Nothing. Even the brilliant infield
Turns brown. Lights out. The circle fades below.
Shucks a'mighty. If you're an eagle, you just go.

The Death of a Public Servant

in memoriam, Herbert Norman

ENVOY ACCUSED OF BEING RED KILLS SELF

Cairo, April 4, 1957 — Canadian Ambassador Herbert Norman
committed suicide early today, apparently because of charges in a
United States Senate subcommittee that he was a Communist.
The Canadian government had denied the charges.

The embassy announced the 48-year-old career diplomat leaped
from a high building. It stated he was an "extremely conscientious
public servant" and that "recent unpleasant publicity and accusa-
tions greatly distressed him."

This is a day when good men die from windows,
Leap from a sill of one of the world's eyes
Into the blind and deaf-and-dumb of time;
Or by ways desperate or ludicrous
Use one of the world's machines for God's,
As George used his gun by the swimming pool
And was found in the flamingo-colored water,
Or John, drowned in a London crater,

Saw a drowned world there before he plunged:
A baby-carriage frame, a plumber's elbow,
Memorials to his dying as he died;
Now you, in Cairo, and I do not know
How that young, dedicated intellect
Was forced away at last from its long service.
Someone in Parliament says you were "killed by slander."
Wounds to your name were mortal to your mind.

Dead friends, who were the servants of this world!
Once there was a place for gentle heroes.
Now they are madmen who, scuttling down corridors,
Eluding guards, climb lavatory walls
And squeeze through air-vents to their liberation,
Where the sensitive concrete receives them
From the world's vast, abstract hate;
So they are smashed to sleep.

Or they, found wandering naked in the woods —
Numbed from the buffets of an autumn storm,
Soaked blissfully in its impersonal furies —
Are wrapped and rescued after a long dark night,
Are bustled into hospitals and baths
While the press explains away their aberrations:
"Needed a rest... and took no holidays..."
But even so, they have managed to catch their death.

I mark the fourth of April on this page,
When the sun came up and glittered on the windows
As you fell away from daylight into heaven:
The muck of Cairo, and a world silenced forever.
A poet, to whom no one cruel or imposing listens,
Disdained by senates, whispers to your dust:
Though you escape from words, whom words pursued,
Take these to your shade: of rage, of grief, of love.

Complex Autumnal

I let the smoke out of the windows
And lift the hair from my ears.
A season of birds and reaping,
A level of light appears.

Sun lies in urns on the terrace
Like the cat on the chimney. Near-
Fall stirs the curtains, narrow

Ribbons of air nip my fingers.
Warm underfoot, the carpet
Reminds my skin I am here.

All things begin together:
Weather and love. The ear
Hears the earth turn; we make an adjustment

To that motion: the dip of the sphere
Into autumn, and rustling music
As the leaves are shaken away...

All things begin together,
Here, as I shake, at the day's
Beginning, with pleasure and fear,

Numb with night's dip and turning
When I weathered love-in-a-sphere,
Like the Siamese cat on the chimney

Mysterious, now, as a vessel,
An ark, or a precious container,
She is smoothing, sunning her fur.

I stand at the window and shiver
As the smoke wreathes out of my hair.
All things begin together:

Weather and love and fear
And the color of leaves, and pleasure.
The waxwings come to the ash trees
That rustle until they are bare.

The birds will wing from the weather
While I stand, still as the harvest,
With the sound of the fall in the air.

What Was in a Name

Thomas Love Peacock! Thomas Love Peacock!
I used to croon, sitting on the pot,
My sympathetic magic, at age three.
These elements in balance captured me:
Love in the middle, on his right hand a saint
And doubter. Gentle à Kempis, Thomas the Rhymer,
Wyatt, Campion, Traherne, came later.

On Love's left hand, the coarse essentials:
Skimp them, and Love, denying, slides away
Into pure Thomas, etiolated sainthood.
Before cock, the satisfying sound of liquid
Which, as it strikes against the enamel basin,
Proclaims a bodily creativity.
Then Love springs eternal; then cock comes

Demonstrating Love. The surname is complete:
Its barbed crest, its thousand eyes, its harsh cries.
Thomas Love Peacock! Thomas Love Peacock!
The person unsung, the person ritually sung.
But that was thirty years ago; a child's loving
Of God, the body, flesh of poetry.
I hail the three-in-one, the one-in-three.

Through a Glass Eye, Lightly

In the laboratory waiting room
containing
one television actor with a teary face
trying a contact lens;
two muscular victims of industrial accidents;
several vain women — I was one of them —
came Deborah, four, to pick up her glass eye.

It was a long day:
Deborah waiting for the blood vessels
painted
on her iris to dry.
Her mother said that, holding Deborah
when she was born,
"First I inspected her, from toes to navel,
then stopped at her head..."
We wondered why
the inspection hadn't gone the other way.
"Looking into her eye
was like looking into a volcano:

"Her vacant pupil
went whirling down, down to the foundation
of the world...
When she was three months old they took it out.
She giggled when she went under
the anaesthetic.
Forty-five minutes later she came back
happy!...
The gas wore off, she found the hole in her face

(you know, it never bled?),
stayed happy, even when I went to pieces.
She's five, in June.

"Deborah, you get right down
from there, or I'll have to slap!"
Laughing, Deborah climbed into the lap
of one vain lady, who
had been discontented with her own beauty.
Now she held on to Deborah, looked her steadily
in the empty eye.

The Suburbans

Forgetting sounds that we no longer hear —
Nightingale, silent for a century:
How touch that bubbling throat, let it touch us
In cardboard-sided suburbs, where the glades
And birds gave way to lawns, fake weathervanes
Topping antennae, or a wrought-iron rooster
Mutely presiding over third-class mail? —
We live on ironed land like cemeteries,
Those famous levelers of human contours.

But cemeteries are a green relief;
Used-car and drive-in movie lots alike
Enaisle and regulate the gaudy junk
That runs us, in a "Park" that is no park.
Our greens kept up for doomed Executives;
Though golf embalms its land, as libraries
Preserve an acre for the mind to play
When, laboring at its trash, the trapped eye leaps,
Beholding greensward, or the written word.

What common symbols dominate our work?
"Perpetual care"; the library steps with lions
More free than moving kinsmen in the zoos;
The seagull is our bird, who eats our loot,
Adores our garbage, but can rise above it —
Clean scavenger, picks clean, gets clean away! —
Past bays and rivers of industrial waste,
Infected oysters, fish bloat, belly-up
In sloughs of sewage, to the open sea.

So much for Nature, carved and animate!
Step in, a minute... But our ankles, brushed
With that swift, intimate electric shock,
Signal the muse: the passing of a cat —
All that remains of tygers, mystery,
Eye-gleam at night, synecdoche for jungle;
We catch her ancient freedom in a cage
Of tidy rhyme. Page the anthologies!
A bridge between our Nature and our Time.

Easily she moves from outer life to inner,
While we, nailed to our domesticity
Like van Gogh to the wall, wild in his frame,
Double in mirrors, that the sinister self
Who moves along with us may own at least
His own reverses, duck behind his molding
When our phones jerk us on a leash of noise.
Hence mirror poems, Alice, The Looking Glass,
Those dull and partial couplings with ourselves.

Our goldfish gazes, our transparent nerves!
As we weave above these little colored stones —
Fish-furniture — bob up for dusty food:
"Just heat and serve"; our empty pear-shaped tones!
Home is a picture window, and our globes
Are mirrors too: we see ourselves outside.
Afraid to become our neighbors, we revolt
In verse: "This proves I'm not the average man."
Only the average poet, which is worse.

The drooping nineteenth-century bard in weeds
On his stone bench, beside a weedy grave,
Might attitudinize, but his tears were free
And easy. He heard authentic birds.
Nobody hid recordings in his woods,
Or draped his waterfalls with neon gauze.
No sign disturbed his orisons, commanding,
"Go to Church This Sunday!" or be damned!
He was comfortably damned when he was born.

But we are saved, from the boring Hell of churches;
We ran to graves for picnics or for peace:
Beer cans on headstones, eggshells in the grass,
"Deposit Trash in Baskets." For release
From hells of public and domestic noise,
We sprawl, although we neither pose nor pray,
Compose our stanzas here, like that dead bard,
But writing poems on poems. Gravely gay,
Our limited salvation is the word.

Not Writing Poems about Children

Once I gave birth to living metaphors.
Not poems now, Ben Jonson, they became themselves.

In despair of poetry, which had fled away,
From loops and chains of children, these were let grow:

"The little one is you all over…"
They fulfill their impulses, not mine.

They invent their own categories,
Clear and arbitrary. No poem needs them.

They need only what they say:
"When I grow up I'm going to marry a tree."

Children do not make up for lost occasions —
"You'd rather kiss that poem than kiss me."

Creation halts, for denials and embraces,
Assurances that no poem replaces them,

Nor, as you knew, Ben, holds the mirror to them,
Nor consoles the parent-artist when they go.

Poems only deprive us of our loss
(Deliberate sacrifice to a cold stanza)

If Art is more durable to us than children,
Or if we, as artists, are more durable than our love.

Ben, I hope you wrote about your dead son
While you were tranced with pain,

Did not offer up those scenes of the infant Isaac in your mind
For the greater poem; but emerged from that swoon

Clutching a page some stranger might have written;
Like a condolence note, cursorily read and tossed aside.

Perhaps at this extremity, nothing improves or worsens.
Talent irrelevant. No poems in stones.

For once, you do not watch yourself
At a desk, covering foolscap. Denied the shameful relief

Of actors, poets, nubile female creatures,
Who save tears like rainwater, for rinsing hair, and mirrors.

Finally, we are left alone with poems,
Children that we cling to, or relinquish

For their own sakes. The metaphor, like love,
Springs from the very separateness of things.

Hera, Hung from the Sky

I hang by my heels from the sky.
The sun, exploded at last,
Hammered his wrath to chains
Forged for my lightest bones.
Once I was warmed to my ears,
Kept close; now blind with fire!
What a child, taking heat for delight
So simply! Scorched within,
I still burn as I swing,
A pendulum kicking in the night,
An alarum at dawn, I deflect
The passage of birds, ring down
The bannering rain. I indict
This body, its ruses, games,
Its plot to unseat the sun.
I pitted my feminine weight
Against God, his terrible throne.
From the great dome of despair,
I groan, I swing, I swing
In unconstellated air.

I had shared a sovereign cloud:
The lesser, the shadowy twin
To my lord. All woman and weight
Of connubial love that sings
Within the cabinet's close
And embracing intimacy.
I threw it all to the skies
In an instant of power, poise —
Arrogant, flushed with his love,

His condescending praise;
From envy of shine and blaze,
Mad, but beautifully mad,
Hypnotized by the gaze
Of self into self, the dream
That woman was great as man —
As humid, as blown with fame,
So great I seemed to be!
I threw myself to the skies
And the sky has cast me down.
I have lost the war of the air:
Half-strangled in my hair,
I dangle, drowned in fire.

Epithalamion

You left me gasping on the shore,
A fabulous fish, all gill
And gilded scales. Such sighs we swore!
As our mirror selves
Slipped back to sea, unsundering, bumped gently there,
The room a bay, and we,
Afloat on lapping, gazes laving,
Glistered in its spume.

And all cerulean
With small, speeding clouds: the ceiling,
Lights beyond eyelids. So you reeled in me,
Reeling.

Our touch was puffed and cloudy now,
As if the most impaled and passionate thought
Was tentative in flesh.
This frail
Smile seemed, in our bodies' wash,
Like a rock-light at sea, glimmering
With all the strength of singleness in space.

Still, you will not turn aside,
Your face fallow, eyes touching.
So I cling to your tendrils of hair,
Our two tides turning
Together: toward and away
With the moon, motionless and sailing.

O my only unleaving lover,
Even in expiring, you reach again.
Thus we may rest, safe in this sealing
As beached, we lie,
Our hulks whitening, sun scaling,
While the small sea-foam dries,
And the sea recedes and the beach accedes,
Our bodies piled like casual timber
Sanded, on this pure, solar lift of hour,
Wreathed in our breathing.

We will exceed ourselves again:
Put out in storms, and pitch our wave on waves.
My soul, you will anticipate my shouting as you rise
Above me to the lunar turn of us,
As skies crack stars upon our symmetries,
Extinguished as they touch this smoky night,
And we exhale again our fume of bliss.

This is my shallow rocking to Orion:
Curling to touch the seaweed at your side.
Wrap my mermaid hair about your wrists
And seal my face upon your resinous eyes.

Foundered on finny wastes, we rest
Till dawn, a gilded layer, lies
Across the pallid sky.
The world's a tinted shell borne up where waves embrace.
Its thin, convolving valve will close and clasp
This love so blessed:
Our sea-life, swooning as it swims, to reach
Tentacular and cleaving arms that touch
A milky flank, a drowned, reviving face.

Persephone Pauses

The lengthened shadow of my hand
Holding a letter from a friend
Tells time: the sun descends again.
So long, so late the light has shone.
Since rising, we have shone with ease:
Perhaps not happiness, but still
A certain comfort from the trees
Whose crests of leaves droop down in tiers,
Their warm trunks veiled by aspen hair,
Their honeyed limbs, the loosened earth
About the roots; while flowers recline
In dusty gardens, rest on weeds,
Those emblems of a passing year.

So be it! As I turn, my train
Is plucked by spikes of summer grass.
No clutch of summer holds me here.
I know, I know. I've gone before.
I glance to my accustomed glass,
The shallow pond, but films of slime
Waver across it, suck the verge
Where blunted marsh frond cuts the air.
But as I stare, the slime divides
Like curtains of old green velour:

I gaze into my gaze once more,
Still veiled in foam. But then, the grim
Tragedian from the other shore
Draws near my shade. Beneath the brim,

In motions formal and austere,
We circle, measure, heel to hem.
He proffers me an iron plate
Of seedy fruit, to match my mouth.

My form encased in some dark stuff
He has bedizened, keeps me hid
Save for that quivering oval, turned
Half-moon, away, away from him
And that excitement of his taste
He suffers, from my flesh withdrawn.

But this unwilling touch of lust
Has moved some gentle part of me
That sleeps in solstice, wakes to dream
Where streams of light and winter join.
He knows me then; I only know
A darkened cheek, a sidelong lower,
My nerves dissolving in the gleam
Of night's theatrical desire,
As always, when antagonists
Are cast into the sensual
Abysses, from a failing will.
This is my dolor, and my dower.

Come then, sweet Hell! I'll name you once
To stir the grasses, rock the pool,
And move the leaves before they fall.
I cast my letter to the breeze
Where paper wings will sprout, and bear
It on to that high messenger
Of sky, who lately dropped it here,

Reminding me, as I decline,
That half my life is spent in light.
I cast my spirit to the air,
But cast it. Summertime, good-night!

The Flower

Two from a pit
Met, as they rose.
For strength, they offered each other their own bright blood to drink.
As cupped hands bumped in haste, there flashed some drops to soil.
Up sprang a rose.

"I used," he said,
"To sow and reap
In passionate haste, flinging the wild seed
Into the noon-hot trench, or where the unbroken, moon-cold ground
Lay cauled in sleep.

"But what I reaped
Was not a crop
Of anemones wildly roiling the contours of the hill.
No ocean of marigolds washed the soil in gold.
What struggled up

"Out of the loam
Was a giant mole
With onion eyes, who spoke: 'Be rich and wise, and dig below
Where coarse roots cut a worm to twins.' So I followed him
Into his hole.

"Into the night
I fell away.
Awash from wounds, I heard him scorning: 'Trail your seed!
Fall as it fell, in a shower of nothing. Lie in the dust you made.'
And so I lay.

"But later woke
And clambered out,
Not so weak as my wounds, meeting another struggler on the way.
We suffered, and were gentled, to give aid. Out of our surge to light
This flower sprouts."

"I dreamed," she said,
"I was with child.
Something fathered a flower in my web of sleep, and then a dream
Within a dream told me I bore and buried it all in one grieving night.
So I woke, wild

"With loss, dug down
To find my fate.
In burrowing, matter and mold gave way. I fell far upon a grave.
Its marking shaft, that must have been the axle of the earth,
Impaled my heart.

"With loamy eyes
That ran, I read
Its epitaph, carved upside down: 'Here lies
No dream of yours. Only the seed of weeds garlands this mourning.'
My wound was dead,

"Deader than I,
The lips a seam
Where no blood sprang. What caused my blood to flow so
                                        sweetly then,
After we climbed together, hand in brimming hand?"
She paused, to dream.

"Listen!" he said.
"Summon your wits!

What bright flare dies from the world if we pluck this flower?
Or if we pass on to our own ways again..."
But milk was streaming from her breast as she bent down
To nourish it.

Columns and Caryatids

I. THE WIFE

"I am Lot's pillar, caught in turning,
Bellowing, resistant, burning
With brine. Fine robes laced with sand,
Solid, soon to be hollowed by tongues of kine."

Solid, solitary salt lick, she
Is soon to be shaped by wind, abstracted,
Smoothed to a sex-shape only.
Large and lonely in the plain,
Rain melting her slowly.

So proud shoulder dips with compliance
Never in life. God's alliance with weather
Eroding her to a spar, a general grief-shape,
A cone, then an egg no bigger than a bead.

"I saw Sodom bleed, Gomorrah smoke.
Empty sockets are a joke of that final vision.
Tongueless, I taste my own salt, taste
God's chastisement and derision."

II. THE MOTHER

"I am God's pillar, caught in raising
My arms like thighs, to brace the wall.
Caught by my own choice,
I willed myself to hold this ceiling.

"He froze me at the moment of decision.
Always I wished to bear weight,
Not in my belly where the seed would light.
That globe is great with stone.
But over me, the weight of endless function,
My thick trunk set for stress,
My face, showing calmly through guano
No strain, my brain sloped by marble curls
To wedge the architrave.

"The world is a womb.
Neither I nor the fetus tires of our position.
My ear is near God, my temples to His temple.
I lift and I listen. I eat God's peace."

III. THE LOVER

"I am your pillar that has fallen.
And now, for centuries of rest
I will regard my breast, my calm hills,
My valley for the stars to travel."

Stripped of all ornament she lies,
Looted alike by conquerors and technicians,
Her curling fingers for an emperor's flower,
Her trinkets in barbarians' museums.
They dust away, but she endures, and smiles,
Accepting ravage as the only tribute
That men can pay to gods, that they would dint them
To raise or decorate themselves, themselves are dinted,
The bruise upon the sense of generations.

So boys will turn from sleep and search the darkness,
Seeking the love their fathers have forgotten.
And they will dream of her who have not known her,
And ache, and ache for that lost limb forever.

The Damnation

Before the adamantine gate, I clear my throat
To summon resonance, collect my epithets and gird my bones,
Prepared to talk my way into Hell.

I beat at the gate till my knuckles turn to cheese.
Rhadamanthus, Minos, Aeacus, I hammer with little words
That thrum in my old, gone pulse, that sting of Tisiphone.

"Let me in! Let me leave the air,
Inhale your sulfurous steam-pits, be massaged with staves.
Best of beasts, I want to burn. Singe my bones!

"Let me lose the shape of self: where is the rack
That rids us of abominable skin?
I want to hear my sockets crack like kindling.

"Can I bend my bones, touch crown to talon in a perfect wheel
Like ancient snake with tail in mouth?
Beset my flesh, its choices. Spend my blood!"

In language stripped from tongue as I wish hot meat from bone,
Verbs active as my standing hair,
I crowd the judges, kneel before the keepers:

"Teach anguish so outrageous that known pain
Will seem as trivial as an ant with one leg gone
Laboring up the mound with a dead fly. Amputate my whine

"So the sound is of wood being sawed in the farther orchard
Mixed with the smell of asphodel, fresh shavings,
And apples tumbled on spongy ground.

"Solder lips shut, melt my north and south.
Distribute my precious organs impartially among the larger dogs.
Rake my remains, to smoke away their age,

"Delivered at last from my thought and my things,
My net weight, my engorged heart,
So humbled that my purposes grow grass.

"Oh, sink me as a germ, a seed,
To Tartarus, where worms are gray..."
The sentence rains on my upraised fists: "Away!

"Here carrion birds swoop down at dark to feast.
Some bulb or bump is left, the prey of love..."
I hear a shape that sucks about the gates

Calling its own name, answering itself;
Then, in a chink, displaying its torn grin
As it preens its pulp.

The old men say, as they turn with a clang of clothes,
"A soul without a self? We've selves to burn!"
And after, only a vapor drifting up.

The Old Gods

After Heinrich Heine

You full-blooming moon!
Turning the ocean to a wash of gold,
So noon and twilight lap the level beaches;
In the blue pallor of a starless heaven
I see clouds move like statues of the Gods:

Great ghosts of mist and marble. No! They're Gods!
The old Greek Gods who ruled the world in joy,
Now abdicated, crowded out,
Parading through the midnight wastes of heaven.

Pantheon of Air! I watch, astounded,
Your giant shapes and mute, mysterious passage.
Ha! There's Kronos, once the King of Heaven,
Who shook Olympus when he shook his hair.
Shock-headed now, he holds and never hurls
The flaccid thunderbolts. Old Zeus,
Old Zeus, you once knew better days,
Enjoying boys, nymphs, hecatombs...
Even the Gods can't live forever.
The young drive out the old, as you drove out
Your Titan relatives, your poor old father.

Here's Hera. How she's fallen
In spite of her anxiety attacks;
Someone else wields the scepter,
You old ex-queen of Heaven.
Your huge eye, scooped out like a statue's,

The limpness of your calla-lily arms:
How could you strike down or trouble
That God-kissed girl, and her God-given Son?

Pallas Athena passes, aegis and all
Her wisdom could not stave off decay.
You too, Aphrodite, transmuted
In reverse, from real gold to ghostly silver,
Still with your amulets, and lovelier
Than real girls. Beauty, you stir me secretly.
If you gave me, once, that liberal body,
I'd die of shock, like the other heroes you endowed...
Dear Lust, you're now the Queen of the cadavers.

Ares, the War God, turns away,
Casts down his terrible eyes;
And old perpetual-adolescent Phoebus
With a rusty lyre, who once livened up those Olympian dinners,
When Hephaistos poured the nectar and waited table;
Poor old cripple! He looks even sadder.
Time, for a long time, has extinguished
The Gods' inextinguishable laughter.

You old Gods, I never cared about you.
I don't feel for the Greeks; I loathe the Romans.
But for you, I sigh. I tremble for you,
Lost Goddesses, dispossessed Gods,
Dead shadows, wandering in the night,
Frail clouds, frayed by the wind.
When I think of those windy deities
Who have beaten you down, and now
Conceal their pleasure at your pain
Under that old-sheep meekness

That is part of their stock-in-trade,
I feel a strange resentment
As terrible as your pride.
I could break down their built-up temples,
Old Gods, and fight on your side:
Fight for your high altars and ambrosial rule,
Altars rebuilt and reeking with sacrificial smoke.
I could even bring myself to kneel,
Call your names, raise my arms, and pray...
After all, when you fought in our little quarrels
You always chose to back the winners.
But I, a man, am more magnanimous:
Now that I've joined the battle of the Gods,
I'll fight on the losing side!

The Apostate

I, Hypocrite Harry, that Hamburg hand-kisser
Who betrayed himself to Jesus for a few lousy Prussian bucks,
A Judas to his race, baptized Christian Heinrich,
Sold out to the Most High, for a safe sinecure
Which never materialized. H. Heine, Ironist

By profession, ate body and blood of crow for this.
Oh, 'twas a veritable black, feathered banquet,
A crow-feast, with self-hate for the first course.
And the entrée? His stomach ate itself.
Then from under his coat, he produced a dripping bouquet

Of ulcers, to adorn the groaning board.
Then the Humbug Herr Professor, Harry the Hoaxer,
Groaned right back. Jews do. Ask any doctor.
Ask Dr. Heine, expert practitioner and self-surgeon
Who could carve his own carcass in public.

Under the chandeliers, on the high-tea tables
Of Her Illustrious Highness; under the hard lights
Of the surgical theater, he pointed to anatomical charts,
Droned out self-explanations as the scalpel flashed.
In one deft move, Harry uncircumcised himself!

Or he hired a hall, and filled it with the high opera
Of his operation, drew the heavy red plush curtains
As he died on the table. But before that drawn-out aria
Milking his death, he had managed to rush backstage,
Crank up the wind-machine, rattle sheets of tin,

Shower down squibs and colophonium, adjust the Devil's cape
Over his surgical uniform, and trim his halo.
A symphony in red, white, and black, he sang his coda
In several voices: wind, heartstrings, and brass.
A whole orchestra, he then conducted himself to death.

He draped the red, white, and black flag over his corpse
Which rose to take bows, shout "Bravo!" "Bis!" and hiss,
Then fall into the pit of hell, while careful Harry
Stood by the flames with his bucket of sand,
Passing out pogroms — er — programs for his Farewell Tour.

So hate Harry. So do him a favor!
Who first wrote *Gelobt sei Jesu Christ*
To conclude a paean to peace. Utopian Harry!
Who dreamed the machines would stop, the streets be clean,
The samite-clad palm-wavers meet with chaste brow-kisses.

I dreamed they saw a huge Christ in the sky,
Holding the sun in His breast: a great Sun-heart
Slowly bleeding on the pure crowd below,
Thrice blessed... Irrepressibly pagan Harry,
That's the Jesus of Mexico, of a Jew enchanted by pantheons.

Then I, Heinrich, wrote *Gelobt sei Jesu Christ*
Again, for the world-as-it-is: "where holy water
Does double duty, washing souls and thinning tea,
And you kiss the crosses, lapdog paws and snooty faces
Of the most high, pious and respectable": Harry, Society's toy,

Prepared to praise Christ, if Her Illustrious Highness
Bestowed a raise in pay. But Honest Harry never did.
Heinrich, fish of Christ, and flesh of Zion,

Harry the cock, crows again at the dawn of Greece.
So Kronos, Jupiter, Venus, Elohim, Christ the Jew,

Bless the Poet, Heinrich, as he blesses you.

Tying One On in Vienna

Variations on a theme by H.H.

I have been, faithfully, to the thirty-nine birthplaces of Beethoven;
To thirty-nine birthplaces of Beethoven have I been.
Reborn, every time, to the wrath of landladies
Who objected to the noise,
He had to move on.
Damn and bless your peripeteia, Beethoven.
I am above your *Meer und Sturm;* I have won my haven
On high, below, in a cozy rathskeller in Vienna.

I tip the whole world down my throat,
Thirsty as Beethoven.
If I were home, I'd float on an ice cube like a polar bear
In my terrible fur, bulky as Beethoven,
Dipping my toes in an ocean of whiskey.
But here is a whole world in a golden brew:
Viennese cathedrals, where Mongol troops, I'm told,
Took potshots at gargoyles, to destroy their evil-eyes —
Never mind: gargoyles will rise again, gargle golden wine,
Giggle in rathskellers; Luther broke things too,
Or his followers did. Give me a golden Pope
Who wallows in artifacts, tithes a thousand villages
For one gold goblet: Oh, I see all the Leos of all the Romes
In this glass: Agamemnon's cup, the brilliant vessels
of Vaphio, with ruminating bulls, bulls grazing,
And bulls chased round and round the bowl by crazy Schliemann.
Turks and Hellenes, Mongols, Shakespearean scholars — Hegel!
Continuity is all!
Changing the petticoat guard at the palace of Paul;
Orange groves, All Souls' Day, Fourth of July parades;

Vienna, Spokane, Los Angeles County — even Hamburg...
And over all others, the face of my lover,
A man with the brain of an angel!

Beloved, thou art fair,
With hair the color of Solomon's beard
And a big head, like Beethoven.
David the Goliath, patron saint of Florence,
Has a navel like a pigeon's swimming pool;
You are the David of the Galleria dell'Accadèmia
Whose navel is a little golden bowl
In which I plunge my nose — Oh, what a heavenly odor!
Landlord, hold me up by the hair
Before I drown!

Der brave Mann! We sit here together
Drinking like brother and sister,
We hug each other like sister and brother
And he speaks to me of the power of love.
I drink to the health of my ex-husband
And other enemies, known and unknown.
I FORGIVE ALL LOUSY POETS
AS THEY SHALL FORGIVE ME.
I weep in an excess of feeling!

Then I cry to him, "Landlord, where are the twelve apostles,
The holy hogsheads, hidden in the back room
Where they preach to the United Nations?
Lead me to them, in their plain wooden jackets,
Looking like Mennonite farmers. Their souls are more radiant
Than the Court of St. James's, than the Fabergé eggs
In the Hermitage Museum...

Purple and Gold! My old High School colors!"
O those grand autumn days, when we crushed Immaculate

Conception,

And the Society of Jesus provided cheerleaders,
Though both teams flopped down on the field to pray
Just before game-time. And I debated the girls from the convent
On, "Resolved: We should have government ownership of railroads"
And God was on my side, the affirmative.
Though I spoke with the tongue of gargoyle and angel,
God and I lost, because the girls of St. Mary's
Kept their skirts over their knees and their hands folded,
While I waved my wild hair, and bit my nails
In an excess of feeling...

Hooray! I'm being fanned by palm trees!
And the scent of orange groves in the sweet San Fernando Valley
Where I spent my childhood;
What an odor of myrrh is rising from a thousand navels!
Reel on, you rivers of the world!
Even the rathskeller door, with its broken hinges
Since the Russian troops hammered it down, looking for girls,
Even the old door, wounded with bayonet marks,
Dances and reels, and my soul staggers for joy,
And we are all healed together, noble Viennese landlord!

He will steer me upstairs to the daylight,
Du braver Ratskellermeister,
And we'll see, though the gargoyles are broken,
There are angels on the roofs of the cathedral,
On all the roofs — see those angels sitting there like pigeons?
Angels of Heine and Rilke, all drunk. Singing,
Hallelujah and Yippee! If there were a sun overhead
It would be red like the nose of a drunkard,

Behind all that Viennese rain, as drunk as Beethoven
Every time he was born. The soul of the world is a nose,
A nose in a navel. The red sun sets in the navel of heaven.
God save a disorderly world, and the wild United Nations!
The twelve holy hogsheads will roll forth on their keg legs
And save us all: poets, Mongolians, landlords & ladies, mad
                                                    musicians.

Hooray for purple and gold, for liquor and angels!

A Muse of Water

We who must act as handmaidens
To our own goddess, turn too fast,
Trip on our hems, to glimpse the muse
Gliding below her lake or sea,
Are left, long-staring after her,
Narcissists by necessity;

Or water-carriers of our young
Till waters burst, and white streams flow
Artesian, from the lifted breast:
Cupbearers then, to tiny gods,
Imperious table-pounders, who
Are final arbiters of thirst.

Fasten the blouse, and mount the steps
From kitchen taps to Royal Barge,
Assume the trident, don the crown,
Command the Water Music now
That men bestow on Virgin Queens;
Or goddessing above the waist,

Appear as swan on Thames or Charles
Where iridescent foam conceals
The paddle-stroke beneath the glide:
Immortal feathers preened in poems!
Not our true, intimate nature, stained
By labor, and the casual tide.

Masters of civilization, you
Who moved to riverbank from cave,

Putting up tents, and deities,
Though every rivulet wander through
The final, unpolluted glades
To cinder-bank and culvert-lip,

And all the pretty chatterers
Still round the pebbles as they pass
Lightly over their watercourse,
And even the calm rivers flow,
We have, while springs and skies renew,
Dry wells, dead seas, and lingering drouth.

Water itself is not enough.
Harness her turbulence to work
For man: fill his reflecting pools.
Drained for his cofferdams, or stored
In reservoirs for his personal use:
Turn switches! Let the fountains play!

And yet these buccaneers still kneel
Trembling at the water's verge:
"Cool River-Goddess, sweet ravine,
Spirit of pool and shade, inspire!"
So he needs poultice for his flesh.
So he needs water for his fire.

We rose in mists and died in clouds
Or sank below the trammeled soil
To silent conduits underground,
Joining the blindfish, and the mole.
A gleam of silver in the shale:
Lost murmur! Subterranean moan!

So flows in dark caves, dries away,
What would have brimmed from bank to bank,
Kissing the fields you turned to stone,
Under the boughs your axes broke.
And you blame streams for thinning out,
Plundered by man's insatiate want?

Rejoice when a faint music rises
Out of a brackish clump of weeds,
Out of the marsh at ocean-side,
Out of the oil-stained river's gleam,
By the long causeways and gray piers
Your civilizing lusts have made.

Discover the deserted beach
Where ghosts of curlews safely wade:
Here the warm shallows lave your feet
Like tawny hair of magdalens.
Here, if you care, and lie full-length,
Is water deep enough to drown.

Afterthoughts of Donna Elvira

You, after all, were good.
Now it is late, you are kind.
Never too late, to my mind.
The mind catches up with the blood.

You, it is good to know,
Now we are not in thrall,
To me were as kind as you would,
Being the same to all.

Those that are true to one
Love not themselves, love none.
Loving the one and many,
You cannot be true to any.

True to your human kind,
You seemed to me too cruel.
Now I am not a fool,
Now that I fear no scorn,

Now that I see, I see
What you have known within:
Whenever we love, we win,
Or else we have never been born.

Plaint of the Poet in an Ignorant Age

I would I had a flower-boy!
I'd sit in the mid of an untamed wood
Away from tame suburbs beyond the trees.
With my botany-boy to fetch and find,
I'd sit in a rocker by a pot of cold coffee
Noodling in a notebook on my knee,
Calling, "Flower-boy, name me that flower!
Read me the tag on that tree!"
But here I sit by an unlit fire
Swizzling three martinis
While a thousand metaphors doze outdoors,
And the no-bird sings in the no-name tree.

I would I had a bug-boy
With a bug-book and a butterfly net,
To bring me Nature in a basket of leaves:
A bug on a leaf by the goldfish bowl;
I'd sit in a rocker, a pocketful of pine-nuts
And a nutcracker knocking my knee,
Cracking nuts, jokes, and crying to my bug-boy,
"Read me the caterpillar on the leaf,
Count the number of nibbled veins
By a tree's light, in fire!"
While I, in my rocker, rolled and called,
A caterpillar crawled on the long-named leaf.

If I had a boy of Latin and Greek
In love with eleven-syllable leaves,
Hanging names like halos on herb and shrub!
A footnote lad, a lexicon boy

Who would run in a wreath around my rocker
To kneel at my chair, at my knee
Saying, "Here is your notebook, here is your pen! —
I have found you a marvelous tree!"
But all I have is a poetry-boy,
A bottle-cap king: he cries,
Thudding from the garden, "What do you call
The no-bird that sings in the no-name tree?"

Birthday Poem for a Childless Man

This is the birthday of your death;
Some odd and forty years ago
The hard light caught you, catching breath
To broach your first, protesting cry.
At birth we leave and enter death,
The bloody pit, the water's tomb;
The knife that cleaves us into love
From love and mother, cuts us back,
Removes the spleen, the gut, the gland,
Till we return to woman's land.

Each form encompassed by the hand
That brought it forth, to soothe the eye
That weeps before the burning light,
To smooth the battered skull, an ear
Turned in against a world of bright
Sensation; in a lapping tide
Of dark, the buried pulses trip.
Caught like a bird, the naked wrist
Flutters in the surgeon's grip.
What woman makes, such men will carve
And shape to fullness, though it starve.

My starveling love, your birthday comes
To mind us of that only cry:
Its bare astonishment at fate,
The cold, the air, the spectrum's shock,
The severance from a throbbing stalk,
The burst of outrage and of pain
That love, who made you, thrust you out.

Because you could not cry again,
I wept, too late! was borne away
In silence, from your clamorous look.

If life unman you at the first,
And all its creatures carry breath
Of carrion, that stinking ghost,
How can you help but turn aside
When love and troubles come to plead?
You suffer, will not suffer me
To bear, to parturiate and bleed.
You will cut down your life instead.
So to be male, of woman born,
You make a birthday of my death.

The Great Blue Heron

M.A.K., September 1880–September 1955

As I wandered on the beach
I saw the heron standing
Sunk in the tattered wings
He wore as a hunchback's coat.
Shadow without a shadow,
Hung on invisible wires
From the top of a canvas day,
What scissors cut him out?
Superimposed on a poster
Of summer by the strand
Of a long-decayed resort,
Poised in the dusty light
Some fifteen summers ago;
I wondered, an empty child,
"Heron, whose ghost are you?"

I stood on the beach alone,
In the sudden chill of the burned.
My thought raced up the path.
Pursuing it, I ran
To my mother in the house
And led her to the scene.
The spectral bird was gone.
But her quick eye saw him drifting
Over the highest pines
On vast, unmoving wings.
Could they be those ashen things,
So grounded, unwieldy, ragged,
A pair of broken arms

That were not made for flight?
In the middle of my loss
I realized she knew:
My mother knew what he was.

O great blue heron, now
That the summer house has burned
So many rockets ago,
So many smokes and fires
And beach-lights and water-glow
Reflecting pinwheel and flare:
The old logs hauled away,
The pines and driftwood cleared
From that bare strip of shore
Where dozens of children play;
Now there is only you
Heavy upon my eye.
Why have you followed me here,
Heavy and far away?
You have stood there patiently
For fifteen summers and snows,
Denser than my repose,
Bleaker than any dream,
Waiting upon the day
When, like gray smoke, a vapor
Floating into the sky,
A handful of paper ashes,
My mother would drift away.

Lovemusic

Come, freighted heart, within this port,
Bring all your bee-collected sweet,
The savor of a liberal night,
The crown of columbine, still-wet,
The muse of days. Bring your delights
To fill the palate and the plate,
To rinse the lips. Unburden, set
Your lilies on my chair of state.

Come, laden love, to this, my cave.
For here we soon may hide and move,
In havens play the courting dove,
And pace the newly altared nave:
This vested place, this heart alive.
With fruit and wine and coupled play,
Each self will give itself away.

Come candidly, consort with me,
And spill our pleasure for a day.
Let love delay, unhurriedly,
This passing taste — I prophesy:
Remembered cinnamon and lime
Will fructify a bleaker time.

The Patient Lovers

Love is an illness still to be,
Still away, another chill.
We shall measure mercury

Of the rising, falling will,
Of the large and resting heart,
Of the body, not quite still,

Still enough to keep the chart
From reflecting what we feel:
We shall be well, and well apart.

Though my body still will start
When from my milky side you steal,
And breathing is a casual art,

And illness we no longer play
Unless we fill the healer's part.
We will be well, and well away

Until our pulse and pallor tell
That we are ill, of being well.

Love Song

for Ruthven Todd

Oh, to fall easily, easily, easily in Love
As nursling birds tumble from the nest
(not — pray — into the dog's jaws).
True lovers of women tend to love
Not grossly, but in gross lots
"Without deduction for tare, tret, or waste,"
(Webster says), love every look,
Think each new taste the best.

Oh, to fall in Love, easily, easily
As a mild child falls to, at the breast
(not as an iron-jawed child clamps on),
To inhale all sweet ambience, breezily
Exhale flowered breath
While rapturously curls the pillowed fist,
Toes clenched in comfort,
Each new taste the best.

O Love, easily, easily, easily to fall
As fledgling bird or child is lost
(within a plot, not acres away),
Only to turn around, and find the haven
That has not moved at all.
Learn lose-and-find without much cost,
Terror smoothed in feathered, ruffled bosom,
And easily, Love, easily to rest.

To My Friend, behind Walls

Who will protect you from the thrust of wings,
The bats, the birds, their rustlings, their clamor?
Frenzied, you scrape at droppings, gauze, and webs,
And scar your naked face with your own claws:

The face of your first self that chokes on plaster
As the old mansion crumbles, crumbles. *Mother!*
My madness hates you! So the tired self-stalker
Creeps through a passage, yearning for the blast.

A thousand fuses gleam like candelabra,
And one poor shaking hand is too confused
To touch them off. Unlit, they rise and hiss,
Writhe and turn black, and spring above Her brow.

Medusa! There are faces in Her hair!
But you are bandaged: mummified and trussed,
Set in the rocker, told to think it over.
You stare at the scarred and cracking nursery walls,

Cannot spit out the gag when father comes,
Smiling and vague, to change his coat for supper.
At the door, his hand flickers a salutation.
He moves, and he is swallowed by The Voice

Murmuring behind walls the obscene endearments,
The sad, domestic lies: *She was bad again.*
And the bats beat on the window; owls and nighthawks
Pounce in the dark on soft young animals.

The wind is an enemy, a branch tapping Her code.
The window thunders, and the harsh bird voices,
The menace of wings... *Nurse, will you hold me?*
So you embrace: *Ah, Love! At last!* Betrayed!

Arms pinioned to your back... the canvas hurts!
Defeat, like a hypodermic, floods your veins.
And the jail is calm and soundproof. Heads in wings,
Or upside-down, they doze behind the walls.

A Poet's Household

three for Theodore Roethke

I.

The stout poet tiptoes
On the lawn. Surprisingly limber
In his thick sweater
Like a middle-aged burglar.
Is the young robin injured?

II.

She bends to feed the geese
Revealing the neck's white curve
Below her coiled hair.
Her husband seems not to watch,
But she shimmers in his poem.

III.

A hush is on the house,
The only noise, a fern
Rustling in a vase.
On the porch, the fierce poet
Is chanting words to himself.

From an Artist's House

for Morris Graves

I.

A bundle of twigs
On the roof. We study pictures:
Nests of hern and crane.
The artist who built this house
Arranged the branches there.

II.

Is the inlaid box
With a gilt hasp concealing
A letter, a jewel?
Within, a bunch of feathers,
The small bones of a bird.

III.

The great gold kakemono
With marvelous tapes and tassels,
Handles of pale bone,
Is a blaze on the wall. Someone
Pinned an oak leaf to the silk.

IV.

Full of withered oranges,
The old, lopsided compote
Reposes on the sill.
Poor crockery, immortal
On twenty sheets of paper.

Linked Verses

for Donald Keene

Read a thousand books!
Consult your dreams! Drink spirits.
Then write your poem.

The poet, tossing pebbles,
Muses on rings with rings.

When the rains descend,
Life, that was buried forever,
Sends up a cool green flame.

What is as new as a toad!
The unborn calls to the born.

Pricked on the furze bush,
You reached for the kindling ax
And forgot the blossom.

So rough, they catch on the silk,
How shall I keep my hands busy?

Gold chrysanthemums
Have the faint, acrid odor
Of Mortality.

Pain, ugliness, old age:
At least they make no demands.

The frost was late this year:
Crystal nips the petals,
As my lover grows impatient.

The blind worm says to his brother,
"Who will need us when we die?"

On a Line from Julian

I have a number and my name is dumb.
Living for death, this paradox I take:
Such a barbarian have I become.

Because historians are growing numb,
They will not say we love what we forsake,
To be a number when a name is dumb.

Our leaders urge us further to succumb.
Our privy hearts in unison must ache,
Says a barbarian. Have I become

A vessel that is empty of aplomb
To ornament the century's mistake,
And be a number when my name is dumb?

Subsisting on a drop of blood, a crumb,
When wine is gone, and bread too hard to break,
A small barbarian have I become.

I can be private in delirium,
Indifferent to the noises that I make.
I have a number, and my name is dumb.
Such a barbarian have I become!

What the Bones Know

Remembering the past
And gloating at it now,
I know the frozen brow
And shaking sides of lust
Will dog me at my death
To catch my ghostly breath.

I think that Yeats was right,
That lust and love are one.
The body of this night
May beggar me to death,
But we are not undone
Who love with all our breath.

I know that Proust was wrong,
His wheeze: love, to survive,
Needs jealousy, and death
And lust, to make it strong
Or goose it back alive.
Proust took away my breath.

The later Yeats was right
To think of sex and death
And nothing else. Why wait
Till we are turning old?
My thoughts are hot and cold.
I do not waste my breath.

To a Visiting Poet in a College Dormitory

Here tame boys fly down the long light of halls
In this late nightmare of your fourth decade:
Medley of shoe-thuds, towel-slaps and horseplay,
Murmurous radios, counterpoint of squalling
Bedsprings and shower-pipes across your ceiling.

Nocturnal soundings turn you back always
To a broken fountain, faces damp as leaves
Stuck to the fountain's lip in autumn, draining
From an era swamped in war's impersonal seas.
Do you sleep empty and long, or cannonading

Through these nautical chambers, having gathered all
Your strength into one battered bowling ball,
Asleep, ramp up and down these corridors of boys
Barely knocking at doors, but bursting into
Identical rooms, like icicles ablaze?

Now, as I hope you sleep, I turn the pages
Of your committed life — rather the notations
Of sensation coaxed and cheated into poems:
Loves are interred three deep, or rise like drowned
Ruined choristers, to flaunt your praises.

Fisher of bodies, when the lure is failing,
Still you proffer the old nibble of boy-bait,
Though nothing comes now, arias or kingdoms;
You may not deny death, nor contrive it soon.
Only escape, your orphanhood outrun,

Run from the glisten of those refracting egos
Where you could love and loathe yourself on sight,
To the worst priesthood, or test-tube remedy
For fratricidal passion! Run from the children
To father men and poems in your mind.

On Rising from the Dead

Lift up in lilac-emerald breath the grail
Of earth again —
                    Thy face
From charred and riven stakes. O
Dionysus...

HART CRANE

Saturday noon: the morning of the mind
Moves through a mist to breakfast: damp from sleep,
Rustic and rude, the partial self comes down
To face a frozen summer, self-imposed;
Then, as the numb shades lift, becomes aware
Of its other half, buried overhead,
A corpse in twisted sheets, a foggy portrait
Smudged in the bathroom mirror — elegies
Sung on the nerves of a pillow-muffled phone.

Nobody's home at home, the house announces.
And the head nods, nobody's home in here.
The bird of dawning silent all day long,
Nobody's home to nobody abroad:
As cars curve past the house, taking themselves
For airings, while the drivers doze within;
Anonymous dogs chivy the ghosts of cats
Safely locked in the basement. Apples nod
Their hard green heads, lost in a blur of leaves.

Last night, in the hot house, the self sang
Its oneness, in reflection of a love.
Now the cold fragments rise, remembering;
As feudal lieges move for a missing King

Shattered on plains of sleep, they summon armies:
The midget fingers, elbows, eyes, and toes,
To patch again the china egg. And horses,
Masculine cavalry of the will, prance, pull
The egg, in cobweb harness, up the hill.

So the self trots upstairs, and reunites
With its lost half, by toweling off the mirror.
Reluctantly, the self confronts the self
Ripped, untimely, from its naked bed,
The winding sheets tossed down the laundry chute.
The room's aroma: whiskey and ripe fruit
Stale with fulfillment, while picked flowers curl
Their lips, like suicides in brackish water,
Soiled Ophelias, whom no breath can fulfill.

Still, air the rooms! though fruit and flowers cry,
"Leave light, leave air to buds! Beyond bloom,
Who cares?" Get thee to a compost heap.
Renew, the self prays to decay. Renew!
And buckles on its shell to meet the day,
Puts off the fantasy these rooms recall,
Of apple-chasing goddesses, a King
Raining his arrows in the laden trees
That, weaponless, drop their pears in sticky grass;

Goes out-of-doors, to its own daylight domain
Where, pomegranate red, a mole on the lawn
Shrieks to the person from its several parts:
A Dionysus, dismembered by the cats
In a community of sharing: "Here! You keep
The head. I love a bloody leg!"
They must have sung in harmony, dragging limbs

About the yard; then left the god unburied,
The raw material of a ritual.

Last night this purring priesthood was caressed
Before the cellar lockup: smelling gamy,
The smoke from incense-fires in their fur;
Dark-jawed from feasting, they had toyed with Kings'
Tossed organs, skinless as the summer moon!
So self and mole shared midnight, and the twain
Lay sundered on their fields. What rose again
To mend its wounds by fading Saturday?
A solar King, a subterranean mole?

Or both? Did severed parts personify
The Prince of Darkness and the Prince of Light?
Kicking, meanwhile, this body from the lawn,
Interring bits below the apple tree
Where the foot turns loose earth around the roots
And tamps it down. But nostrils of the cats
May raise the dead. So be it. What's a grave
But plunder, to a gardener? Or a priest
Rooting up bones of martyrs for display.

The other body takes itself to bed,
Buries itself in sheets as thin as soil,
Dreams of the elevation of the Host:
Mole in a silver chalice; kneels to sup
The blood of the dying, resurrected soul.
But there is leaping in the chancel aisle;
Stale altar flowers toss their heads, and burst
In an orgy of bloom: Communion Sunday,
With Dionysus, singing from the Cross!

THE SIXTIES

Chinese Imitations

for Arthur Waley, in homage

We wrestle with non-being
to force it to yield up being;
we knock upon silence
for an answering music....
FROM THE *WÊN-FU* OF LU CHI

For Jan, in Bar Maria

after Po Chü-i

Though it's true we were young girls when we met,
We have been friends for twenty-five years.
But we still swim strongly, run up the hill from the beach without
                                                 getting too winded.
Here we idle in Ischia, a world away from our birthplace —
That colorless town! — drinking together, sisters of summer.
Now we like to have groups of young men gathered around us.
We are trivial-hearted. We don't want to die any more.

Remember, fifteen years ago, in our twin pinafores
We danced on the boards of the ferry dock at Mukilteo
Mad as yearling mares in the full moon?
Here in the morning moonlight we climbed on a workman's cart
And three young men, shouting and laughing, dragged it up
                                         through the streets of the village.
It is said we have shocked the people of Forio.
They call us Janna and Carolina, those two mad *straniere*.

Singing Aloud

after Po Chü-i

We all have our faults. Mine is trying to write poems.
New scenery, someone I like, anything sets me off!
I hear my own voice going on, like a god or an oracle,
That cello-tone, intuition. That bell-note of wisdom!

And I can't get rid of the tempting tic of pentameter,
Of the urge to impose a form on what I don't understand,
Or that which I have to transform because it's too grim as it is.
But age is improving me: Now, when I finish a poem

I no longer rush out to impose it on friendly colleagues.
I climb through the park to the reservoir, peer down at my own
                                                    reflection,
Shake a blossoming branch so I am covered with petals,
Each petal a metaphor...

By the time we reach middle life, we've all been deserted and
                                                    robbed.
But flowers and grass and animals keep me warm.
And I remind myself to become philosophic:
We are meant to be stripped down, to prepare us for something
                                                    better,

And, often, I sing aloud. As I grow older
I give way to innocent folly more and more often.
The squirrels and rabbits chime in with inaudible voices.
I feel sure that the birds make an effort to be antiphonal.

When I go to the zoo, the primates and I, in communion,
Hoot at each other, or signal with earthy gestures.
We must move farther out of town, we musical birds and animals,
Or they'll lock us up like the apes, and control us forever.

Amusing Our Daughters

after Po Chü-i,
for Robert Creeley

We don't lack people here on the Northern coast,
But they are people one meets, not people one cares for.
So I bundle my daughters into the car
And with my brother poets, go to visit you, brother.

Here come your guests! A swarm of strangers and children;
But the strangers write verses, the children are daughters like yours.
We bed down on mattresses, cots, roll up on the floor:
Outside, burly old fruit trees in mist and rain;
In every room, bundles asleep like larvae.

We waken and count our daughters. Otherwise, nothing happens.
You feed them sweet rolls and melon, drive them all to the zoo;
Patiently, patiently, ever the father, you answer their questions.
Later, we eat again, drink, listen to poems.
Nothing occurs, though we are aware you have three daughters
Who last year had four. But even death becomes part of our ease:
Poems, parenthood, sorrow, all we have learned
From these of tenderness, holds us together
In the center of life, entertaining daughters
By firelight, with cake and songs.

You, my brother, are a good and violent drinker,
Good at reciting short-line or long-line poems.
In time we will lose all our daughters, you and I,
Be temperate, venerable, content to stay in one place,
Sending our messages over the mountains and waters.

Hiding Our Love

from a poem by Emperor Wu-ti

Never believe I leave you
From any desire to go.
Never believe I live so far away
Except from necessity.
After a whole day of separation
Still your dark fragrance clings to my skin.
I carry your letter everywhere.
The sash of my dress wraps twice around my waist.
I wish it bound the two of us together.

Do you know that we both conceal our love
Because of prior sorrow, superstitious fear?
We are two citizens of a savage era
Schooled in disguises and in self-command,
Hiding our aromatic, vulnerable love.

Night Sounds

based on themes in the *Tzu Yeh*

The moonlight on my bed keeps me awake;
Living alone now, aware of the voices of evening,
A child weeping at nightmares, the faint love-cries of a woman,
Everything tinged by terror or nostalgia.

No heavy, impassive back to nudge with one foot
While coaxing, "Wake up and hold me,"
When the moon's creamy beauty is transformed
Into a map of impersonal desolation.

But, restless in this mock dawn of moonlight
That so chills the spirit, I alter our history:
You were never able to lie quite peacefully at my side,
Not the night through. Always withholding something.

Awake before morning, restless and uneasy,
Trying not to disturb me, you would leave my bed
While I lay there rigidly, feigning sleep.
Still — the night was nearly over, the light not as cold
As a full cup of moonlight.

And there were the lovely times when, to the skies' cold *No*
You cried to me, *Yes!* Impaled me with affirmation.
Now when I call out in fear, not in love, there is no answer.
Nothing speaks in the dark but the distant voices,
A child with the moon on his face, a dog's hollow cadence.

Summer near the River

themes from the *Tzu Yeh* and
the *Book of Songs*

I have carried my pillow to the windowsill
And try to sleep, with my damp arms crossed upon it,
But no breeze stirs the tepid morning.
Only I stir... Come, tease me a little!
With such cold passion, so little teasing play,
How long can we endure our life together?

No use. I put on your long dressing-gown;
The untied sash trails over the dusty floor.
I kneel by the window, prop up your shaving mirror
And pluck my eyebrows.
I don't care if the robe slides open
Revealing a crescent of belly, a tan thigh.
I can accuse that nonexistent breeze...

I am as monogamous as the North Star,
But I don't want you to know it. You'd only take advantage.
While you are as fickle as spring sunlight.
All right, sleep! The cat means more to you than I.
I can rouse you, but then you swagger out.
I glimpse you from the window, striding toward the river.

When you return, reeking of fish and beer,
There is salt dew in your hair. Where have you been?
Your clothes weren't that wrinkled hours ago, when you left.
You couldn't have loved someone else, after loving me!

I sulk and sigh, dawdling by the window.
Later, when you hold me in your arms
It seems, for a moment, the river ceases flowing.

The Skein

from a poem by Emperor Wu-ti

Moonlight through my gauze curtains
Turns them to nets for snaring wild birds,
Turns them into woven traps, into shrouds.
The old, restless grief keeps me awake.
I wander around, holding a scarf or a shawl;
In the muffled moonlight I wander around
Folding it carefully, shaking it out again.
Everyone says my old lover is happy.
I wish they said he was coming back to me.
I hesitate here, my scarf like a skein of yarn
Binding my two hands loosely
                that would reach for paper and pen.
So I memorize these lines,
Dew on the scarf, dappling my nightdress also.
O love long gone, it is raining in our room!
So I memorize these lines,
                without salutation, without close.

Winter Song

on a line from Arthur Waley

So I go on, tediously on and on...
We are separated, finally, not by death but life.
We cling to the dead, but the living break away.

On my birthday, the waxwings arrive in the garden,
Strip the trees bare as my barren heart.
I put out suet and bread for December birds:
Hung from evergreen branches, greasy gray
Ornaments for the rites of the winter solstice.

How can you and I meet face to face
After our triumphant love?
After our failure?

Since this isolation, it is always cold.
My clothes don't fit. My hair refuses to obey.
And, for the first time, I permit
These little anarchies of flesh and object.
Together, they flick me toward some final defeat.

Thinking of you, I am suddenly old...
A mute spectator as the months wind by.
I have tried to put you out of my mind forever.

Home isn't here. It went away with you,
Disappearing in the space of a breath,
In the time one takes to open a foreknown letter.
My fists are bruised from beating on the ground.
There are clouds between me and the watery light.

Truly, I try to flourish, to find pleasure
Without an endless reference to you
Who made the days and years seem worth enduring.

A Month in Summer

A Month in Summer

FIRST DAY

Several years ago, I wrote haiku in this way:

> The frost was late this year:
> Crystal nips the petals
> As my lover grows impatient.

I have come to prefer the four-line form which Nobuyuki Yuasa has used in translating Issa because, as he says, it comes closer to approximating the natural rhythm of English speech:

> Let down the curtain!
> Hamlet dies each night
> But is always revived.
> Love, too, requires genius.

Perhaps that can stand, also, as my attempt to put "O my prophetic soul!" into haiku.

SECOND DAY

> The drama of love:
> Scenes, intermissions
> Played by two actors,
> Their own spectators.

THIRD DAY

Strange how the tedium of love makes women babble, while it reduces men to a dour silence. As my voice skipped along the surfaces of communication like a water bug, below it I sensed his quiet: the murky depths of the pond.

Alone, I play a Telemann concerto on the phonograph. A rather pedantic German note on the slipcase speaks of "the curious, upward-stumbling theme." Can we be upward-stumbling? If so, there is hope for us.

> When you go away
> I play records till dawn
> To drown the echoes
> Of my own voice.

FOURTH DAY

As a reaction from trying to please, one becomes reckless and resentful:

> Lights in every room.
> I turned on more!
> You sat with one hand
> Shading your eyes.

FIFTH DAY

I listen to myself being deliberately annoying, deliberately irritating. I know so well, now, what he hates; I can so easily provoke it. It is a kind of furious attempt to rouse us both from the inert boredom with which we regard our life together. I'd like to sting him into madness, as if I were one of the Erinyes. I don't believe he is capable of understanding why I behave this way.

A party at which we play our customary roles. Later, when the guests go home, he says, "Let's have a serious talk." Invariably, he wants to have elaborate discussions only when I am dead with fatigue, and incapable of listening or responding. So I beg off. Reckless, impatient, I hurry him away.

SEVENTH DAY

Some friends come to visit for a few hours. My daughter Laurel picked roses for them, dozen after dozen, until the garden was stripped of ripening flowers. It was a relatively easy winter. The aphids seemed to be under control this year. One must not allow one's self to become superstitious about the tremendous, massive florescence of roses, nor about the great numbers of pregnant women. It doesn't necessarily mean that the days of the world are numbered; merely that the life-impulse is putting forth an extra effort, just in case.

EIGHTH DAY

We agree not to see each other for a while. Now for a period of bravado, while we pretend that we have no need for that total, mutual dependence which has been habitual for so long.

NINTH DAY

Sometimes it's best to run away for a little.

TENTH DAY

I decided to return the visit of my friends. So, with my two daughters, I drove south. When we arrived, we saw the flowers Laurel had picked for them three days earlier. We had packed the masses of roses — white, yellow, and heat-faded pink — into a ten-gallon jar. The bouquet is still a large, fresh globe, in spite of the warmth of a four-hour drive and the passing of thirsty days.

> Roses should always
> Rest in glass containers
> Revealing the pattern
> Of packed thorns and stems.

How happy one can seem — even to one's self — in the presence of others!

ELEVENTH DAY

> On the porch two squirrels,
> Half-grown and chubby,
> Play at making love.
> And we parents smile.

TWELFTH DAY

In the afternoon, my daughters and my father and I go out on a friend's boat, to the river that seems as vast as a sea. My old father stays in the cabin while the rest of the adults brace their feet on the deck and drink the spray. Laurel, eleven, sits inside with him and takes his hand, and says, "Are you all right, Grandpa?" I am touched by her gentle and tactful solicitude. And I reflect that there is a difference of over seventy years in their ages.

THIRTEENTH DAY

We came home last night. I drove slowly, with a cargo of two sleeping children. After they were in bed, I took presents to his house, as it was his birthday. But it looked as if he had retired for the night, so I left the gifts on the screen-porch.

> The shadow of leaves
> On your door, at night...
> I'm a young girl again,
> Tiptoeing home.

The pattern of the maple, etched by the streetlamp shining against the side of his house, reminded me of my own home, years ago. The silhouettes of leaves and whiplike branches of our old white birch would be flickering on the porch when I came home late and alone. Perhaps, too, that same sense of desolation I felt then: a young girl in a small town, without congenial friends, with aging parents. Lovers as yet unmet, in the far-off cities of my imagination...

FOURTEENTH DAY

He telephoned to ask if I would mind if he exchanged the present I had given him. I knew when I picked it out that he wouldn't care for it. Even in this perversity I'm not being original, but am behaving like every woman mismanaging every love affair on record. I suppose that what we want is to be given a cuff, and told to behave ourselves!

FIFTEENTH DAY

School is out for the summer. The children will be away for a few weeks, and I can concentrate all of my time and attention on being unhappy. One should always end a love affair in summer, when one's social life is at an ebb, and the sun is shining. Sunlight provides the excuse for dark glasses to hide swollen eyelids, and permits the important events of one's life to take place unwitnessed, as in Greek tragedy.

> Alone in my house
> I can make gross noises
> Like a caught hare or stoat
> Or a woman in labor.

SIXTEENTH DAY

Nearly every night I dream of my mother, dead these four years. I remember reading an account by a well-known doctor, himself the victim of the agonizing disease which had been his specialty, saying that in extreme pain we all call for our mothers.

> I dream of the dead,
> Kind, brilliant, and comforting.
> The lost return to us
> When we are lost.

SEVENTEENTH DAY

Inertia, planned and involuntary. Do things come to an end because we no longer have the energy to pursue them, or does the prescience of this ending drain us of energy?

EIGHTEENTH DAY

> The pleasure of pain:
> It destroys pretension.
> We abandon effort
> And live lying down.

Inertia.

One of the profound consolations in reading the works of Japanese men of letters is their frank acknowledgment of neurotic sloth. Or the overwhelming impulse, when faced with hurt or conflict, to stay in bed under the covers!

Make a gigantic effort. Surely there are at least three or four persons, out of the four hundred thousand inhabitants of this city, whom I would care to see.

Later: I drove out to visit two artist friends. One of them is painting butterbur, but isn't fond of the name of it. I am reminded of the episode in Issa's journal when an eleven-year-old priest named Takamaru slips while crossing a bridge, and is drowned. When his body is discovered, wedged between two rocks, "even the sleeves of those unused to weep were wet with tears when they discovered in his pocket a few blossoms of butterbur—just picked—perhaps intended as a happy present for his parents...."

> *For G.*
> Your paintings of butterbur
> Might be called "Colt's Foot"
> Or, simply, "Homage
> To Takamaru."

That should be suitably obscure!

G. is angry and impatient with his work: "They just look *pretty* and *cheap!*" he storms, and has to be restrained from doing away with them.

> You hate the paintings
> Made with such love.
> Not you who are mad
> But a mad century!

TWENTY-FIRST DAY

Is it suffering which defeminizes? Or the sense that one is relinquishing sexual love, perhaps forever?

> Neutered and wistful,
> My spinster cat
> Stands on my chest
> And laps up my tears.

Each morning I am wakened by my own weeping and the rasp, rasp of the little cat's tongue across my cheek.

TWENTY-SECOND DAY

I run across my friend on the street and we talk for a bit. He urges me into a nearby "greasy spoon" for a cup of coffee. We sit at a table smeared with food and cluttered with soiled dishes. A water glass holds cigarette stubs and wet ashes. I am feeling quite faint. No one waits on us. I get up to run away, but he insists that I sit down again. We analyze, very calmly, very objectively, the faults we find in each other. How trivial they are! Idiotic! Don't we dare to broach the larger topics? And love — doesn't it endure somewhere peacefully, like an underground river, beneath all this dust and meaningless commotion on the surface?

However, we both seem relieved of some tension by this exchange, and part amiably.

TWENTY-THIRD DAY

> No, I am *not*
> A cricket in a matchbox,
> Nor are you a boy,
> To keep pets in your pocket.

We meet. We talk. And so? Nothing changes.

TWENTY-FOURTH DAY

An acquaintance reproaches me: "You shouldn't give him up. The world is overrun with lost, lonely women. Make any compromise."

I am too arrogant to take something over nothing. But I well know that all my arrogance is going to be flayed out of me. I am going to be stripped and flayed of all of it. *He* doesn't know that he is going to do this to me; he protests violently when I tell him so. But I know it.

TWENTY-FIFTH DAY

> Strange how the range
> Of possibility dwindles.
> Imagination fails us
> When we need her most.

There should be so many alternative courses of action. Instead, self-destruction becomes finally comprehensible.

The terror of loss:
Not the grief of a wet branch
In autumn, but the absolute
Arctic desolation.

One simply lies in the dark contemplating loss, as if it were luminous: in itself a kind of mystic experience.

TWENTY-SIXTH DAY

Do I see him approaching? Instinctively, I flinch, duck my head, crook an arm across my face. I hurry past, and don't really know if he saw me or not.

Your handsomeness. I find it
An irrelevant fact
To file away carefully
For my old age.

The other day I caught a glimpse of him playing the pinball machine in the same coffee shop where we met last week. Are *his* days such a wasteland then?

TWENTY-SEVENTH DAY

Seen through tears
This moonlight
Is no more poignant
Than a saucer of cream.

Why the artifice of this *haibun*, which I have appropriated from a culture which doesn't belong to me? Perhaps to lose *me*. Perhaps because the only way to deal with sorrow is to find a form in which to contain it. And, at last, surely it is time to study restraint?

A tanka:

> I stayed up all night
> Till the sky turned to saffron
> Behind black mountains.
>
> I saw the color of hell
> Has its own kind of beauty.

TWENTY-NINTH DAY

I was playing the Telemann concerto over and over. I bought two copies and gave one to my friend. Now I am reduced to wondering whether we are listening to the same record at the same time of night.

> The music I play
> This summer and fall:
> Will I hear it at sixty
> And be ready to die?

Perhaps at the extremes of happiness or unhappiness, one should take care that only inferior works of art will be contaminated by nostalgia. And, after all, it is well known that a cheap popular song can arouse through its associations a more violent reaction than the greatest composition.

It's all over.

> I realize now
> The dialectic error:
> Not love against death,
> But hope, the bulwark.

Holding his letter, barely skimmed, in my hand, I drove to the house of my only intimate friend. She was not at home. I caught a glimpse of myself reflected in a window: a reeling ghost. Suddenly G., the artist, appeared before me. Though in ten years we've hardly exchanged a personal word, I took his hand and held it very tightly in both of mine, and he supported me along the street to my car.

Much later, at G.'s house, I saw the other copy of the Telemann, which I had given my friend, lying on the table. So, the links are broken.

Nothing remains.

And the worst, unimaginable until now: it is as if nothing had ever been.

"Is that what is meant by dwelling in unreality? And here too I end my words."

Pro Femina

Pro Femina

ONE

From Sappho to myself, consider the fate of women.
How unwomanly to discuss it! Like a noose or an albatross necktie
The clinical sobriquet hangs us: codpiece coveters.
Never mind these epithets; I myself have collected some honeys.
Juvenal set us apart in denouncing our vices
Which had grown, in part, from having been set apart:
Women abused their spouses, cuckolded them, even plotted
To poison them. Sensing, behind the violence of his manner —
"Think I'm crazy or drunk?" — his emotional stake in us,
As we forgive Strindberg and Nietzsche, we forgive all those
Who cannot forget us. We *are* hyenas. Yes, we admit it.

While men have politely debated free will, we have howled for it,
Howl still, pacing the centuries, tragedy heroines.
Some who sat quietly in the corner with their embroidery
Were Defarges, stabbing the wool with the names of their ancient
Oppressors, who ruled by the divine right of the male —
I'm impatient of interruptions! I'm aware there were millions
Of mutes for every Saint Joan or sainted Jane Austen,
Who, vague-eyed and acquiescent, worshiped God as a man.
I'm not concerned with those cabbageheads, not truly feminine
But neutered by labor. I mean real women, like *you* and like *me*.

Freed in fact, not in custom, lifted from furrow and scullery,
Not obliged, now, to be the pot for the annual chicken,
Have we begun to arrive in time? With our well-known
Respect for life because it hurts so much to come out with it;
Disdainful of "sovereignty," "national honor," and other abstractions;

We can say, like the ancient Chinese to successive waves of invaders,
"Relax, and let us absorb *you.* You can learn temperance
In a more temperate climate." Give us just a few decades
Of grace, to encourage the fine art of acquiescence
And we might save the race. Meanwhile, observe our creative chaos,
Flux, efflorescence — whatever you care to call it!

TWO

I take as my theme "The Independent Woman,"
Independent but maimed: observe the exigent neckties
Choking violet writers; the sad slacks of stipple-faced matrons;
Indigo intellectuals, crop-haired and callus-toed,
Cute spectacles, chewed cuticles, aced out by full-time beauties
In the race for a male. Retreating to drabness, bad manners,
And sleeping with manuscripts. Forgive our transgressions
Of old gallantries as we hitch in chairs, light our own cigarettes,
Not expecting your care, having forfeited it by trying to get even.

But we need dependency, cosseting, and well-treatment.
So do men sometimes. Why don't they admit it?
We will be cows for a while, because babies howl for us,
Be kittens or bitches, who want to eat grass now and then
For the sake of our health. But the role of pastoral heroine
Is not permanent, Jack. We want to get back to the meeting.

Knitting booties and brows, tartars or termagants, ancient
Fertility symbols, chained to our cycle, released
Only in part by devices of hygiene and personal daintiness,
Strapped into our girdles, held down, yet uplifted by man's
Ingenious constructions, holding coiffures in a breeze,
Hobbled and swathed in whimsy, tripping on feminine
Shoes with fool heels, losing our lipsticks, you, me,
In ephemeral stockings, clutching our handbags and packages.

Our masks, always in peril of smearing or cracking,
In need of continuous check in the mirror or silverware,
Keep us in thrall to ourselves, concerned with our surfaces.
Look at man's uniform drabness, his impersonal envelope!
Over chicken wrists or meek shoulders, a formal, hard-fibered
                                        assurance.
The drape of the male is designed to achieve self-forgetfulness.

So, Sister, forget yourself a few times and see where it gets you:
Up the creek, alone with your talent, sans everything else.
You can wait for the menopause, and catch up on your reading.
So primp, preen, prink, pluck, and prize your flesh,
All posturings! All ravishment! All sensibility!
Meanwhile, have you used your mind today?
What pomegranate raised you from the dead,
Springing, full-grown, from your own head, Athena?

THREE

I will speak about women of letters, for I'm in the racket.
Our biggest successes to date? Old maids to a woman.
And our saddest conspicuous failures? The married spinsters
On loan to the husbands they treated like surrogate fathers.
Think of that crew of self-pitiers, not-very-distant,
Who carried the torch for themselves and got first-degree burns.
Or the sad sonneteers, toast-and-teasdales we loved at thirteen;
Middle-aged virgins seducing the puerile anthologists
Through lust-of-the-mind; barbiturate-drenched Camilles
With continuous periods, murmuring softly on sofas
When poetry wasn't a craft but a sickly effluvium,
The air thick with incense, musk, and emotional blackmail.

I suppose they reacted from an earlier womanly modesty
When too many girls were scabs to their stricken sisterhood,
Impugning our sex to stay in good with the men,
Commencing their insecure bluster. How they must have swaggered
When women themselves endorsed their own inferiority!
Vestals, vassals, and vessels, rolled into several,
They took notes in rolling syllabics, in careful journals,
Aiming to please a posterity that despises them.
But we'll always have traitors who swear that a woman surrenders
Her Supreme Function, by equating Art with aggression
And failure with Femininity. Still, it's just as unfair
To equate Art with Femininity, like a prettily packaged commodity
When we are the custodians of the world's best-kept secret:
Merely the private lives of one-half of humanity.

But even with masculine dominance, we mares and mistresses
Produced some sleek saboteuses, making their cracks
Which the porridge-brained males of the day were too thick to
                                                    perceive,
Mistaking young hornets for perfectly harmless bumblebees.
Being thought innocuous rouses some women to frenzy;
They try to be ugly by aping the ways of men
And succeed. Swearing, sucking cigars and scorching the bedspread,

Slopping straight shots, eyes blotted, vanity-blown
In the expectation of glory: *she writes like a man!*
This drives other women mad in a mist of chiffon.
(One poetess draped her gauze over red flannels, a practical feminist.)

But we're emerging from all that, more or less,
Except for some ladylike laggards and Quarterly priestesses
Who flog men for fun, and kick women to maim competition.
Now, if we struggle abnormally, we may almost seem normal;

If we submerge our self-pity in disciplined industry;
If we stand up and be hated, and swear not to sleep with editors;
If we regard ourselves formally, respecting our true limitations
Without making an unseemly show of trying to unfreeze our assets;
Keeping our heads and our pride while remaining unmarried;
And if wedded, kill guilt in its tracks when we stack up the dishes
And defect to the typewriter. And if mothers, believe in the luck of
our children,
Whom we forbid to devour us, whom we shall not devour,
And the luck of our husbands and lovers, who keep free women.

THE SEVENTIES

Where I've Been All My Life

I.

Sirs, in our youth you love the sight of us.
Older, you fall in love with what we've seen,
Would lose yourselves by living in our lives.
I'll spin you tales, play the Arabian girl;
Working close, alone in the blond arena,
Flourish my cape, the cloth on the camera.
For women learn to be a holy show.

I'll tell you where I've been, not what I am:
In Rotterdam, womb where my people sprang,
I find my face, my father, everywhere.
New cousins I must stoop to greet, the get
Of tall, whey-colored burghers, sturdy dams,
As children fed on tulip bulbs and dirt,
Tugged at dry dugs and sucked at winter's rind.

My cousins, dwarfed by war! Your forms rebuke
The butcher and the bystander alike.
To ease you I can't shrink this big Dutch frame
Got of more comfortable ancestors.
But from my Southern side I pluck a phrase,
"I'll carry you." And it means "rest in me,"
To hold you as I may, in my mind's womb.

But snap the album, get the guidebook out!
Rotterdam: her raw, gray waterfront,
Zadkine's memorial burning on the quay;
This bronze is mortal, gaping in defeat,
The form that wombed it split to let it be.

It mends; he lurches up, in blood reborn,
The empty heavens his eternal frame.

II.

Move to my room beside the Golden Horn
Where minarets strike fire against the sky.
The architecture: breasts and phalluses.
Where are the words to say that words are lies?
Yeats lied. And here Byzantium lies dead.
Constantinople? Syllables in a text.
Istanbul. Real. Embalmed in dancing dust.

Everywhere the dark-brown past gives way
To the beige of progress, that wide vacant lot.
Turkey without coffee! Endlessly we sip tea
From bud vases, and I lust for the guide,
A sultry, serious, pedantic boy
In a tight brown suit, thirsting to get out
Of the triple city weighing on his mind.

Oh, he was doomed, doomed like the dogs
On Dog Island, in the sea,
Netted and dumped and exiled, left to die,
Then skinned. We heard imaginary canine howls,
Like the rustlings of a thousand gauzy girls,
Film-eyed cattle, perishing of ennui
In abandoned harems where he guided me.

Meanwhile the Faithful, prostrate and intoning,
Stare into the light as blind as death,
Knowing for sure their end is instant Heaven.
We Infidels concede them Paradise,

Having seen heaven-as-harem, a eunuch God
In charge: the virgin slowly fattening to blubber.
Love, become feminized, tickles like a feather.

The saints of Art? Sophia, that vast barn
Holds no small Savior waiting to get born.
The formal scribble on the assaulted walls —
Five hundred years of crossing out His name!
Some famous, glittering pebbles mark the place
As God's most grandiose sarcophagus.
Decay, decay. And the mind, a fetus, dies.

III.

Return me to the airfield near Shanghai
Where I am very young: shy, apprehensive,
Seated like Sheba on a baggage mountain
Waiting for the first adventure to begin.
The train will glide through fields of rice and men,
Bodies like thongs, and glorious genitals,
Not alien as Chinese, but Adam-strange.

Rejoiced by her first look at naked men,
Her soul swims out the window of the train!
She goes where newborn daughters clog the creeks;
Bank-porticoes are strewn with starving rags.
Here the old dragon, China, thrashes, dying.
But the ancient, virile music of the race
Is rising, drenched in gongs and howls of dogs

Islanded, the sighs of walled-up women
Dreaming of peasants in their prisoning fields...
But we break out of the harem of history!

No longer that young foreigner on the train,
I listen like a bird, although I ruminate
Like a cow, in my pale Holland body, riven
By love and children. These eyes are what they see.

Come die with me in the mosques of Rotterdam.

The Dying Goddess

The love goddess, alas, grows frailer.
She still has her devotees
But their hearts are not whole.
They follow young boys
From the corners of their eyes.
They become embarrassed
By their residual myths.
Odd cults crop up, involving midgets,
Partial castration, dismemberment of children.
The goddess wrings her hands; they think it vanity
And it is, partly.

Sometimes, in her precincts
Young men bow curly heads.
She sends them packing
Indulgently, with blown kisses.
There are those who pray endlessly,
Stretched full-length with their eyes shut,
Imploring her, "Mother!"
She taps her toe at these. A wise goddess
Knows her own children.

On occasion, her head raises
Almost expectantly: a man steps forward.
She takes one step forward,
They exchange wistful glances.
He is only passing.
When he comes to the place
Of no destination
He takes glass after glass

As her image wavers.
In her own mirror the image wavers.
She turns her face from the smokeless brazier.

The Copulating Gods

Brushing back the curls from your famous brow,
Lingering over the prominent temple vein
Purple as Aegean columns in the dawn,
Calm now, I ponder how self-consciously
The gods must fornicate.
It is that sense of unseen witness:
Those mortals with whom we couple or have coupled,
Clinging to our swan-suits, our bull-skins,
Our masquerades in coin and shrubbery.

We were their religion before they were born.
The spectacle of our carnality
Confused them into spiritual lust.
The headboard of our bed became their altar,
Rare nectar, shared, a common sacrament.
The wet drapery of our sheets, molded
To noble thighs, is made the basis
For a whole new aesthetic:
God is revealed as the first genius.

Men continue to invent our histories,
Deny our equal pleasure in each other.
Clubfoot, nymphomaniac, they dub us,
Then fabricate the net that God will cast
Over our raptures: we, trussed up like goats,
Paraded past the searchlights of the sky
By God himself, the ringmaster and cuckold,
Amidst a thunderous laughter and applause.

Tracing again the bones of your famous face,
I know we are not their history but our myth.
Heaven prevents time; and our astral raptures
Float buoyant in the universe. Come, kiss!
Come, swoon again, we who invented dying
And the whole alchemy of resurrection.
They will concoct a scripture explaining this.

The Way We Write Letters

for Robert Peterson

We must lie long in the weeds
In places like Palo Alto or Perugia,
Get lost to find ourselves, get going *soon.*
But none of the old Hearth & Home;
Be a Logan or Creeley, all arrowheads
And .22 cartridges studded and strewn inside,
Find new places to rest and nest. Get looser;
Get back to (you said) daytime drinking, mu-
Sic of Telemann, Schütz, Buxtehude.
Don't keep your house in order.
If you have any further suggestions for
Improving chaos, please write or wire.

We should lie long in the woods, full of light.
Old friends get published again, though losing
Their moon & vinegar. Write me soon (I said).
Meanwhile, find a new place too,
Where air, not character, is cool.
Not Sausalito. San Gimignano?
There, despite psychiatry, towers simply *are*
In a piercing, lyric, prodigal confusion,
Regulated. Well, remember Heller in Paradise.
Madness & you (we both said). Stay sane and annoyed,
Drunk in the daytime. Call your book *Home for the Night.*
But don't go home tomorrow. Write me instead
From the meadow. Turn on the poem & the light.

The Italian Kittens

for Jan, again

The saggy-bellied cat of Bar Maria,
Alley-gray, all female self-deprecation:
Pendulous lean sides sway as she prowls
And scavenges beneath the café tables
Undulating among limbs, shaved (non-Italian)
Or in foreign flannel. One would say
She connotes classic malnutrition, not fecundity.
Yet that waif, lapping up spilled Campari
Or teasing the leprous goldfish in the fountain,
Slides into maternity one day.

She is called Carolina. Delightedly the waiters
Point to my appellation and her litter: three,
Two girls and a boy, duplicating my own endeavors.
What could be more tender or more flattering than
To call them, though unpronounceable, after my distant brood?
Perturbed though they are, the staff of the bar
And the vocal hangers-on, that no child of mine
Bears a Saint's name, an exception is made. We cheer,
Toasting the kittens, the mother, and one another.
"Teary with mutual concord" describes our mood.

Three days later, the plump waiter named Tonino
Leads me from the umbrella-blooming terrace
To the kitchen side: Fish churn in tubs
Awaiting supper (ours); a carpet of spoiled grapes
Popping beneath our feet; old lettuce leaves on flagstones
Ground to calligraphy of translucent green:
The nether regions, dank with vice and ptomaine.

I inhale Italy. He beckons, I hang back.
But he urges me to gaze into a bucket
Where I find three kittens drowned, my quondam family.

Streets of Pearl and Gold

'Tis not what it once was, the World;
But a rude heap together hurl'd....

ANDREW MARVELL

I.

Within, walls white as canvas stretched to stain;
A tabula rasa clean as a stripped bed.
The painter's order: jars and brushes neat,
Harmoniously fixed, like palette clots.
Here, perilous in this secret nest, he paces,
Naked and fierce, dressed only in his paint;
His place condemned, pinched nearer by the beast,
The lover streaked with motley, seeing white,
Would cuff the ball and hammer with his fist
But hides instead, frowns, grappling with art:
Waves and flames and clouds and wounds and rags.
While I sit careless on the bed; I float
Posing as Venus in a pearly boat.
How wide we dream! His picturing and mine,
As the light glitters, deepening our breath
Until we sink for pearls through profound seas,
Swimming before the funeral of the earth.

II.

Outside, the buildings kneel as if yielding up
To the levelers their infirm confessions:
Not rats or roaches in the wainscot
Nor the old staled odors of man's functioning
But that they were chalice of our history,

And this, a pastoral Dutch village. Here
In a black-shuttered tavern, clarks and squires
In linsey-woolsey, plotted revolution!

Yea, the streets were steep with mud and dung
From which we raised ourselves a dwelling-place,
On sober frames affixed a frontispiece.
Later, these first buildings failed in form
When they admitted to their broken cells
Child-sweat and chilblain, women laboring
Hook-shouldered, early deformed by the machine:
A house of light become a cave of pain.

Now cornice, fretwork, sagging pediment,
Outliving purity and sin, each warrant signed,
Tell more than Bowery faces of our fate.
The stain is mortal on their livid meat,
Emptier than this periled wood and stone.
A lover carved here, priding in his skill,
Above the old eye-levels, garland, gargoyle,
In the time of the artisan, when our land was small.

III.

Sun dust. Noon is noiseless. Stink of fish
From Fulton, all the produce gone by ten
Save for squashed jelly, viscid scales
Rusting and iridescent. Seasoning sprinkled
On the cooked street.

A wino crawls onto a briny tray,
Lies down in inches of leftover sea.
Curling, crustacean-red, he dozes his nondeath away.

Nearby. The pier where we watch trawlers:
Mending their nets, men sweat, look up, scowl, smile;
Held still a moment, beetles caught in crystal.
The River is brown jelly in the sun.

Between the air and water flies the Bridge:
The twang of her long azure strings...
Below us, grass grows over boards and water;
AMERICA, THE DEAD IN CHRIST RISE FIRST
On bulkheads scrawled unevenly, fuzzing chalk
Xs in rows, the childlike mark of love.

IV.

Retreat to darkness, two dark flights away!
Tin ceilings, thinly blue: pale rippling.
All afternoon the water undulates...

The sky is silent. For the wino in the tray.
He has not moved, or died.

We rouse in the opal twilight, open eyes:
Dust, a marble crust ground underfoot;
Splintering sills crumble, frame the street
Laid like a whip across the backs of blasted lots
Near rubble mountains raised by dying men.

Bits of the old town lean on the August air,
Wait blindly for the X of the builder-killers,
Their multitudinous eyes taped out.

Racks of white crosses fenestrate the night,
Before the two hairs cross in the last bombsight.

And who are we, for whom our country cares?
America makes crosses of us all.
Each artist in his fortress: boiling oil
A weapon still. Seething across his canvases, a fury
Flung over white, ripped out: the X in paint.

v.

Art is this marveling fury of spurned love.
Caught in this present, impatient of histories,
Even your own, while you mourn what vanishes.
Who endures, rootless? But our roots are strewn
On every pavement, smashed or drowned in brine.

Observe the world with desperate affection;
Snatch up your brush to catch it, fix it all
On canvases which, stacked against a wall,
Dozen on dozen, are crumbling unseen.
Paint out the day and you will keep the time:

Exhaust fumes, and a building's trembling dust,
Fish entrails, wino-reek, and attic waste,
The shapes below the names on billboard signs,
And — what the bums find early — paint the dirt
Which we all come to: paint the old dirt sleep.

So stamp your canvas with the X of loss,
Art mutilated, stained with abuse and rage.
But mark it also as the cross of love
Who holds this woman-flesh, touch it alive,
As I try to keep us, here upon this page.

The Good Author

for Bernard Malamud

Contrary to the views
A few days earlier
Of a fading Irish poet
Who flared into the room
With Rimbaud round his shoulder
But with hair and spirit
Receding, too much the wise
Predator not to know it,
You told us to be good.
Meaning: pure in spirit,
To strive for purity.
"Oh, play as much as you like!
But remember that an author
Is one who labors daily
Putting words to paper,
Not a man who wrote a book,"
You concluded, quietly, gravely.

We were aware as we walked
Through the campus in the snow
Of a game of hare and hound:
We found him chasing her
In tighter and tighter circles,
The innocent one flying
From wily nose and jaws.
Then he cracked the diameter,
And the only rule she knew,
To plunge her to the ground.

We could not save her, nor
Quickly enough turn away,
Fists over ears, lids clenched
From the brilliant agony.
And now your calm tones linger,
But tinctured with her cry.
Though I shall not wed the image
To any word you say.

Two Poets by the Lake

for James Wright

I.

Here lakeshore modulated to a cove;
Mud-hens, ducks, and grebes came coasting near our hands.
A few aggressive gulls snatched at stale loaves
We had not yet broken, drove the others back
As we cast our bread on February waters.

You had turned away from the chrome-trimmed car,
The too-neat frozen lawns across the street;
Mailbox and fireplug on the parking strip
Like squat fraternal twins, regarding us.

Pale with cold, and the forcing of emotion,
You shook off chrome, and crumbs, the century,
And bade me enter your chill pastoral.

You failed, I failed. We fed the waterfowl,
Stayed as we came, shaken, disconsolate,
In hope that something further might be said,
It was told now, a cold story, unresolved;
The raw scream of a gull ripped the sky's gray caul.

Vacuous, I gazed into the lake
Reflecting various vain waterfowl
As I could not, would not, mirror you.
How the vapor of your voice rose overhead!

The word made visible, a trance, an ectoplasm,
A sign, in smoke, to the skeptical believer
Who said, "It's no use, Tom. Let's go on home."

II.

What a bucolic poem you wrote then!
Postbox and plug were gone; a moderate season;
A country lake, not town. The selective artist
Erased gulls, mallards, coots, and candy-wrappers,
Laid bedding grass upon the muddy shore.

We lie down side by side, are lost in love
Instead of simply lost. We go home to each other:
And so, fulfilled, though time and place are gone,
Though we have not touched, except on paper.

Do you still look for the lady of the lake?
Or walk, waist-deep, into the quaking waters,
Fracturing your reflection as you go?

III.

I add a coda to your poem here:
Where we paraded our rapt self-dismay,
Muffled and breathy, numb-lipped and morose,
Wildlife has fled. No more
Articulate doubts and moldy crusts of bread.

A hydroplane has sliced across your voice;
The passive, silvery bay, churned to morass.
Pits have been dug, where the wide-backed hulls
Nest before racing, bed in grease and noise.

Then, summoned to the starting line,
Take off like a pack of bloodhounds baying
Each time the hulls hit water as they fly
Past shoals of bystanders, tireless and morbid, waiting
By our shallows, for a death or agony.

They face, as we did not, a final mating:
Boat slams into boat, buoy, or debris.
A cushion, or a sodden book of verse
One drunken lover drops from his canoe
Can toss three thousand horses. Fatality!

Now raw, but moribund, in this midwinter,
Still the deserted pits, the barren bank
Represent a violent coming-together,
Given the man, the water, the event.

While we are true neither to life nor nature,
But perhaps to each other as we write:
Your sensuous pastoral, or my murky weather,
The laying of the past, line upon line.
The balked need urgent in your words, and mine.

Poem, Small and Delible

We have been picketing Woolworth's.

> This page, some day, under the Poetry Decoder
> Set for 20, Midcentury, Western, White, Decline,
> A brown tatter pinned beneath a lens
> Will stall here: What is the verb "to picket"?
> And what, a Woolworth? A form of primitive market?
> Perhaps they weighed and sorted fleece, then sold it.

We have been picketing Woolworth's

> It is mysterious to many, even now:
> Thirty-six people sweating and circling
> Woolworth's on a summer's day, in a Northern town.
> Three spectators ask: What *Is* Segregation?
> You Should Be Ashamed!!! SIT-INS. What's them?
> Laboriously picking out syllables

From our homemade posters, picketing Woolworth's

> Notes for the student: Woolworth's, one of a series
> Of regional emporia, privately owned, and under
> A centralized management, designed to cater
> To mass taste and income... Picket: See *Pike*, a weapon.
> (2) A pointed or sharpened stake, a peg or pale.
> Or, (3) A sentry, set to guard an army.

And so we walked with words impaled on stakes:

SUPPORT OUR SOUTHERN BRETHREN.

BOYCOTT WOOLWORTH'S.

(From *Boycott,* a notorious Irish captain.)
Sit-ins? But the words are baffling, as arcane
As poems. Who cares, lady? I'd picket Woolworth's
Any day, on general principles. Indignation:
Why don't you people leave poor old Woolworth's alone?

We, paying our homage to Mohandas Gandhi,

Cast our handwritten signs, our unwritten poems,
On his pyre. Here the decoder won't stutter
Nor the lens hesitate. They will know who *he* was,
And that Art and Action, mostly incompatible,
Could support each other now and then. *Voici
Que j'ai dessein encore d'un petit poème délébile
Picketing Woolworth's.*

Lines to Accompany Flowers for Eve

who took heroin, then sleeping pills,
and who lies in a New York hospital

The florist was told, cyclamen or azalea;
White in either case, for you are pale
As they are, "blooming early and profusely"
Though the azalea grows in sandier soil,
Needing less care; while cyclamen's fleshy tubers
Are adored, yes, rooted out by some.
One flourishes in aridness, while the other
Feeds the love which devours.

But what has flung you here for salvaging
From a city's dereliction, this New York?
A world against whose finger-and-breath-marked windows
These weak flares may be set.
Our only bulwark is the frailest cover:
Lovers touch from terror of being alone.
The urban surface: tough and granular,
Poor ground for the affections to take root.

Left to our own devices, we devise
Such curious deaths, comas, or mutilations!
You may buy peace, white, in sugary tincture,
No way of knowing its strength, or your own,
Until you lie quite still, your perfect limbs
In meditation: the spirit rouses, flutters
Like a handkerchief at a cell window, signaling,
Self-amazed, its willingness to endure.

The thing to cling to is the sense of expectation.
Who knows what may occur in the next breath?
In the pallor of another morning we neither
Anticipated nor wanted! Eve, waken to flowers
Unforeseen, from someone you don't even know.
Azalea or cyclamen... we live in wonder,
Blaze in a cycle of passion and apprehension
Though once we lay and waited for a death.

The First of June Again

Dateline Saigon: Marines wait in the rain
For the Buddhists to rise.
It's monsoon time: Marines in the water's rush
Turn their carbines upside down
To keep the barrels dry.

We wait — and the season pauses in midstream:
Suddenly, Buddhists, in the steam and hush,
Spring like mushrooms from the cracked wet pavement.
Some priests levitate; one, "an ungainly jumping-jack
In his saffron robes," leaps in the air, gesticulating.
All is silent, for a spreading moment.
Then one Marine lobs a grenade...

The pattern is set. The circle breaks, reforms;
When a cluster is dense enough to be worthwhile
Riot-police fling tear gas. We bystanders loiter and cry.
At least we give them that:
The Vietnamese are pleased to see us cry.

Meanwhile, this very day, in *The New York Times,*
Mr. Reston says, "War has a life of its own.
Officials may hesitate, but machines produce.
Men argue and loiter, but the training camps
And factories meet their quotas,
And the ships sail on time."

Today, along the Pacific Coast, the redwoods fall.
When you've seen one, you've seen 'em all,
Says the Governor of California.

Around these red wounds and amputated stumps
The magic fungus rings are springing up.

Smashed by the logger's boot, they return next season.
And the timber-Gestapo are only obeying orders.
Orders for redwood siding are piling up.
Burls can be polished to a fine patine.
They would make lamp-bases for the shades
Of Ilse Koch.

But when we loiter near a national park,
Counting the rings on those great clocks of time
The loggers have laid bare,
Is there anywhere a break or hesitation in the ring
That reveals a civilization so dismayed
And so dismaying, that its children wanted it to stop?

Tawny we rise, one more time, in our broken circles,
Children of the giant mushroom, blind
From its blaze, choked by its pillar of smoke.
Caught here, pinned down by our own malaise.
As the gods and oracles warned us for centuries,
Presumption is punished.
We were not ready for their toys.

Here in the California rain an action detains us:
An ungainly jumping-jack in his peculiar clothes leaps up.
With a wild whoop, we follow him. Come, jumping-jack,
Poor Jackself!
And the National Guard and the civil police
Turn their rifles right-side up.

        1966, 1967, 1968, 1969, 1970, and on and on...

Season of Lovers and Assassins

Safe from the wild storms off Cape Hatteras,
Hastily stripped, in the warm surf we embrace.

The storm we made has flung us to the sand.
A force not thought has plunged each into each.

Trailing our clothes like seaweed up the beach,
We swim to sleep, and drown, entwined in dreams.

The other ocean wakes us, where a gun
Struck, as we slept, a caring public man.

From early dawn, zoo noises bruise our ears
Played on TV's gray window to the news.

Blood fills the famous brain. The rains descend
(your gentle hands), a continent of tears.

One passionate harsh light has been put out.
Numbly we move to the noontime of our love:

The strip of rain-pocked shore gleams pallidly.
Fragments of broken palm-frond fly like knives

Through tropic wind. Soon we bear star-shaped wounds,
Stigmata of all passion-driven lives.

We leave this island, safety, to our fate,
Wrapt in a caul of vulnerability,

Marked lovers now, the moony night is ours,
Surf-sounds reminding us that good decay

Surrounds us: force which pounds on flesh or stone,
The slow assassination of the years.

The Wars in Sweden

The streets of Stockholm are churning with guerrillas.
Shouting fierce chants of war, they vomit in doorways.
Blond Indians wear beaded bands across their brows;
Deerskin and fringe adorn them, cindery moccasins
Soften the icy sidewalks where they war-dance,
Then regroup for a final assault on the spirit of Santa Claus.

All wars are concentrated here; this is a nerve center
Where revolutions communicate via satellite: Hanoi with Biafra.
Pigs of the Greek junta kick Chicago hippies in the groin,
Then amputate their hair while pronouncing sentence.
The citizen armies of Stockholm brandish tin cups
For the justified causes. At night on TV, all blood is gray.

In this sculptured city there are no monuments to war,
Only the stale air of moral victory. Forget you sold iron ore
To Hitler, while the Danish King wore a yellow armband reading

JUDEN,

And the bitter Finns won for weeks in the snows of Lake Ladoga.
Instead, you deplore America. How sorry you are for New York,
Her torn inhabitants, her labyrinthine racial tunnels!

Progressive film-directors offer ice-bound sanctuary
To our deserters, while exporting films that make intercourse boring,
Hoping, perhaps, to cool off the West. Care-packages of snow
May be next, stamped in little molds of Chairman Mao.
Bestowing your winter purity on the world, poor Sweden!
Being the conscience of the white race isn't much fun.

Voyager

for Charles Gullans

I.

Digging my claws in sand, I crawled ashore.
Children stopped their play to stare. One boy
Threw me his coat, then fled. I fell asleep
Easily, on this mild, familiar strand.
Women came running, hauled me up, then clung
Like faded pennons to my broken rigging.
Homeward they lugged the light bones of my legend.

But they were weak, and stumbled in the sand...
Did all of you journey with me in your minds,
Aged and disabled crones? At our last parting
We tumbled in the sand, and you were bitter girls
Flinging farewells at us, like pelting stones
At a retreating army. We had seemed brilliant,
Sure of our rendezvous — but you commenced our exile.

For nightmare weeks we searched our neighbor's coast
Looking to join the force that was arrayed
To march against those traitors to the Peace.
We never heard. Did they depart without us?
Did a tidal wave obliterate the camp,
The many thousand men, the tents, the stallions,
The muscled armorers hammering at the forge?

Weapons stacked beside the saffron tents
High as the ridgepole; whole sheep on the spits
Sputtering fat that flared the fires for miles;

150

Camp-sounds: the creak of leather saddles, hooves
On hard-packed ground, men's curses, yapping dogs.
The cold soft voice of that great General:
Did he burn or drown? Is he in hiding now?

Wine of my province! Tasting it again
I taste my own blood, sweet when I sucked a scratch
In boyhood. Yet the aftertaste is sour,
Spoilt by an old man's breath, death in his throat.
And now I spill the cup. My hands are stiff
As a galley-slave's, and split from brine and rowing,
Smooth when I left, commander of the fleet.

II.

I gave the orders that we must abandon
The search for armies that abandoned us.
Like hounds grown lean from looking, we raced back
Across the fastest, brightest autumn sea!
Sights were inaccurate: one long ribbon beach
A long mirage, seducing us from the North,
Our true direction, toward a curving bay

Shaped like a siren's mouth. The Navigator
Hunted our home beyond another cove
So like the one we turned to all our lives
We feared that Heaven's hand had scooped you up,
Moved huts and livestock, children's prints in sand
Clean from the place, and set you down on grass
And daisies, in pale meadows of the dead.

We disembarked to search those teasing hills
Whose contours were familiar as our wives'.

But gradually the verdure of the slopes
Turned tropical, and we were jungle-bound.
A bird screamed like a brother; near the ground
A deadly, chuckling voice from ferns and moss.
Roots toiled our feet like snakes, became snakes.

All life voracious, fearsome, ravenous!
Great orchids dipped and gulped: and soldiers vanished
Silently, where they stood. Only the clang
Of a dropped shield on a log, or the soft hinge
Of closing flower jaws... we could not tell.
A few pulled back in time, but never whole.
As we wallowed on, we smelled our rot.

The rain descended, not quick jungle storms
But seas upended. And the land joined in,
All elements reversing: skies dropped mud
Like excrements of Gods... and we, whipped blind
And putrid, fled to the immaculate sea.
So we believed. Staggering, caked like apes
With soil, we sensed the rains' diminishing.

Still we were puppets to the dirt. We whirled
Choking in storms of all the vast world's dust.
How many last words strangled in a cough?
We fell to the ground, to join our dust to dust.
The breeze turned sweet and whistled us awake.
We rose like the dead in vestments of white dust
But could not praise the landscape. There was none.

Only the land we stood on, like the deck
Of the universe, lost in seas of vacant space;
Laughing, with barren minds and eyes, we stared:

Scarecrow confronting scarecrow in a field
Banging our arms against our smoking sides.
And so we danced like grains of emery
Polishing the round lens of the world.

    III.

The Navigator fumbled at a rag
Which was a map, its rivers silted up.
We followed him, till, drowning in the sand,
He said he needed water under him
To chase the stars that wriggled in the sky
Like jellyfish. But with his closing eyes
He sighted spars, or trees, or picks for teeth...

Perspective lied: a camel was a cat.
But, singing folly and mad hope aloud,
He died too soon. For if we hadn't killed him
We could have cursed him as we dragged him up
To scrape his snout over the rotten planking
Of the one remaining ship, her side stove in,
And knock his bones across that broken deck.

Despair turned lyric, and we moved like dancers:
One man fingered a rusty nail, another
Sifted a cornucopia of wheatlike sand
That overflowed the hold, and lay there humming.
For weeks, unlaboring, we watched the season alter,
Till winter fell on us like crashing armor
And the living used the dead for food and shelter.

In Spring a friendly caïque picked us up.
We voyaged from isle to isle, all so alike

I could repeat one story for all. No doubt I will,
The gaffer huddled in his moldy corner,
A bore to his descendants, mouthing lies.
So now you face the Hero, breath to breath,
And know no more than he what victory was.

On a Line from Sophocles

I see you cruel, you find me less than fair.
Too kind to keep apart, we two brutes meet.
Time, time, my friend, makes havoc everywhere.

Our stammers left to hunger in the air
Like smoke or music, turn the weather sweet:
To seek us, cruel; to find us, less than fair.

Testing our own reflections unaware
Each caught an image that was once conceit.
Time, time, my friend, makes havoc everywhere.

Eyes lewd for spotting death in life declare
That fallen flesh reveals the skull: complete.
I see you. Cruel. You find me less than fair.

The sacking of the skin, the ashen hair —
But more than surfaces compound the cheat!
Time, time, my friend, makes havoc *everywhere*.

The years betray our vows to keep and care.
O traitors! Ugly in this last defeat,
I find you cruel, you see me less than fair.
Time, time, my friend, makes havoc everywhere.

A Long Line of Doctors

Mother, picked for jury duty, managed to get through
A life of Voltaire in three volumes. Anyway, she knew
Before she half-heard a word, the dentist was guilty.

As a seminarist whose collar is his calling
Chokes up without it, baring his naked neck,
The little, furtive dentist is led across the deck,
Mounts the plank, renders a nervous cough.
Mother frowns, turns a page, flicks a flyspeck
With her fingernail. She will push him off!

Call to her, Voltaire, amid the wreck
Of her fair-mindedness; descended from a line
Of stiff physicians: dentists are beyond
The iron palings, the respectable brass plate,
Illegible Latin script, the chaste degrees.
Freezing, she acknowledges the mechanic, welder, wielder
Of pliers, hacker, hawker, barber — Spit it out, please.
Worst of all, this dentist advertises.

Gliding through Volume II with an easy breaststroke,
Never beyond her depth, she glimpses him,
Formerly Painless, all his lifelike bridges
Swept away; tasting brine as the testimony
Rises: how he chased his siren girl receptionist,
Purse-lipped, like a starlet playing nurse
With her doll's kit, round and round the little lab
Where full balconies of plaster teeth
Grinned at the clinch.

New musical chimes
Score their dalliance as the reception room fills.
Pulling away at last from his mastic Nereid,
He admits a patient; still unstrung,
Stares past the tiny whirlpool at her, combing
Her silvery hair over his silver tools, runs the drill —
Mark this! — the drill through his victim's tongue.

Mother took all his easy payments, led the eleven
Crewmembers, docile, to her adamantine view:
He was doomed, doomed, doomed, by birth, profession,
Practice, appearance, personal habits, loves...
And now his patient, swollen-mouthed with cancer!

Doves

Never cooed like Mother pronouncing sentence.
She shut Voltaire with a bang, having come out even,
The last page during the final, smiling ballot,
The judge, supererogated, studying the docket
As Mother, with eleven good men in her pocket
And a French philosopher in her reticule, swept out.

Nice Mrs. Nemesis, did she ever look back
At love's fool, clinging to his uneasy chair,
Gripping the arms, because she had swooped down,
And strapped him in, to drill him away, then say,
"Spit out your life, right there,"

Imposing her own version of the Deity
Who, as the true idolaters well know,
Has a general practice, instructs in Hygiene & Deportment,
Invents diseases for His cure and care:
She knows him indispensable. Like Voltaire.

Dixit Insipiens

At first, it was only a trickle
Of eminent men, with their astrolabes and armillae,
Who passed cautious notes to each other, obscurely worded.
Of course the terrible news leaked out
And the peasants were agitated.
Moans arose from the windowless hovels.
Men, hardly human, shouldering crude farm implements,
Gathered in knots along the roads and raved:
Storm the great houses! Smash the laboratory,
The retorts, the lenses — instruments of Satan.
But the minions of the manors
Lashed them back from the bronze gates,
Back to the fetid darkness, where they scoured their knees,
Praying for us.

The magnificent correspondence between Madame A.
And the more eminent, though less notorious,
Monsieur B. reveals a breathtaking indifference
To You: not even the target of a bilious epigram.
They move intently toward their prime concern:
Which voice, this time, will loose
Its thunderbolt? The straggling troops of revolution
Must be rallied yet again.
In perfect confidence of their powers,
As if they, who after all are people of flesh and bone,
Despite their attainments, had replaced You;
Not by storming the throne room, nor by those manifestos
They so supremely compose.
You were swept out, and they swept in, that's all.

Out there, on the edge of the familiar world,
Are knots of men, burned dark as our own peasants
Used to be, but better armed, we know;
We armed them.
From time to time they bang their heads on the sand
And shout, unintelligibly, of You.
Their version of You, of course, quite different
From the blandness You metamorphosed into
Over the centuries, progressively edited.

Holy war! Can they be in earnest?
After all, this isn't the fourteenth century.
Is it the uneasiness we feel, or the remnants
Of ancestral superstition, which makes us ask ourselves,
Can this be Your planned revenge?

How can You be vengeful when You don't exist?
If only the weight of centuries
Wasn't on Your side.
If only disbelief was more like faith.

Semele Recycled

After you left me forever,
I was broken into pieces,
and all the pieces flung into the river.
Then the legs crawled ashore
and aimlessly wandered the dusty cow-track.
They became, for a while, a simple roadside shrine:
A tiny table set up between the thighs
held a dusty candle, weed-and-fieldflower chains
placed reverently there by children and old women.
My knees were hung with tin triangular medals
to cure all forms of hysterical disease.

After I died forever in the river,
my torso floated, bloated in the stream,
catching on logs or stones among the eddies.
White water foamed around it, then dislodged it;
after a whirlwind trip, it bumped ashore.
A grizzled old man who scavenged along the banks
had already rescued my arms and put them by,
knowing everything has its uses, sooner or later.

When he found my torso, he called it his canoe,
and, using my arms as paddles,
he rowed me up and down the scummy river.
When catfish nibbled my fingers he scooped them up
and blessed his reusable bait.
Clumsy but serviceable, that canoe!
The trail of blood that was its wake
attracted the carp and eels, and the river turtle,
easily landed, dazed by my tasty red.

A young lad found my head among the rushes
and placed it on a dry stone.
He carefully combed my hair with a bit of shell
and set small offerings before it
which the birds and rats obligingly stole at night,
so it seemed I ate.
And the breeze wound through my mouth and empty sockets
so my lungs would sigh, and my dead tongue mutter.
Attached to my throat like a sacred necklace
was a circlet of small snails.
Soon the villagers came to consult my oracular head
with its waterweed crown.
Seers found occupation, interpreting sighs,
and their papyrus rolls accumulated.

Meanwhile, young boys retrieved my eyes
they used for marbles in a simple game
till somebody's pretty sister snatched at them
and set them, for luck, in her bridal diadem.
Poor girl! When her future groom caught sight of her,
all eyes, he crossed himself in horror,
and stumbled away in haste
through her dowered meadows.

What then of my heart and organs,
my sacred slit
which loved you best of all?
They were caught in a fisherman's net
and tossed at night into a pen for swine.
But they shone so by moonlight that the sows stampeded,
trampled one another in fear, to get away.
And the fisherman's wife, who had thirteen living children
and was contemptuous of holy love,
raked the rest of me onto the compost heap.

Then in their various places and helpful functions,
the altar, oracle, offal, canoe and oars
learned the wild rumor of your return.
The altar leapt up, and ran to the canoe,
scattering candle grease and wilted grasses.
Arms sprang to their sockets, blind hands with nibbled nails
groped their way, aided by loud lamentation,
to the bed of the bride, snatched up those unlucky eyes
from her discarded veil and diadem,
and rammed them home. Oh, what a bright day it was!
This empty body danced on the riverbank.
Hollow, it called and searched among the fields
for those parts that steamed and simmered in the sun,
and never would have found them.

But then your great voice rang out under the skies
my name! — and all those private names
for the parts and places that had loved you best.
And they stirred in their nest of hay and dung.
The distraught old ladies chasing their lost altar,
and the seers pursuing my skull, their lost employment,
and the tumbling boys, who wanted the magic marbles,
and the runaway groom, and the fisherman's thirteen children
set up such a clamor, with their cries of "Miracle!"
that our two bodies met like a thunderclap
in midday — right at the corner of that wretched field
with its broken fenceposts and startled, skinny cattle.
We fell in a heap on the compost heap
and all our loving parts made love at once,
while the bystanders cheered and prayed and hid their eyes
and then went decently about their business.

And here it is, moonlight again; we've bathed in the river
and are sweet and wholesome once more.
We kneel side by side in the sand;
we worship each other in whispers.
But the inner parts remember fermenting hay,
the comfortable odor of dung, the animal incense,
and passion, its bloody labor,
its birth and rebirth and decay.

The Blessing

for Ashley

I.

Daughter-my-mother
you have observed my worst.
Holding me together at your expense
has made you burn cool.

So did I in childhood:
nursed her old hurts and doubts,
myself made cool to shallowness.
She grew out as I grew in.
At midpoint, our furies met.

My mother's dust has rested
for fifteen years
in the front hall closet
because we couldn't bear to bury it.
Her dust-lined, dust-coated urn
squats among the size-eleven overshoes.
My father, who never forgets
his overshoes,
has forgotten that.

Hysterical-tongued daughter
of a dead marriage,
you shed hot tears in the bed
of that benign old woman
whose fierce joy you were:
tantrums in her closet

164

taking upon yourself the guilt
the split parents never felt.

Child and old woman
soothing each other,
sharing the same face
in a span of seventy years,
the same mother wit.

    II.

I must go home, says my father,
his mind straying;
*this is a hard time
for your mother.* But she's been dead
these fifteen years.
Daughter and daughter, we sit
on either side.
Whose? Which? He's not sure.
After long silence,
don't press me, he says.

Mother, hysterical-tongued,
age and grace burned away
your excesses, left
that lavender-sweet child
who turned up the thermostat
on her electric blanket, folded
her hands on her breast.
You had dreamed death
as a silver prince:
like marrying Nehru, you said.

Dearest, does your dust hum
in the front hall closet —
this is a hard time for me —
among umbrella points,
the canes, and overshoes
of that cold climate?

Each week she denies it,
my blithe mother
in that green, cloud-free landscape
where we whisper our dream-secrets
to each other.

III.

Daughter, you lived through
my difficult affairs
as I tried to console
your burnt-out childhood.
We coped with our fathers,
compared notes
on the old one and the cold one,
learned to moderate our hates.
Risible in suffering,
we grew up together.

Mother-my-daughter
I have been blessed
on both sides of my life.
Forgive me if sometimes
like my fading father
I see you as one.

166

Not that I confuse
your two identities
as he does, taking off
or putting on his overshoes,
but my own role:

I lean on the bosom
of that double mother,
the ghost by night, the girl by day;
I between my
two mild furies,
alone but comforted.

And I will whisper blithely
in your dreams
when you are as old as I,
my hard time over.
Meanwhile, keep warm
your love, your bed,
and your wise heart and head,
my good daughter.

Dangerous Games

I fly a black kite on a long string.
As I reel it in,
I see it is a tame bat.
You say it's you.

You fly a white kite, but the string snaps.
As it flutters down,
You see it is a cabbage butterfly.
I say it's I.

You invented this game,
Its terms, its terminology.
I supplied the string,
Giving you the frayed length
So I could escape.

I flew a black kite, let go the string,
But the thing darted down
Straight for my long hair
To be entangled there.

You flew a white kite that ran away.
You chased it with your bat sonar.
But you found only a cabbage butterfly
Trembling on an aphid-riddled leaf.

Race Relations

for D.B.

I sang in the sun
of my white oasis
as you broke stone

Then I sang and paraded
for the distant martyrs
loving the unknown

They lay still in the sun
of Sharpeville and Selma
while you broke stone

When you fled tyranny
facedown in the street
signing stones with your blood

Far away I fell silent
in my white oasis
ringed with smoke and guns

Martyred in safety
I sighed for lost causes
You bled on   You bled on

Now I recommence singing
in a tentative voice
loving the unknown

I sing in the sun
and storm of the world
to the breakers of stone

You are sentenced to life
in the guilt of freedom
in the prison of memory

Haunted by brothers
who still break stone
I am sentenced to wait

And our love-hate duet
is drowned by the drum
of the breakers of stone

Children

What good are children anyhow?
> They only break your heart.

The one that bore your fondest hopes
> will never amount to anything.

The one you slaved to give the chances you never had
> rejects them with contempt.

They won't take care of you in your old age.
> They don't even write home.

They don't follow in your footsteps.
They don't avoid your mistakes.
It's impossible to save them from pain.
> And of course they never listen.

Remember how you hung on the lips
> of your father or grandfather,

Begging for the old stories:
> "Again! Tell it again!
> What was it like 'in olden times'?"

We have good stories too:
> funny, instructive, pathetic.

Forget it. Write them down for your friends.
Your friends, with whom you have that unspoken pact:
Don't ask me about my children, and I won't inquire of yours.

Remember how we used to exchange infant pictures?
How we boasted of cute sayings? How we...
> Forget it.

Put away those scrapbooks, with the rusted flute in the closet,
> with the soiled ballet slippers.

Tear up the clumsy Valentines.

Tear up every crayoned scrap that says, "I love you, Mama."
They don't want us to keep these mementos:
                     they find them embarrassing,
These relics of dependent love,
The orange crayon that didn't dare write, "I hate you."
Forget their birthdays, as they forget yours.

Perhaps because they never finish anything,
                     not a book, not a school,
Their politics are cruel and sentimental:
Some monster of depravity
                     who destroyed millions with his smile,
Who shadowed our youth with terror,
                     is a hero to them.
Now he smiles benignly from their walls.

Because they are historyless, they don't believe in history:
                     Stalin wasn't so bad.
                     The Holocaust didn't really happen.
                     Roosevelt was a phony.
But the worst of it is:
                     they don't believe we ever believed;
They don't believe we ever had ideals.
They don't believe that we were ever poor.
They don't believe that we were passionate
                     — or that we are passionate today!
Forget it. Don't torture yourself.
                     You still have some life to salvage.
Get divorced. Go on a diet.
Take up the career you dropped for them twenty years ago.
Go back to the schools they deserted, and sign up for courses:
Study Tranquility 101; take Meditation; enroll for Renewal.

Remember those older friends we used to envy,
              brilliant and glittering with beauty,
Who refused to have children,
              not about to sacrifice their careers;
Who refused the mess, the entrapment,
              as we toiled over chores and homework,
              worried about measles and money —
Have you seen them lately?
They no longer converse in sparkling cadenzas.
They are obsessed with their little dog
              who piddles on the Oriental rug,
              who throws up on the bedspread.

They don't notice his bad breath;
His incessant yapping doesn't seem to disturb them.
To be honest about it,
              the whole apartment smells!
And the way they babble to him in pet names
              instead of talk of Milton, Chaucer, Dante.
The way they caress him makes you fairly ill;
              the way they call him, "Baby."

In the First Stanza,

first, I tell you who I am:
shadowed, reflective, small
pool in an unknown glade.
It is easy to be a poet,
brim with transparent water.
In autumn, the leaves blow down
over the ruffled surface,
sink to rest, then resume their cycle.

In the second stanza, you laugh,
skipping pebbles across my surface,
charmed by the spreading circles.
In the trees' perpetual twilight
you are alone with the poet.
Gently, you shake your head.
You know me as turbulent ocean
clouded with thunder and drama.

In the third stanza, I die.
Still, I insist on composing
as my throes go on and on.
I clench the pen in my teeth
making those furious scratches
that you will see, much later,
as graceful calligraphy:
drift of sails that sketch my horizon.

My hands, in the fourth stanza,
with the agonized clutch of the dying,
draw your hand beneath the covers.

I beg you to travel my body
till you find the forest glade.
Then your hand, like a leaf in autumn,
is pulled into the pool.
The rest of you doesn't believe it.

The fifth stanza begins
with water, and quiet laughter.
Then I die, I really die.
You pick up this piece of paper.
You read it aloud and explain me,
my profile cast in prose.
It drops from your hand like a leaf.
This is all part of the cycle.

Then, in the final stanza,
I tell you who I am.

Food of Love

Eating is touch carried to the bitter end.

SAMUEL BUTLER II

I'm going to murder you with love;
I'm going to suffocate you with embraces;
I'm going to hug you, bone by bone,
Till you're dead all over.
Then I will dine on your delectable marrow.

You will become my personal Sahara;
I'll sun myself in you, then with one swallow
Drain your remaining brackish well.
With my female blade I'll carve my name
In your most aspiring palm
Before I chop it down.
Then I'll inhale your last oasis whole.

But in the total desert you become
You'll see me stretch, horizon to horizon,
Opulent mirage!
Wisteria balconies dripping cyclamen.
Vistas ablaze with crystal, laced in gold.

So you will summon each dry grain of sand
And move toward me in undulating dunes
Till you arrive at sudden ultramarine:
A Mediterranean to stroke your dusty shores;
Obstinate verdure, creeping inland, fast renudes
Your barrens; succulents spring up everywhere,
Surprising life! And I will be that green.

When you are fed and watered, flourishing
With shoots entwining trellis, dome, and spire,
Till you are resurrected field in bloom,
I will devour you, my natural food,
My host, my final supper on the earth,
And you'll begin to die again.

Running Away from Home

Most people from Idaho are crazed rednecks
Grown stunted in ugly shadows of brick spires,
Corrupted by fat priests in puberty,
High from the dry altitudes of Catholic towns.

Spooked by plaster madonnas, switched by sadistic nuns,
Given sex instruction by dirty old men in skirts,
Recoiling from flesh-colored calendars, bloody gods,
Still we run off at the mouth, we keep on running.

Like those rattling roadsters with vomit-stained backseats,
Used condoms tucked beneath floor-mats,
That careened down hairpin turns through the blinding rain
Just in time to hit early mass in Coeur d'Alene!

Dear Phil, Dear Jack, Dear Tom, Dear Jim,
Whose car had a detachable steering-wheel;
He'd hand it to his scared, protesting girl,
Saying, "Okay, *you* drive" — steering with his knees;

Jim drove Daddy's Buick over the railroad tracks,
Piss-drunk, just ahead of the Great Northern freight
Barreling its way through the dawn, straight for Spokane.
Oh, the great times in Wallace & Kellogg, the good clean fun!

Dear Sally, Dear Beth, Dear Patsy, Dear Eileen,
Pale, faceless girls, my best friends at thirteen,
Knelt on cold stone, with chilblained knees, to pray,
"Dear God, Dear Christ! Don't let him go All The Way!"

Oh, the black Cadillacs skidding around corners
With their freight of drunken Jesuit businessmen!
Beautiful daughters of lumber-kings avoided the giant
Nuptial Mass at St. Joseph's, and fled into nunneries.

The rest live at home; bad girls who survived abortions,
Used Protestant diaphragms, or refused the sacred obligation
Of the marriage bed, scolded by beat-off priests,
After five in five years, by Bill, or Dick, or Ted.

I know your secrets; you turn up drunk by ten AM.
At the Beauty Shoppe, kids sent breakfastless to school.
You knew that you were doomed by seventeen.
Why should your innocent daughters fare better than you?

Young, you live on in me; even the blessed dead:
Tom slammed into a fire hydrant on his Indian Chief
And died castrated; Jim, fool, fell four stories from the roof
Of his jock fraternity at Ag. & Tech.;

And the pure losers, cracked up in training planes
In Utah; or shot by a nervous rookie at Fort Lewis;
At least they cheated the white-coiffed ambulance chasers
And deathbed bedevilers, and died in war in peace.

II.

Some people from Oregon are mad orphans
Who claim to hail from Stratford-upon-Sodom.
They speak fake BBC; they are Unitarian fairies,
In the Yang group or the Yin group, no Middle Way.

Some stay Catholic junkies, incense sniffers who
Scrawl JESUS SAVES on urinal walls, between engagements;
Or white disciples of Black Muslims; balding blonds
Who shave their pubic hair, or heads, for Buddha.

I find you in secondhand bookstores or dirty movies,
Bent halos like fedoras, pulled well down,
Bogarts of buggery. We can't resist the furtive questions:
Are you a writer too? How did you get out?

We still carry those Rosary scars, more like a herpes
Simplex than a stigmata: give us a nice long fit
Of depression; give us a good bout of self-hate;
Give us enough Pope, we pun, and we'll hang.

Hung, well hung, or hungover, in the world's most durable
Morning after, we'd sooner keep the mote and lose the eye.
Move over, Tonio Kröger, you never attended
Our Lady of Sorrows, or Northwestern High!

Some people from Washington State are great poetasters,
Imbibers of anything, so long as it makes us sick
Enough to forget our sickness, and carry on
From the Carry Out: Hostess Winkies and Wild Duck.

We "relate," as they say, to Indians, bravest of cowards
Furtively cadging drinks with a shit-faced grin:
Outcasts who carry our past like a 90 lb. calcified fetus
We park in the bus-station locker, and run like sin.

Boozers and bounders, cracked-up cracker-barrel jockeys,
We frequent greasy bistros: Piraeus and Marseilles;

As we wait for our rip-off pimps, we scribble on napkins
Deathful verse we trust our executors to descry.

Wills. We are will-less. As we have breath, we are willful
And wishful, trusting that Great Archangel who Still Cares,
Who presides at the table set up for celestial Bingo.
We try to focus our eyes and fill in the squares.

III.

Some people from Spokane are insane salesmen
Peddling encyclopedias from door to door,
Trying to earn enough to flee to the happy farm
Before they jump from the Bridge or murder Mom;

Or cut up their children with sanctified bread-knives
Screaming, "You are Isaac, and I am Abraham!"
But it's too late. They are the salutary failures
Who keep God from getting a swelled head.

Some shoot themselves in hotel rooms, after gazing
At chromos of the Scenic Route through the Cascades
Via Northern Pacific, or the old Milwaukee & St. Paul:
Those trains that won't stop rattling in our skulls!

First they construct crude crosses out of Band-Aids
And stick them to the mirror; then rip pages
From the Gideon Bible, roll that great final joint,
A roach from Revelations, as they lie dying.

Bang! It's all over. Race through Purgatory,
At last unencumbered by desperate manuscripts

In the salesman's sample-case, along with the dirty shirts.
After Spokane, what horrors lurk in Hell?

IV.

I think continually of those who are truly crazy:
Some people from Montana are put away;
They shake their manacles in a broken dance,
With eyes blue-rimmed as a Picasso clown's.

Still chaste, but nude, hands shield their organs
Like the original Mom & Dad, after the Fall;
Or they dabble brown frescoes on the walls
Of solitary: their Ajanta and Lascaux.

While the ones that got away display giant kidneys
At the spiral skating-rink of Frank L. Wright,
Or framed vermin in the flammable Museum
Of Modern Mart. But they're still Missoula

In their craft and sullen ebbing, Great Falls & Butte.
Meanwhile, Mondrian O'Leary squints at the light
Staining the white radiance of his well-barred cell,
Till ferocious blurs bump each other in Dodgem cars.

Oh, that broken-down fun-house in Natatorium Park
Held the only fun the boy Mondrian ever knew!
Now seven-humped, mutated radioactive Chinook salmon
Taint the white radiance of O'Leary's brain.

O mad Medical Lake, I hear you have reformed;
No longer, Sunday afternoon, the tripper's joy.

Watch the nuts weep! or endlessly nibble fingers.
Funny, huh? The white ruin of muscular men

Twisting bars like Gargantua; lewd Carusos,
Maimed Chanticleers, running off at the scars.
They hoot their arias through the rhythmic clashing
Of garbage-can lids that serve as dinner trays;

Inmates are slopped, while fascinated on-
Lookers watch Mrs. Hurley, somebody's grandma,
Eating gravy with her bare hands. Just animals, Rosetta.
She's not *your* mother. Don't let it get you.

Suddenly, Mr. Vincente, who with his eleven brothers
Built roads through the Spokane Valley
Where Italians moved like dreams of Martha Graham
As they laid asphalt over subterranean rivers,

Spots a distant cousin, Leonard, an architect
Until seventh grade, who seems to know him:
Leonard displays, by way of greeting,
His only piece of personal adornment:

How the tourists squeal! Watch them fumble at coat, and fly!
Girdled and ginghamed relatives disperse
Back to the touring car, the picnic basket
With its homemade grappa in giraffe-necked bottles.

As sun-scarred men urge olive children on,
Grandma Hurley, who thought the treat was for her,
Shyly waves her gravy-dappled fingers,
Couple-colored as her old brindled cat.

Enough of this madness! It's already in the past.
Now they are stabbed full of sopers, numbed & lobotomized
In the privacy of their own heads. It's easier for the chaplain:
They're nodding. If you consent to be saved, just nod for God.

It's never over, old church of our claustrophobia!
Church of the barren towns, the vast unbearable sky,
Church of the Western plains, our first glimpse of brilliance,
Church of our innocent incense, there is no good-bye.

Church of the coloring-book, crude crayon of childhood,
Thank God at last you seem to be splitting apart.
But you live for at least as long as our maimed generation
Lives to curse your blessed plaster bleeding heart.

A Muse

"The baby was wakened from her afternoon nap today by a fierce wind blowing up and rain.... She danced around a few times and came to me speaking with her little face close to me,

"'When the wind blows in your eyes and makes a *turble* song in your ears, you *cry out,* and biz around like this,' and she was off on another little dance. She lacks four days of being two years and five months old today." That is my forty-seven-year-old mother speaking, of me, her first and only child. She is a woman "liberated" by necessity if not by choice. Losing her mother at thirteen (Grandmother had just given birth to a son whose cleft palate split his face open from nose to chin: her sixth living child among a number of miscarriages and a baby, Little Will, lost at one and a half from scarlet fever; "she just turned her face to the wall and died," Mother said), she raised her younger brothers and took care of her father; earned a B.A. from Boulder and a doctorate from Stanford in biology, which she taught at Mills and San Francisco State; she lived a bohemian life in San Francisco while contributing most of her earnings to send three brothers through college; at some point (my chronology is a bit shaky here, as all this information was conveyed orally, and in scraps) she studied art and philosophy at Harvard, with Dow and Santayana respectively; she ran the first federally sponsored drug clinic in New York City in a Rockefeller home that is now the site of the Museum of Modern Art; she was an organizer for the IWW and assisted Anna Louise Strong on her paper, *The Union Record,* in Seattle during the terrible management-Pinkerton strife around 1918; and when she met my father in Spokane, in her midforties, she was working for the government, investigating the conditions of women in the mines and lumber camps of the Northwest. But now, all that energy, all that talent, all that passion, is focused on maternity, on me.

I am already, from mother's evidence, a genius. The truth that nearly all children from the ages of around three to six are geniuses is something of which she has firsthand knowledge — brothers, social work, teaching kindergarten — but that information is carefully compartmentalized, kept from herself, and me.

You can see that I am rife with possibility; a dancer, yes, and it may be a choreographer, and a poet, a poet who dances to her own music, her own words. In the tradition of the revered Isadora.

A year and a half later, I am visiting "the San" with mother at Christmas. "The San" is a charitable tuberculosis sanitarium that my grandfather runs for the State of California, assisted by two of my mother's brothers, one a doctor, one a ne'er-do-well with the thickened speech and twisted lip of a crudely mended cleft palate. I *remember* the following scene for reasons that will become obvious:

Grandfather is in his easy chair, listening to the radio. Bob and Charles, my uncles, are painting a bookcase Chinese red. I smell the lacquer as I write these words. My mother is watching me intently as I mess around with a paper and crayons, struggling to form letters of the alphabet. Laboriously, I form the letters A, R, T, in what might generously be called a crooked line, and hold it up for Mama's approval. Sensation. *Her first word!* In her wonderfully dramatic way, my mother announces that this proves my extraordinary gifts; further, it proves that I am *fated* to become an artist. Do I remember (see, hear, smell) this episode so vividly because I realize that at that moment my fate was sealed? I think not. I remember it because I was entirely aware at the time that the conjunction of the letters A, R, T, was wholly accidental. I believe that I tried to mumble something to that effect at the time, but of course nobody paid any attention. I remember the incident, friends, because I have suffered from a bad conscience ever since. I have never believed that I was what my mother (and thus everyone who was to follow) thought I was. Of course, nobody could have been. Do I blame my mother? No. Do I blame me? Don't we all?

In the scrapbook in which my mother carefully mounted every example of my burgeoning genius (and which I haven't quite had the heart to throw on the dump, much as I am tempted), we come across a "poem" composed when I was just five, which runs as follows:

> My breath runs in front of me.
> I am running after it.
> I am catching my breath.

What this garden-variety bit of talent reveals is that I have been, almost from birth, irresistibly drawn to the bad pun. Another example, twenty days later (yes, each of these *immortelles* is carefully dated): I am splashing and shouting in the tub. My father, as usual, tells me not to disturb him. I reply that, "I'm a wet Democrat, making a speech." ("Wet," O younger generation, was the label for an anti-Prohibitionist.) The Greeks exposed children like this on a hillside, especially girls, but I regret to say that I was positively encouraged along these lines, and tendencies developed that I have never quite been able to eradicate. Encouraged by my mother, that is. My father just wanted quiet, obedience, and a captive audience for him to read aloud to when his law practice didn't allow enough scope for his histrionic energies.

In retailing the excesses of a spoilt childhood, it is difficult to avoid irony, but from now on, I shall try: I'm not sure from any of the foregoing if you get the picture of my mother as a lovable woman. She was, intensely lovable, by virtue of her ambient charm, her looks (though tending to fat in her fifties, which I found comfy, and so did the men who came to dinner and who promptly fell for her, her style, and her cuisine), her considerable abilities as a raconteuse, and above all, her concern for the unfortunates of this world, a concern so unforced, sensitive, opulent in its manifestations that she was widely beloved by people who barely knew her. It is hard to leave out the thousand examples that illustrate these qualities, but I must cling to this chronicle of the "making" of a poet — for make me she did, in all senses, not excluding the sexual. I suppose the greatest testimony to her seductive lovableness is that I really forgive her for the unending overestimation and exploitation of my abilities, which drove me mad, and which I was powerless to abate.

The next stage was one of outings, picnics, and play-parties at home when, as well-equipped with the paraphernalia of creation, pen, pencils, scissors, as any artist could have wished, I and she collaborated. So, in going through the infamous scrapbook, I am often puzzled to determine which was her contribution, which mine. As a general rule, if the end product looks suspiciously good, I suspect her fine and innocent Italian hand. During and after this period, I was beneficiary of lessons in every conceivable branch of the arts (except ballroom dancing, where my adamant refusal to be trapped in a long hall with unwilling members of the opposite sex was, for some reason, honored). What I really needed, from the cornucopia of my mother's own gifts, although I might have resisted at the time — being lazy, quick, and self-confident — was Latin and Greek, Mother having had eight years of one and eleven of the other. The discipline would have been priceless, and the illumination of my later life equally so. My mother's habitual self-denigration seemed to poison her for the things at which she was truly brilliant: languages, mathematics, bridge, the sciences. I was trained away from all of the above, and steered, God help me, toward "creativity." Creativity, the thing, above all, which life had denied her. I was to be fulfilled where she had been crippled. It didn't occur to me that what she was trying to create was a mirror-image of herself.

There was this capable, energetic, worldly woman, settled at last in marriage, to "a wonderful man," twenty-five years after her friends had given her up for lost, with a surprise baby that somehow crept in between marriage and menopause, and stuck — after years in San Francisco, Cambridge, New York, after befriending and being friended by artists, writers, radicals, the length and breadth of the land — in an archetypal small American town of the twenties. Why, I ask, was maternity enough for a woman who had done, and seen, and been, as much as she had? Why was I chosen to live the life she wanted, when she might well have gone on to live it herself? I can only surmise part of the answer. She had worked, worked, worked, largely for others, since the age of thirteen. Exceptionally sensitive and, beneath the charm and bravado, riddled with self-doubt, she had been dealt many a buffet by life, and many a low blow. She was tired. And, to herself, she was old. When I try to make sense of it, the cliché of a frail bird, battered by storms at sea, who finds safe haven, seems appropriate.

But why, after a few peaceful and probably boring years, when she had recovered her stamina, her nervous energy, did she not strike out again, and add a new career to the multifarious occupations of the past? My father wouldn't have opposed it. I think he would have welcomed it in fact, because he, too, had more of her neurotic concern showered upon him than he could have wanted. But he could, and did, escape to the office, into books (play quietly, now; your father's reading), leaving me to bear the brunt. Do I blame my father? You bet.

Most children, when told to "play quietly," know what to do, but I was sexually backward, so I wrote. I mean I really wrote, as distinct from saying things that my mother the amanuensis took down. Don't fear that I shall drag you through the scrapbook page by page, from the innocent effusions of infancy, through the assisted inspirations of childhood, to the eruptions of adolescence. Although it is tempting to prove that I made some advances from what you have read thus far, I am restrained by the awareness that until I reached about the age of twenty-nine (except for a couple of accidents we call "given" poems), I wrote nothing that would appeal to the adult mind, other than that of the authoress of my being.

Those early poems were written for her. They were given to her partly from love, partly as a bribe. The implicit barter: my poems, a partial invasion of my privacy, in exchange for some control over the rest of my life. Naive hope!

When I went to college, I managed to get as far away from Spokane, and her, as possible, short of wading into the Atlantic Ocean, pursued by her anxious, demanding biweekly letters. Enchanting letters, I discover now, when I come across them. Then they were read in a blur of guilt and tossed into the depths of my closet along with the unwashed laundry.

There, in the midst of many talented and well-educated girls, I discovered that I was less remarkable than I had been raised to believe. All those lessons in dancing, theatre, piano, singing, drawing, painting, modeling; the plays I had written and produced for my parents, Mrs. Anderson the laundress, and my playmates; the handmade books, the poems by the dozen, the parodies, the serials, the songs — what did they prove? Not that I was in any way exceptional, but that my mother was.

Though I loved college, and studied with reasonable diligence, I dropped my "accomplishments" one by one. Painting and sculpting and drawing went first, and forever. Then the piano. Then singing. There was one last outburst: I wrote a sort of play, the music for it, choreographed it, and danced and acted in it, in collaboration with my college mates, and then retired from public life.

I published one poem in *The New Yorker*, then got a job dealing, among other things, with Indian labor statistics. I did not go back home except for short and infrequent vacations. Eventually I got married. I published one poem in *The Atlantic* and got pregnant again. I had three children in three years. I got divorced. My mother died. And then my serious life as a poet began. At last I could write, without pressure, without blackmail, without bargains, without the hot breath of her expectations.

I wrote the poems for her. I still do.

Dream of a Large Lady

The large lady laboriously climbs
        down the ladder from a gun emplacement.

She had gone up to contemplate
        the blue view
                and to damage the gun.

She has done neither
        for the view was a baize haze
and the rooted gun immovable in stone.

        So she climbs down the shaky ladder
                with a few rungs missing
carrying her mostly uneaten
        picnic lunch

of which she has consumed a single
        hard-boiled egg
                leaving the shell
not as litter but as symbolism
        on the sullen gun
                in its gray rotunda.

At the foot of the ladder she finds sand;
        and one brown, shuttered house
from which another lady
        stares.

This one wears a blurry face
        and an orange dress

matching her orange hair
        in a bun.

The large lady perforates along the beach
        on her high-heeled pumps
                by the water's verge,
as a large, pale waterbird might do.

        When she reaches her own cottage
           near the bay,
she finds a letter from the strange orange lady
        in its crisp white envelope
                lying on the table:

"I am an admirer of your poesy,
        so I am baking you a fresh peach pie,"
              the nice note reads.

"Do come to my house near the bay,"
        she speaks in her head,
              "orange lady who admires my poesy.

"We will sit here quietly, in twilight,
        and drink a cup of carefully brewed tea."

With a sigh, she puts aside the memory
        of the gray gun she could only decorate
           but not destroy.

Though clear in her eye she holds a vision:
        the thin, ceremonious shell
           of her eaten egg
painted by the sun against the sky.

Reading Your Poems in Your House
While You Are Away

for Richard Shelton

This morning my first roadrunner
paused on the dry wall you built
right outside your window.
A couple of playful jackrabbits
bounded among the cactus
under a chilly sun.

The mountains are mirage-like
as if they had just leaked
from one of your poems
and the god over there
had puffed them full of air
to float on a blur of sage
and desert broom.

Insubstantial mountains!
I found their serious weight
inside your books.
I found the serious roadrunner
not cartoonlike at all
with a tail full of adverbs.

I follow the dry wall
as it twists from page to page,
the glowing yellow stones
spontaneous but neat
nested together, held by your sweat;

rabbits, your cactus garden,
saguaro, living tombstones on the lawns;
dogs that serially howled at dawn,
your big white dog — when a coyote screamed.
And the bitter dark.

You remember I told you
after our night on the desert
I never see the first full moon
without thinking of you?

And your perfect poem about history:
How do you like nesting
in someone else's life?

Remember this when you come home:
One day, as you pause in composing,
a phrase of mine will leap into your stanza.
Just as, in writing this,
I borrow the words that belong to you
and give them back, like moonlight.

Postcards from Rotterdam

I.

Came such a long way
To find you —
Now only a channel
Separates us.
It is enough.

We are divided by water.
I shed one tear.

II.

Waited for your letter
Until I lost interest.
Then it arrived,
Full of protestations.

Ah no, friend, you woo us with words
Just once.
Then you must lay your body
On the line.
And it isn't here.

III.

I thought
When the moon was full again
I would be in your arms.

But I'm not.

I'm in somebody else's arms.
We don't even glance
At the moon.

IV.

Having wonderful time
Coming in from the town.

Having wonderful time
Contemplating the bidet.

Having wonderful time
With the shutters drawn.

Having wonderful time
Converting silver into dross.

Having wonderful time walking around
With a five-pound key in my purse

And a plastic flask full of Holland gin.
I shed one tear.

Wish you were here.
Love,
           Carolyn.

For My Daughter

Ashley's twenty-fifth birthday

It was lingering summer
when you announced your birth,
as you were rapt in me,
rapt in a field-flower haze
of those last, listless days
the waters burst
in a summer storm:
Like Beethoven
your bold overture began.

It was sterile winter
in the birth-room zoo;
animals clung to the bars,
humped and yelled
as the fogs blew
through our primate skulls.
From a far distant self
I dreamily overheard
the worst, visceral howl.

Eyes opened to autumn
overnight: the trees
red against blazing blue
framed by a Lutheran wall.
You were brought in to me
so pitiably small
and unbelievably red
as if God had dyed

the leaves and you
with the same Mercurochrome.

Your young new parents,
terrified,
held on to each other
as they cried.
Later, your father
returned, with a stern smile,
handed me gold chrysanthemums
wrapped in damp newspaper
smelling of earth and death
and man-inflicted pain.
I held my breath that night
to the light sound of rain
and prayed you to grow.

From that time, you took
each season in your stride.
Still, when an ideal passion
for man or justice seizes
your fierce imagination
that birth-day glow is kindled
on your cheek and brow.

Now, as you have reached
your quarter-century,
with that same pristine fear
and undiminished pride
I thank your star, and you.

For Sappho/After Sappho

in memoriam, S.L.M.B.

I.

and you sang eloquently
for my pleasure
before I knew
you were girl or boy

> at the moment
> dawn awoke me
> you were in my bed

not sister   not lover
fierce though you were
a small cat
with thorny claws

> any daughter
> seeking comfort

you asked what you could give
to one who you thought
possessed everything

> then you forgot giving
> and tried to take
> blindly seeking the breast

what to do but hold you
lost innocent...

we love whatever
caresses us
in need or pleasure
a debt a favor
a desperation

you were already
a speaking instrument
I loved the speaker
loved the voice
as it broke my heart with pity

breath immortal
the words nothing
articulate poems
not pertinent   the breath
everything

you the green shoot
I the ripe earth
not yours to possess
alas   not yours

II.

the punch bowl was full
a boy flirted
in our drunken dance
you dripped sweat
trembling shook your body
you tried to kill him
black darts shot from your eyes

and the company laughed
at your desperation

someone took you away
you lay on the grass
retching   then spewed your love
over the bed of crocus buds

we led you home
where I confronted
your mother's picture
my face enameled

I have a slender daughter
a golden flower
your eyes are dark as olive pits
not for me to devour
child   no child of mine

you screamed after me
Aphrodite!   not giving
as with a sweep of my cloak
I fled skyward...

the full moon is shining
in the spring twilight
your face more pallid
than dry grass
and vomit-stained
still you are the evening star

most beautiful star
you will die a virgin

Aphrodite thick-armed and middle-aged
loving the love of men
yet mourns you

III.

when I lost you
where did you go
only the fragments of your poems
mourn you as I mourn you

and the unwritten poems leapt with you
over the cliff-side

hyacinth hair   rising
in the rush of wind

hyacinth shattered
a dark stain on the ground
yet wine   some drops
some essence
has been distilled

this mouth drinks thirstily
as it chokes on the dust of your death

IV.

yet I hold you in midair
androgynous child of dream
offshoot of muses

my thought holds you
straight-browed and piercing-eyed
breastless as a boy
as light of foot

       wandering in that world
       beyond this   and before

but for now you forget it all
in Lethe
I too am treacherous   I forget everything
mind and limbs loosen
in the arms of a stranger
searching for Lethe

       but you dart through the future
       which is memory
       your boy's voice shouting out
       the remainder of your poems
       of which I know
       simply beginnings

words heard a thousand times
in the echoing night
across the sea-foam

       separating us
       for this moment only

October 1973

Last night I dreamed I ran through the streets of New York
Looking for help for you, Nicanor.
But my few friends who are rich or influential
were temporarily absent from their penthouses or hotel suites.
They had gone to the opera, or flown for the weekend to Bermuda.
At last I found one or two of them at home,
preparing for social engagements,
absently smiling, as they tried on gown after gown
until heaps of rich, beautiful fabric were strewn
over the chairs and sofas. They posed before mirrors,
with their diamonds and trinkets and floor-length furs.
Smiling at me from the mirror, they vaguely promised help.
They became distracted — by constantly ringing phones,
by obsequious secretaries, bustling in with packages,
flowers, messages, all the paraphernalia,
all part of the uninterruptible rounds of the rich,
the nice rich, smiling soothingly, as they touched their hair
or picked up their phone extensions.
Absently patting my arm, they smiled, "It will be all right."

Dusk fell on the city as I ran, naked, weeping, into the streets.
I ran to the home of Barbara, my friend,
Who, as a young girl, rescued four Loyalist soldiers
from a Spanish prison;
in her teenage sweater set and saddle shoes and knee socks,
she drove an old car sagging with Loyalist pamphlets
across the Pyrenees all the way to Paris without being caught.
And not long ago, she helped save a group of men
from Franco's sentence of death.

In my dream, Barbara telephones Barcelona.
I realize this isn't quite right,
but I just stand there paralyzed, as one does in dreams.
Then, dimly, from the other end of the line,
through the chatter of international operators,
we hear artillery fire, the faint tones of lost men,
cracked voices singing, "Los Quatros Generales" through the
pulsations
of the great, twisted cable under the ocean.
Agonía, agonía, sueño, fermente y sueño.
Este es el mundo, amigo, agonía, agonía.

"No, Barbara!" I scream. "We are not back there.
That's the old revolution. Call up the new one."
Though I know that, every day,
your friends, Nicanor, telephone Santiago,
where the number rings and rings and rings
with never an answer. And now the rings
are turning into knells:

The church bells of Santiago
tolling the funeral of Neruda, his poems looted,
his autobiography stolen, his books desecrated
in his house on Isla Negra.
And among the smashed glass, the broken furniture,
his desk overturned, the ruined books strewn over the floor,
lie the great floral wreaths from the Swedish academy,
the wreaths from Paris, South Asia, the whole world over.
And the bells toll on...
Then I tell Barbara to hang up the phone.

She dials the number again, then turns to me, smiling,
smiling like an angel:

"He is there." Trembling, I take the phone from her,
and hear your voice, Nicanor,
sad, humorous, infinitely disillusioned,
infinitely consoling:
"Dear Carolyn..." It *is* Nicanor!
And the connection is broken, because I wake up,
in this white room, in this white silence,
            in this backwater of silence
on this Isla Blanca:
            Nicanor, Nicanor,
are you, too, silent under the earth,
            Brother? Brother?

THE EIGHTIES

Afternoon Happiness

for John

At a party I spy a handsome psychiatrist,
And wish, as we all do, to get her advice for free.
Doctor, I'll say, I'm supposed to be a poet.
All life's awfulness has been grist to me.
We learn that happiness is a Chinese meal,
While sorrow is a nourishment forever.
My new environment is California Dreamer.
I'm fearful I'm forgetting how to brood.
And, Doctor, another thing has got me worried:
I'm not drinking as much as I should...

At home, I want to write a happy poem
On love, or a love poem of happiness.
But they won't do, the tensions of every day,
The rub, the minor abrasions of any two
Who share one space. Ah, there's no substitute for tragedy!
But in this chapter, tragedy belongs
To that other life, the old life before *us*.
Here is my aphorism of the day:
Happy people are monogamous,
Even in California. So how does the poem play

Without the paraphernalia of betrayal and loss?
I don't have a jealous eye or fear
And neither do you. In truth, I'm fond
Of your ex-mate, whom I name "my wife-in-law."
My former husband, that old disaster, is now just funny,
So laugh we do, in what Cyril Connolly
Has called the endless, nocturnal conversation

Of marriage. Which may be the best part.
Darling, must I love you in light verse
Without the tribute of profoundest art?

Of course it won't last. You will break my heart
Or I yours, by dying. I could weep over that.
But now it seems forced, here in these heaven hills,
The mourning doves mourning, the squirrels mating,
My old cat warm in my lap, here on our terrace
As from below comes a musical cursing
As you mend my favorite plate. Later of course
I could pick a fight; there is always material in that.
But we don't come from fighting people, those
Who scream out red-hot iambs in their hate.

No, love, the heavy poem will have to come
From *temps perdu*, fertile with pain, or perhaps
Detonated by terrors far beyond this place
Where the world rends itself, and its tainted waters
Rise in the east to erode our safety here.
Much as I want to gather a lifetime thrift
And craft, my cunning skills tied in a knot for you,
There is only this useless happiness as gift.

Medicine

for W.S., MD

The practice of medicine
Is not what it was
In my grandfather's time.

I remember him telling me
Of weeks that went by
When he would be paid
Only in chickens
Or only potatoes;

Of treating the families
Of striking miners
In Montrose or Telluride
Who could not pay at all;
Of delivering babies
(A total of twenty)
For a tribe of dirt farmers
Who paid one new-laid egg
Or a cup of springwater:

After sweating a breech birth
And twins at that,
At five in the morning
It was mighty good water.

When, fifty years later,
He came back to the mountains
Middle-aged babies
Ran up in the street

Crying, Doc! Doc! eyes streaming,
Tried to kiss his old hands.

No, the practice of medicine
Is not what it was,
But it has its moments:

That morning in surgery
I regained consciousness
A little too early
And found the doctor
Kissing my hand,
Whispering, whispering,
It's all right, darling,
You're going to live.

How It Passes

Tomorrow I'll begin to cook like Mother:
All the dishes I love, which take her
Such hours to prepare:
The easy dishes that are so difficult
Like finnan haddie and beef stew
"That I wouldn't be ashamed to serve a king";
Her applesauce, bread pudding, lemon sponge,
All the sweet nursery foods
That prove I had a happy childhood.

Starting tomorrow, I'll be brave like Father,
Now that I don't have those recurring nightmares
Of jackboots on the stairs, the splintered door
            just before dawn,
And the fascists dragging Daddy out of bed,
Dragging him down the steps by his wonderful hair;
The screams as his spine cracks when he hits cement.
Then they make him brush his teeth with his own shit.
Though I know this is the price of bravery,
Of believing in justice and never telling lies,
And of being Benjamin, the best beloved.

I'll begin tomorrow. I'll learn how to work
Like my brilliant friends who speak in tongues,
Who drink and crack up, but keep on working,
While I waste my time in reading, reading, reading
The words of my brilliant and not-so-brilliant friends.
I promise to increase production, gather up
            all those beginnings
Of abandoned novels, whose insights astound me

As I contemplate their fading paragraphs.
I'll reveal how ambitious I have been in secret!

There is plenty of time.
I'll find the starter button soon.
After all, young women are meant to meander,
Bemused by fantasies of future loves.
It's just that I'm so sleepy tonight, so tired…
And when I wake up tomorrow, I'll be old.
And when night comes tomorrow,
It won't go away.

After Bashō

Tentatively, you
slip onstage this evening,
pallid, famous moon.

Threatening Letter

I understand youre writing your autobiography youd better be careful remember Im a published author & can strike back I can get printed here for example & you cant anyway the children tell me I dont figure in it they dont either but if you omit your wife & children what can you possibly have to say of any interest nothing absolutely nothing has happened to you except us.

I suppose you will use the excuse I am writing this for my children even though they don't figure in it you will have chapter headings such as my reading in which you will discuss montaigne & stendhal no poetry philosophy or fiction since 1940 you said once i formed all my ideas in school now i dont have to think about them any more its just confusing & deflects me from my purpose that was one of the moments when I realized I have married a nut.

Other chapters will deal with your interest in politics & outdoor sports the latter including your career as a middleweight in college to falling off a mountain at age fifty-nine really at your age no one can say youve been inconsistent Ill bet you still carry that wornout clipping of kiplings if in your wallet.

The unifying principle behind all this is pain if it hurts it must be good for you everything from getting your teeth knocked out at twenty to freezing your balls at 12000 feet I have a great title for you mr negative incapability why not call it my non-life.

Just remember dont go back & put in anything about me I have refrained from writing about you for twenty years mainly from boredom but also because our years together have faded like an old kodachrome in sunlight remember me in the blue bikini on the bear rug with the baby you stretched out at my feet but if you should want to get nasty I feel sure I could resurrect some details & where memory fails invent so just hold down the old paranoia which would contaminate everything you said anyway & keep on including me out & I promise to ignore you when I write mine.

Cupid and Venus

translated from the Scots of Mark Alexander Boyd
(1563–1601)

From bar to bar, from curb to curb I run,
From greasy alley walls I ricochet,
Blown over by my feeble fantasies
Till I drop like a roach from the linoleum.

Two gods guide me: one with a white cane,
Yes, he's a kid brought up to be a bum;
The gutter spawned the other one, a dame
Who roars like a rhino as she comes and comes.

A man pursues unhappiness forever,
Spewing out poems to drunks in the saloon,
And jacking off in the men's room in between.
But it's twice as bad to fool yourself that love
Leads anywhere: chasing that mad cunt up the stairs
As the kid, her blind pimp, eggs me on.

Antique Father

there is something
        you want urgently
                to communicate
                    to me

it is in your eyes
        of ancient
                glacier water

I wait
        I try to listen
                try to tolerate
your terrible silence

                speak   Father

I believe you believe
        I am ready

                we are both tense

I with expectancy
        and the terror you once
                inspired in me

quelling all queries
        of my childhood

not the terror with which we
                    (I over your shoulder)
                                    gaze into the pit
eternity

                          Father speak
from the last edge
            where all folly
                        became wisdom
becomes folly again

            self-quelled   I listen
                      but the lesson
is your nervous silence
                alone on the edge
more than you want to tell
            you don't want
                      to tell
your grave secret

            stern and reticent
                    you cannot say
that I cannot know

            now will never know
                  if you ever knew

Fanny

Part Four of "Pro Femina"

At Samoa, hardly unpacked, I commenced planting,
When I'd opened the chicken crates, built the Cochins a coop.
The Reverend Mr. Claxton called, found me covered with mud,
My clothes torn, my hair in a wad, my bare feet bleeding.
I had started the buffalo grass in the new-made clearing.
The next day the priest paid a visit. Civil but restless,
I was dying to plant the alfalfa seed — gave him a packet.

That evening I paced up and down, dropping melon seeds,
Tomatoes and bush lima beans here and there
Where I thought they would grow. We were short of food now,
So I cooked up a mess of fat little parrots, disturbed
At the way they suggested cages and swings and stands...
An excellent meal. I have been told the dodo survived here,
And yearn for a pet on a string. And I built the pig-house.

I had brought sweet coconut seed from Savage Island.
I planted kidney potatoes in small earthen hills.
Sowed seeds of eggplant in numerous boxes of soil,
Tomato and artichoke too; half-a-dozen fine pineapple
Sent over by Mr. Carruthers, the island solicitor.
As fast as we eat them, we plant the tops.
The kitchen a shack near the house. I made bread in the rain.

October, 1890. I have been here nearly a month;
Put in corn, peas, onions, radishes, lettuce. Lima beans
Are already coming up. The ripening cantaloupe were stolen.
Carruthers gave me mint root and grenadilla
Like a bouquet; he delivered a load of trees,

Two mangoes among them. I set them out in a heavy rain,
Then rounded off the afternoon sowing Indian corn.

Louis has called me a peasant. How I brooded!
Confided it to you, diary, then crossed it out.
Peasant because I delve in the earth, the earth I own.
Confiding my seed and root — I too a creator?
My heart melts over a bed of young peas. A blossom
On the rose tree is like a poem by my son.
My hurt healed by its cause, I go on planting.

No one else works much. The natives take it easy;
The colonials keep their shops, and a shortage of customers.
The mail comes four times a month, and the gossip all day.
The bars are crowded with amateur politicians,
Office-seekers I named the earwig consul and king:
Big talkers, with small-time conspirators drinking them in.
Mr. Carruthers and I picked a site for the kitchen garden.

I was planting a new lot of corn and pumpkin
When a young chief arrived, laden with pineapple plants.
I set them out as I talked to him on the way home.
Rats and a wild hen ate the corn. Lettuce got too much sun.
So I dug a new patch up the road; in the fragrant evening
I confided to Louis, a puff of the sweetest scent
Blows back as I cast away a handful of so-called weeds!

It still hurts, his remark that I have the soul of a peasant.
My vanity, like a newly felled tree, lies prone and bleeding.
I clear the weeds near the house for planting maize.
Sweet corn and peas are showing. I send for more seeds.
I clean out the potatoes, which had rotted in their hills.
Of course, RLS is not idle; he is writing *A Footnote to History:*
How the great powers combine to carve up these islands.

I discovered the ylang-ylang tree: a base for perfume,
Though it suggested to me the odor of boots.
Another tree is scented like pepper and spice,
And one terrible tree, I am forced to say,
Smells like ordure… It nearly made me ill.
Breadfruit is plentiful. I found a banana grove,
Began clearing it instantly, and worked till I was dizzy.

The garden looks like a graveyard: beds shaped like tombs.
I plant cabbage which I loathe, so the British won't tease me
For not growing it. But behold! in the hedge
Among citron and lime, many lemon trees, in full bearing.
Still, I will fall to brooding before the mirror,
Though Louis says he finds the peasant class "interesting."
He is forty today. I am ten years his senior.

On the cleared land, the green mummy-apple,
Male and female, is springing up everywhere.
I discover wild ginger, turmeric, something like sugar.
Roots of orange, breadfruit and mango, seeds of cacao
Came with a shipment from Sydney; also eleven
Young navel orange trees. The strawberry plants are rotten.
I am given a handful of bees. I plant more pineapple.

All fall I am cursed with asthma, rheumatics, a painful ear.
Christmas. A hurricane. And the New Year begins.
Louis describes it divinely to Henry James.
Mr. Carruthers' gift pineapple starts to fruit.
I set out one precious rhubarb plant, pause to gloat
At the ripe tomatoes, the flourishing long-podded beans.
But the neighbors' horses break in and trample the corn.

Sometimes, when planting, a strange subterranean rumble
—Volcanic? — vexes the earth beneath this peasant haunch.

I rise up from my furrow, knuckle smooth my brow
As I sniff the air, suddenly chemical, a sulphurous fume.
Louis insisted on going to Sydney, fell ill again.
His mother comes back with him, finds me on my knees.
The old lady's heart leaps! Alas, I am planting, not praying.

We both rise at five-thirty, after dreaming of weeds.
Louis describes to me endless vivid deeps:
Dreams of nettle-stings, stabs from the citron's thorns,
The ants' fiery bites, the resistance of mud and slime,
The evasions of wormy roots, the dead weight of heat
In the sudden puffs of air... Louis writes till nine,
Then if he's well enough, he helps with the weeding.

He writes Colvin, keeper of prints at the British Museum,
"I know pleasure still... with a thousand faces,
None perfect, a thousand tongues, all broken,
A thousand hands, all with scratching nails...
High among joys, I place this delight of weeding,
Out here alone by the garrulous water, under the silence
Of the high wind, broken by sounds of birds."

The shock of bird-calls, laughing and whistling!
They mimic his name till it seems, he says,
"The birds re-live the business of my day."
But the rain continues to fall on birds and weeds.
The new servants fooled around with the ice machine
As the house leaked and listed. Mildew spread its failure.
Mrs. S. gave me some nuts, and went back to Australia.

Green peppers, eggplant, tomatoes are flourishing,
Asparagus also. The celery does to season soup.
Avocados grow at a rate that is almost frightening.

Coconuts too. I read about Stanley and Livingstone.
I cured my five ulcers with calomel, wished I could tell
Stanley the remedy. Instead, I made perfume.
The servants feared devils, so I planted the orange grove alone.

For two months I misplaced this diary...
War is in the air, talk of killing all whites.
I bought coffee trees, rose trees, and Indian beans,
Then went to Fiji to rest, and to get more seeds
From a former Kew gardener. An Indian in a shop
Told me how to raise Persian melon and cauliflower
And a radish that turns into a turnip when it grows up.

I came home to a burgeoning world: cacao, custard squash.
The new house was finished, and painted peacock blue.
The jealous old cat bit off the new cat's toes.
My mother-in-law returned with her Bible and lady's maid;
My daughter, her family, and my son Lloyd came too.
The relatives had a terrible row. Mrs. S. refused
To pray with the servants. I threw up my hands!

My diary entries grow farther and farther apart.
I wrote life was a strain. Later, someone crossed it out.
In pain again, from an aneurysm inside my head...
I planted more and more cacao, and a form of cherry tree,
Tobacco and rubber, taught how by Mr. Sketchley.
I planted more cacao through an epidemic of 'flu.
Three hundred seeds in baskets broke through the ground.

I get almost no time to write. I have been planting...
Four kinds of cabbage are doing very well.
Mr. Haggard, the land commissioner, come to dine,
Points out a weed which makes excellent eating

Cooked like asparagus. I shall try it very soon.
Now, when the Reverend Mr. Claxton comes to call,
I refuse to see him. I am tired of the Claxtons.

The political situation grows grim. I rage at Louis
Who toasts, "Her Blessed Majesty the Queen," then aggressively
Throbbing, turns to my American son
To say he may drink to the President *afterward*
If he likes. I am writing this down
Hoping Louis will see it later, and be ashamed
Of his childishness and bad taste. (This will be erased.)

Because war is near, the Germans stop growing cacao.
Captain Hufnagel offers me all the seeds I can use.
So now we are blazing with cacao fever,
The whole family infected. Six hundred plants set out!
The verandah tracked with mud, and the cacao litter.
Mrs. S. upset by the mess. Twelve hundred cacaos planted.
Joe, my son-in-law, planted his thousandth tree today.

The tree onions make large bulbs but don't want to seed.
Most vigorous: sunflower, watermelon — weeds!
The jelly from berries out of the bush is delicious;
Lovely perfume from massoi, citron, vanilla, and gum.
The peanuts are weeded while Joe plays on his flute.
I plant cabbage by moonlight, set out more cacao.
The heart of a death's-head moth beats a tattoo in my hand.

Planted coffee all day, and breadfruit, five beauties…
Planted coffee the better part of the day, eight plants.
In the nursery, three times that many. Planted coffee…
Painted the storm shutters. Planted coffee all morning.
I found a heap of old bones in a bush near the sty;

Two heads and a body: a warrior died with his prize.
Louis gave the bones a funeral and a burial.

A series of hurricanes: Louis writes to *The Times*
Of "the foul colonial politics." I send to New York for seeds:
Southern Cross cabbage, eggplant, sweet potato
And two thousand custard apples. Louis' own seed,
David Balfour, is growing. I wrote nothing
From June till the end of this year; too busy planting.
The Samoan princes are getting nearer to war.

It pains me to write this: my son-in-law has gone native
In a spectacular way. Belle is divorcing him.
Austin, my grandson, is in school in Monterey.
I have not, I believe, mentioned Mrs. Stevenson recently.
She has gone back to Scotland. The first breadfruit bore.
Belle and I go on sketching expeditions
To the hostile Samoan camps, stop in town for ginger beer.

Mr. Haggard begged us to stay in town
Because he bitterly wanted women to protect.
I suggested to him that I and my daughter
Could hide under his table and hand him cartridges
At the window, to complete the romantic effect.
It is clear that Mr. Haggard is Ryder's brother!
He said, "You'd sell your life for a bunch of banana trees."

I've given permission to most of the "boys"
To go to the races. Lloyd has put up the lawn tennis things.
Mr. Gurr, the neighbor, rushes in to say war has begun.
We all race to the mission. Eleven heads have been taken.
Later: Mr. Dine's cousin received a head smeared with black
(The custom is to return them to the bereaved).
He washed it off and discovered it was his brother.

He sat there, holding his brother's head in his hands,
Kissing it, bathing it with his tears. A scandal arose
Because the heads of three girls have been taken as well
(Unheard of before in Samoa), returned wrapped in silk to their kin.
At Malie, the warriors danced a head-hunter's pantomime;
The men who had taken heads carried great lumps of raw pork
Between their teeth, cut in the semblance of heads.

I stopped writing this. Too hysterical with migraine.
Also, people find where I hide it, and strike things out.
Our favorite chief is exiled for life. The war winds down.
Louis works on his masterpiece, *The Weir of Hermiston*.
Well, I've kept him alive for eight more years,
While his dear friends would have condemned him to fog and rain
So they might enjoy his glorious talk in London,

Though it be the end of him. Fine friends! except for James.
Later: At six, Louis helped with the mayonnaise,
When he put both hands to his head, said, "Oh, what a pain!
Do I look strange?" I said no, not wanting to frighten him.
He was never conscious again. In two hours he died.
Tonight, the chiefs with their axes are digging a path
To the top of the mountain. They will dig his grave.

I will leave here as soon as I can, and never return,
Except to be buried beside him. I will live like a gipsy
In my wild, ragged clothes, until I am old, old.
I will have pretty gardens wherever I am,
But never breadfruit, custard apples, grenadilla, cacao,
Pineapple, ylang-ylang, citron, mango, cacao,
Never again succumb to the fever of planting.

Exodus

We are coming down the pike,
All of us, in no particular order,
Not grouped by age, Wanda and Val, her fourth husband,
Sallie Swift, the fellows who play bridge
Every Thursday, at Mason's Grill, in the back,
Two of them named George,
We are all coming down the pike.

Somebody whose face I can't make out
Is carrying old Mrs. Sandow, wrapped in a pink afghan;
Her little pink toes peep out from the hem
Of her cotton nightie like pink pea pods,
As pink as her little old scalp showing through.
Be careful, Mister, don't lose ahold of her.
She has to come down the pike.

Maybelle and Ruth walk together, holding hands;
Maybelle wears tennis shorts and a sweatband
As she strides along sturdily in her golf-shoes;
Ruth has on something flimsy,
Already ripped, and sling-backs, for God's sake.
But right now they are both coming down the pike.

Richard had to leave his piano; he looks sort of unfinished;
His long pale fingers wave like anemone
Or is it amoeba I mean?
He's artistic, but would never have been
Of the first rank, though he's changed his name three times.
He doesn't like the mob he's with,

But you can't be picky
When you're coming down the pike.

One of the monitors wants us to move faster,
But you can't really organize this crowd.
The latch on the birdcage was loose so the budgie escaped
About two miles back, but Mrs. Rappaport still lugs his cage:
She's expecting the budgie to catch up any minute.
Its name was Sweetie. I can't stand pet names
And sentimentality at a time like this
When we should be concentrating all our efforts
On getting down the pike.

Who would have thought we would all be walking,
Except of course for Mrs. Sandow, and Dolly Bliss
In her motorized wheelchair and her upswept hairdo.
Someone has piled six hatboxes on her lap;
She can hardly see over, poor lady, it isn't fair,
And who needs picture hats at a time like this.
But they are probably full of other things,
The kind of useless stuff you grab up in a panic
When there's no time to think or plan,
And you've got ten minutes before they order you down the pike.

Bill Watkins is sore that he wasn't chosen monitor
Because he lacks leadership qualities.
But he rushes up and down the lines anyhow
And snaps like a sheepdog. The Ruddy family,
All eight of them redheads, has dropped out for a picnic,
Using a burnt-out car
As a table. Not me, I'm saving my sandwiches.
The Ruddys were always feckless; they won't laugh tomorrow
When they run out of food on the pike.

Of course Al Fitch has nothing, not even a pocketknife
Let alone a gun.
He had to get Morrie Phelps to shoot his dog for him.
No pets! You can see the reason for that,
Although nobody fussed about the budgie.
I expect there's a few smuggled cats
Inside some of the children's jackets.
But old Al Fitch, he just strolls along
With his hands in his pockets, whistling "Goodnight Irene."

My husband says I shouldn't waste my breath
Describing us, but save it for the hike
Ahead; we're just like people anywhere
Though we may act crazier right now.
Maybelle drags Ruth along faster and faster
Though she's stumbling and sobbing, and has already fallen twice.
Richard, who's been so careful of his hands,
Just hit Al, and told him to whistle something else
Like Bach: one of the hymns he wrote, that we could sing.
Will you be trying to sing, wherever you are,
As you come down the pike?

To My Friend Who Rhymes with Peace

For a while my mother was a believer in Coué,
so as a child I chanted, "Every day
in every way, I am getting better and better."
Later in my youth
Mother moved on to The Church of Truth
which Mrs. Weinstein led, and at her nod
we sang, "Be still and know that I am God."

Though it's been years since I believed in me
with that utter childlike faith, I believe in you.
I believe that every day in every way
you are getting better and better;
and if the world is saved, it will be saved
by the likes of you.
Now I am able to be still and know
God *is* us, because so clearly, God is in you.

Whether or not you're here
your husky, girlish voice breathes in my ear
its passion to rescue man from his nightmare
of torture and killing, and the old despair
which tempts us to abandon dreams of peace.
I hear your summoning to work and prayer,
the throb of your indomitable heart, Denise.

For Jan As the End Draws Near

We never believed in safety,
certainly not in numbers
and little more alone.

Picking peas in California
was our old jest of how we'd end our days
when we knew there was no providence,
not any.

We didn't need a reason to be foolish!
Now it turns out that serious theorists
were more improvident than we.

The ones with everything to lose
will mind it most.

I whisper this in some uncertainty:
I don't believe that they grow peas
in California, even on the coast.

Who knows? There may not be a California.

To us it meant a hellish kind of heaven,
a kind that unbelievers could believe in;
a warm land, where we would be
companionable crones

in our little shack, a stinking stove,
a basin of warm water for cracked feet,

each other's hands to stroke
our twisted spines;

our twin grins cracking leather
as we dish out dinner
on our pie-tin plates.

Well, we were a pair of feckless girls!
Depression children, idealists, and dreamers
as our parents and grandparents were.

Of the two of us, you had the darker view.
As it turns out, it wasn't dark enough.

Now the sun shines bright in California
as I shell peas for supper.
Our old-crone fantasies have moved much closer
to an obscure isle in Greece
though we well know that there's no hiding place
down here.

Meanwhile, we've had nearly forty years
to crack our dismal jokes and love each other.
This was our providence, this was our wisdom.
The present is this poem, O my dear.

Thrall

The room is sparsely furnished:
A chair, a table, and a father.

He sits in the chair by the window.
There are books on the table.
The time is always just past lunch.

You tiptoe past as he eats his apple
And reads. He looks up, angry.
He has heard your asthmatic breathing.

He will read for years without looking up
Until your childhood is safely over:

Smells, untidiness, and boring questions;
Blood, from the first skinned knees
To the first stained thighs;
The foolish tears of adolescent love.

One day he looks up, pleased
At the finished product,
Now he is ready to love you!

So he coaxes you in the voice reserved
For reading Keats. You agree to everything.

Drilled in silence and duty,
You will give him no cause for reproach.
He will boast of you to strangers.

When the afternoon is older
Shadows in a smaller room
Fall on the bed, the books, the father.

You read aloud to him
"La Belle Dame sans Merci."
You feed him his medicine.
You tell him you love him.

You wait for his eyes to close at last
So you may write this poem.

Bitch

Now, when he and I meet, after all these years,
I say to the bitch inside me, don't start growling.
He isn't a trespasser anymore,
Just an old acquaintance tipping his hat.
My voice says, "Nice to see you,"
As the bitch starts to bark hysterically.
He isn't an enemy now,
Where are your manners, I say, as I say,
"How are the children? They must be growing up."
At a kind word from him, a look like the old days,
The bitch changes her tone: she begins to whimper.
She wants to snuggle up to him, to cringe.
Down, girl! Keep your distance
Or I'll give you a taste of the choke-chain.
"Fine, I'm just fine," I tell him.
She slobbers and grovels.
After all, I am her mistress. She is basically loyal.
It's just that she remembers how she came running
Each evening, when she heard his step;
How she lay at his feet and looked up adoringly
Though he was absorbed in his paper;
Or, bored with her devotion, ordered her to the kitchen
Until he was ready to play.
But the small careless kindnesses
When he'd had a good day, or a couple of drinks,
Come back to her now, seem more important
Than the casual cruelties, the ultimate dismissal.
"It's nice to know you are doing so well," I say.
He couldn't have taken you with him;
You were too demonstrative, too clumsy,

Not like the well-groomed pets of his new friends.
"Give my regards to your wife," I say. You gag
As I drag you off by the scruff,
Saying, "Good-bye! Good-bye! Nice to have seen you again."

Promising Author

Driving on the road to Stinson Beach
I remember your witty gap-toothed face
Half-ruined in a dozen shore-leave brawls,
And the straw hair and softening gut
Of a beat-up scarecrow out of Oz.

I drove this road with you
Some sixteen years ago
Skidding on curves between the pepper trees.
You whipped the wheel as though it were a helm
And laughed at my nauseated pleas.

Once at the beach you made the finest soup
I've ever tasted: scallops, peas, and leeks,
And I pictured you, the cook on some old tramp
Scudding through Conrad seas,
A boy still dazzled by his luck and grace.

Later that week, in Sausalito's
Bar with no name, I watched you curl your lip
As you ran down every writer in the place,
Unkinder with each drink,
Till I fled up the hill to the French Hotel.

After that you married Beth, so rich
She bought you monogrammed silk shirts,
A dozen at a clip,
You wore as you sneered at your shabby friends
Who had lent you money.

You became glib as any Grub Street hack,
Then demanded help
To write the novel you would never write:
As I turned you from the door
You cursed me, and I cursed you back.

Once I believed you were the great white shark,
Slick predator, with tough scarred hide.
But now I know you were a small sea-lion,
Vulnerable, whiskery, afraid,
Who wept for mercy as you died.

The Glass

Your body tolls the hour,
The hands spin round and round.
Your face, the focus of light,
Will burn me to the ground.

Losing ourselves in love
Beneath this counterpane,
Unwinding from its womb
To the all-consuming now,

All day today I die,
I die eternally,
Losing myself in joy.
By one touch you put out time.

The Light

To wake embedded in warm weight of limbs
Never till now so wholly in repose,
Then to detach your body, strand by strand
From his; but slumbering, murmurous a moment
He confidently drowns again. His arms
Gather you closer, stirring to take leave,
The birds' hushed rapture ushering the dawn.
But hesitate before you break his bonds:

Suspend this moment, see beyond the hour
His form, so tenderly alone and calm,
Yet clinging to that sensual catacomb
Where we embrace eternally in last night.
You rational marvel! As if will were all,
As if this image could be kept or doomed
By what you choose. While still he hems you round
His closed eye holds you faster than your sight.

The Gift

Gift of another day!
To hold in velvet glove
This heavy force of love,
Of you alive in me.

Gift of another noon,
Its crest of tenderness:
In touching we converse,
Thrill in our joy-spent bones.

Gift, as the light declines
Of her reviving powers.
You drench me in new wines.
I fill my hands with flowers.

Gift of another moon,
The perfect O of love
For your single arrow, bowman,
Feather and shaft and eye,

Before we are drawn away
Back into the cold
Scald of the world again
Let us rest, hold, stay.

Heart's Limbo

I thrust my heart, in danger of decay
through lack of use,
into the freezer-compartment, deep
among the ice-cubes, rolls ready to brown 'n' serve,
the concentrated juice.

I had to remember not to diet on it.
It wasn't raspberry yogurt.
I had to remember not to feed it to the cat
when I ran out of tuna.
I had to remember not to thaw and fry it.
The liver it resembled
lay on another shelf.

It rested there in its crystal sheath, not breathing,
preserved for posterity.

Suddenly I needed my heart in a hurry.
I offered it to you, cold and dripping,
incompletely thawed.
You didn't even wash its blood from your fingertips.
As it numbed them, you asked me to kiss your hands.
You were not even visibly frightened
when it began to throb with love.

Maimed, vicious as a ferret mutilated
by an iron trap set for bigger game,
dangerous, smooth as a young stone-bathing serpent,
nude, vulnerable as a new-hatched bird,
now my heart rests in your warm fingers' cage.

Console and heal my heart with gentleness.
Quicken its beat with your caresses.
Be passionate! Be bold!
Give me your heart to hold.

My Good Father

PIERONE'S INC.

RIVERSIDE AND POST — SPOKANE, WASHINGTON 99201

Carolyn Kizer
1401 LeRoy Avenue
Berkeley, California 94708

Dear Carolyn:

I'm attempting to put together a Study Club paper on the subject of your father Ben. I make no bones about my literary abilities, but he has long fascinated me, and at least one benefit of the paper will fall to me: some of my curiosities about him may be satisfied.

My source will be those enormous files your lawyer laid in my office, the *Review-Chronicle* files on him, and some local interviewing.

But I need some insights that the above cannot provide. I want to know more intimate facts about him. He came across as supremely structured, intelligent, polite but always somewhat remote. What was he like to you? How close could he or would he get, was he tactile, did he understand you? Did he have any fears about himself? Was he as strong as he appeared? Was he a loving husband?

Whatever is convenient and comfortable for you to send I'll appreciate.

Bob Pierone

MEN'S CLOTHING, FURNISHINGS AND SPORTSWEAR

FEATURING HICKEY-FREEMAN

Kizer, Benjamin Hamilton, lawyer; b. Champaign County, Ohio, Oct. 29, 1878; s., Benjamin Franklin and Mary Louise (Hamilton) K.; LL. B., U. Mich., 1902; LL. D., Linfield Coll., McMinnville, Oreg., Reed Coll., Portland, Oreg.; m. Helen Bullis, May 19, 1915 (dec. Sept. 1919); m. 2d Mabel Ashley, Mar. 12, 1921 (dec. Oct. 1955); 1 dau., Carolyn Ashley (Mrs. John Marshall Woodbridge). Admitted to Mich. bar, 1902, Wash. bar, 1902, U.S. Supreme Ct. Appeals, 9 th Circuit, 1942–44; dir. China Office, UNRRA, 1944–46; Walker-Ames prof. internat. relations U. Wash., 1946–47, Pres. Spokane City Plan Commn. 1928–44; chmn. Wash. Planning Council, 1933–44; chmn. Pacific N. W. Regional Planning Commn.; former pres. Am. Soc. Planning Ofcls.; chmn. World Affairs Council of Inland Empire. Assoc.; chmn. W. coast lumber commn. Nat. War Labor Bd.; Wash. Chmn. Crusade for Freedom 1950; chmn. Rhodes Scholars Exam. Com. for 6 Pacific N. W. States 1932–64. Bd. regents Reed Coll. Portland. Recipient Auspicious Star, Grand Cordon (China). Mem. Am. Wash. (past pres.), Spokane County (past pres.) bar assns. Phi Beta Kappa, Order of Coif. Author: The U.S. Canadian Northwest. Home: Culmstock Arms Apts., Spokane WA 99201.

(Benjamin Kizer died on April 8, 1978, in his 100th year.)

Dear Bob,

I'm glad to sit down and think about the questions you asked in your letter about Dad. They were the kind a good biographer would be concerned with. "Supremely structured, intelligent, polite but always somewhat remote," you said. So he appeared to all but his intimates. Add "authoritarian and severe," and you get a pretty close approximation of how he appeared to that stranger, his child. After his death, his longtime secretary told me that for about the first six years of my life he referred to me as "Mabel's baby," a rather unusual parthenogenetic attitude! Despite having a younger brother and sister, he seemed to view me much as an early Renaissance painter saw a child: as an adult in miniature. One was expected to be a wholly rational person: no tantrums, no tears, no noisy outbursts whether of shouting, laughing, or sneezing! As a father, you'll appreciate that this attitude was, to say the least, unrealistic. And for a number of years it obscured for me the fact that he was the most loving, demonstrative, and affectionate husband and father.

Two things should be remembered: first, that he was nearly fifty when I was born. He required — demanded — a tranquil household, where nothing should be permitted to disturb his constant activity of thinking and reading. Second, he hadn't much of a childhood himself. As a small boy on the farm in Ohio, he was expected to work, like everyone else. And when he came to Spokane, still a child, the death of his father required him to leave school and work again: selling newspapers on the streets of Spokane, to support his mother, brother, and sister. A forced maturity then, at least a decade before anyone of our generation was expected to behave like an adult. Only the most rigorous of self-discipline saw him through this terrible period. (Of this, and the price he paid for it, more anon.)

Partly as a result of his attitude toward me, I learned to write and read as early as humanly possible. Then, my going to school, and learning things, and getting good marks, began to give us something in common. He was very conscientious about doing things with me during these years (whether prodded by my mother or not, I do not know): taking me for walks and talks (I was expected to discuss intelligently recent Supreme Court decisions at around the age of eight or so), learning to ice skate with me, buying me a bike, going on picnics and expeditions into the country — all activities which I think he genuinely enjoyed. My fear of him diminished, but didn't altogether evaporate until I was around thirty and he was around eighty. Disciplining me was pathetically easy: all he needed to do was speak my name, in what I later discovered was his courtroom voice, and I was quelled. Of course, communication between us was still imperfect. I remember the time in my childhood when he was angriest with me. Like many episodes in the rocky history of parent-child relations, this one grew out of a misunderstanding. During Hoover's first campaign, both of my parents were enthusiastic; my mother, in particular, worked very hard for his election. They were soon disillusioned. Because we were an intensely political household, I was quite aware of this. It was borne in upon me that the name "Roosevelt" was being bruited about in accents of mingled doubt and hope. I knew that Roosevelt was a Democrat, that we had been Republicans, and that we were changing sides. In the middle of a dinner party, with interesting out-of-town guests, one of them asked if we were Democrats or Republicans. "Oh," I interjected breezily, "we veer with the wind." Now at the age of seven or so, precocious as I undoubtedly was (precocity was a survival trait in my relations with my father), I had no idea of the negative implications of this phrase, which indeed I found pleasant and expressive. My father was livid. I have suppressed what he said, but I know that I withered like a violet in an ice-storm.

This little episode also illustrates what was wrong with my upbringing in another respect: Like all bright only children of elderly parents, I was expected to provide the floor-show for visitors. And, like all children, I was thrilled by praise, and tried to top myself: louder, if not funnier. Suddenly the petted and exploited one heard the voice of thunder, and saw the long, bony finger of doom. I assure you, this is not just a writer's hyperbole. If there are still any among those present who were ever on the wrong side of my father in a courtroom, they will recall, all too vividly, what a viscera-shriveling experience it could be. With no prior warning, the kind and indulgent father could turn in an instant into the terror of the courtroom. A verbally battered child, I never knew what hit me. In later life, when I saw the same treatment meted out to members of the House Un-American Activities Committee and other villains of the '50s, to even more devastating effect, I almost forgave him.

I remember, in his early nineties he said an extraordinary thing to me: "The last thing we learn about ourselves is our effect." I think this remark well illustrates his special genius. How he affected others may have been one of the last things he learned, but he went on trying.

Husbandhood is perhaps the finest example of how, in him, the conscious learning-process went on, almost until the end. My mother, until she met my father in her mid-forties, had had a difficult and damaging life. Curiously — or perhaps not so curiously — my grandfather Ashley was very like my father. A figure cold, austere and frightening to his children, and seen as kind and indulgent only later. Unfortunately my mother did not have the shelter I did. She lost her own mother when she was barely entering adolescence, and soon acquired the proverbially cruel stepmother. (I have no idea what this lady was like in reality.) While finishing her own schooling (a Ph.D. in Biology from Stanford in 1904 — pretty unusual for a woman in those days, even in these), and for long years afterward, she was making a major financial contribution to the education of her younger brothers and stepbrothers. She worked, worked, worked, at a variety of fascinating jobs, which I will forbear from describing as this is his story, not hers. Politically, she was a radical, and sexually she was liberated, but alas, I fear, not liberated enough not to feel guilty. Not too many years before she met my father — she was forty — she had a devastating love affair with a fascinating, worldly and eminent man of the Hemingway *macho* type. From this, she declined into tuberculosis, as so many women before her have done. Tuberculosis! That great escape-hatch. How do we get along without it?

So I think it must have been a weary and chastened lady who collapsed into my father's arms, on a bench on the mezzanine of the Davenport Hotel, just two weeks after they had met, and agreed to marry him. (In later years, we would make short, sentimental pilgrimages to that bench. Daddy used to joke with Mr. Davenport about buying it.) My father always claimed that he fell in love with her over the telephone, before he ever saw her. "Her voice was ever soft, / Gentle and low, an excellent thing in a woman," he would quote again and again, with never-diminishing pleasure. For Daddy, if a thing was good, it stayed good. His middle name was fidelity.

Periodically, during their marriage, I heard the oft-repeated re-frain, "If only we had met twenty years earlier!" Then they would variously collapse in ruefulness and laughter, one voice or the other confessing that, in youth, they had been far too willful and stubborn to have made a go of it. But life had taught a great deal to both of them, supremely intelligent as they both were. Hard lessons, harsh lessons, absorbed in loss and pain.

Unlike Mother, Father had been married before. At the age of thirty-six, he began writing fan letters to Helen Bullis, then the po-etry critic for the *New York Times Book Review*. Helen was a con-firmed spinster, seven years older than he, devoted to her aging and crippled mother, with all thought of matrimony, if it had ever en-tered her mind, put well behind her. On the strength of a handful of letters and a snapshot, father proposed. Incredulous, Helen dis-posed. Father bided his time. In due course, Helen wrote him that her mother was desperately ill. Father hopped on a train for New York. He arrived just in time to catch the body, so to speak. He com-forted the bereaved, took care of all the funeral arrangements with wonderful competence, I'm sure, and generally made himself useful, if not indispensable. Poor Helen never had a chance. Triumphantly, he returned to Spokane with his captured bride. From his stand-point, it was a long honeymoon, terminated by Helen's death, only four years and four months later.

They had a mutual joy in horseback riding. One day, Helen's horse puffed out his belly when the saddle was being cinched; later, the saddle slipped under the horse, and he kicked her to death before my father could reach them. Ben was absolutely devastated. To tell how devastated, I need only mention that he, most rational of men, dabbled in spiritualism for a while, finally to turn in disgust from its palpable charlatanry. From the autumn of 1919 to the harsh spring of 1921, my father was a man in mourning, a man whose brightening prospects had turned to the dark night of the soul. It was the thought of this bereaved, forsaken man that prompted Norman

Coleman, President of Reed College, to suggest to my mother that she phone Ben Kizer when she visited Spokane in the course of her work.

Let's pause for a moment, and consider Mr. Rational, as you, and I, knew him. How impulsive can one get? To propose to a woman never seen nor spoken to; and to another, whose voice one fell for over the telephone, a scant two weeks after meeting! And, in both cases, to be supremely right. To love both women with a passion that never diminished, never faded. Consider further: Both these handsome, intelligent, intellectual women were into their forties. Now we must return, for a moment, to that little boy selling newspapers. By his account, young Ben used to rouse himself at four AM so that he might gather up his early edition of the paper and haunt the entrances of the saloons and whorehouses, where the emerging customers, genial and loaded, might carelessly toss a dollar to a little boy instead of the expected nickel. Now we all know, by hearsay and reading, what a tough little frontier town Spokane was in the '80s, a hundred years ago. Its primary purpose was to service the loggers and miners come to town on a toot, to rake the money from their burning pockets by whatever means. When Daddy would tell of those days as a poor newsie, counting every penny that he brought home to pour into his devout Methodist mother's lap, I'd recall these lines of Blake:

> But most through midnight streets I hear
> How the youthful harlot's curse
> Blasts the new-born infant's tear
> And blights with plagues the marriage hearse.

What was blighted in Ben, and kept him a virgin until thirty-seven, was the notion that the flesh alone, prettiness alone, soiled and profaned as it was by need and booze and money, was not enough for him. That the fastidious young puritan could grow into a mature man who positively reveled in sexual love, is a minor miracle.

But what about "nice girls" in Spokane? Like the kind his brother married: nice, respectable, unread and rather stupid. No, for Ben it had to be everything. He never betrayed a flicker of interest in beautiful dumb women. But I'm afraid he never had any interest in homely intelligent ones either! In my memory, the two women who really turned him on were Mme. Pandit, sister of Nehru, and Mme. Sun Yat-sen, both ladies well along in life, both beautiful and diamond-bright. If required to choose between the company of women and that of men, he would unhesitatingly choose the former.

In his eighties, he became pally with some of the nuns at Fort Wright College of the Holy Names. I came to visit him one time when he was still bubbling with pleasure over an evening he had just spent there. Mother Superior, knowing how he detested amateur performances of any kind (to the extent that he never attended any musical or dramatic event at school in which I took part), had assured him that the young woman pianist who was to perform was indeed exceptional. And indeed she had been. It seemed there had been a party afterward, at which he'd clearly had a wonderful time.

"How many people were there, Daddy?" I inquired.

"Oh, about forty, I guess."

"And how many other men?"

"Hm..." He thought for a while. "I guess... there weren't *any!*" He hadn't noticed. His total absence of what we now call "sexism" was one of the qualities for which I cherished him.

In case I'm making Ben sound a little too good to be true, I hasten to add that he was an undoubted "leg man." How he loathed the advent of slacks and jeans! He could not refrain from moans and sighs when I and his granddaughters lounged around in these convenient garments. And what joy he took in the mini-skirt! His nurses told me that, well into his nineties, when a young lady visited him wearing a scrap of skirt that barely cleared her crotch, he was riveted to the spot. He and his heroes, Oliver Wendell Holmes and Benjamin Franklin, had a lot more in common than what went on upstairs.

But to get back to Ben and that wounded bird of passage, my mother (who, incidentally, had great legs): How tenderly he watched over her, alert to the slightest nuance that would indicate that her perpetual self-dissatisfaction had gained the upper hand! How he lavished praise on her, discriminating praise that she could not turn aside, as she habitually did when complimented by outsiders! And he found something to praise in her, something with which to cajole her or please her, *every day* of their married life of thirty-four years. Oh, they quarreled, hotly. Mother would rush to the bedroom and shut the door. When he'd cooled down, Ben would compose a note, and slip it under the door. Sullen, reluctant, Mother would emerge. But he noticed that she'd put on lipstick and smoothed her hair. A little tease, a little hug, and a smile would break through the mask, unwilling at first, then radiant and wholehearted. Mother told me that my father was always the first to patch up a quarrel, that the sun was never permitted to go down upon her wrath, or his. He was a wonderful husband, and she freely admitted it. Whether or not she was ever "in love" with him remains a question. And it's not a question to which children can give an authoritative answer. I know she believed him to be the finest man in all her not inconsiderable experience. And I have to agree with that. I never knew him to have a venal or self-serving moment. I never heard him tell a fib, much less a lie — to himself, or to anyone else. He was, in an old-fashioned phrase which I cherish because of him, "the soul of honor."

He was a man who performed numberless acts of charity and generosity without the necessity of telling anyone about them. Mother and I found out only by accident, and there must be thousands of incidents known only to him and the recipient of his kindness. And he knew how to perform an act of charity without shame to the recipient. Once, when he was in his eighties, I wandered into his law office, to find him confronted by an Italian matriarch, in rusty black, obviously creaking with poverty and age. Something about water rights, which he had settled to her obvious relief. Dad waved me to the chair. Suddenly, anxiety was chasing gratitude right off her old, creased face. "And-a what do I owe-a you, Meester Kizer?" she asked, clutching her old cracked leather coin purse. Daddy put the tips of his fingers together and took it under advisement. "Well, Mrs. Giovanni," he said, courteous as always, "I'm afraid I'll have to charge you twenty cents." Relief flooded her face. With fingers as cracked as her wallet, she extracted two dimes, which he gravely accepted, and proceeded to enter in his little black book. We shook hands all around, and Dad and I sailed out to lunch.

Faults? Of course. With the exceptions noted above, of his concern for my mother and other needy people, he was the most self-absorbed — call it "narcissistic" if you will, if that quality can be present without a trace of vanity about his exterior person — human being that I have ever known. He didn't have to tell anyone of his good deeds because the only person whose exorbitantly high standards he had to satisfy was himself. He was absolutely — and I mean *absolutely* — indifferent to what people thought of him. He knew that people smiled when he walked downtown in the rain wearing a woman's plastic babushka on his enormous head (no hat would fit it). He simply didn't give a curse. Allied to this indifference was that he was perfectly secure in his masculinity. I think this must be attributed to a mother who uncritically adored him and a sister who idolized him (and who was lost to him when she died early, in childbirth, to his evergreen sorrow). That's not enough to explain it, of course, but it's the best I can do.

I think, if the truth must be told, he didn't care very much for very many people. He deeply loved a few men friends, and needless to say, outlived them all: Norman Coleman, George Greenwood, Joel Ferris, Connor Malott, Richard Hargreaves, Stanley Webster, Bishop Cross — nearly all of them members of the Study Club. But for several generations this town was full of people who idolized him, whose names he could barely remember, and quickly forgot.

To him, people were chiefly important as vehicles by which he could express his passion for abstractions, abstractions for which he gaily marched into battle, chanting his war chant: truth, justice, equity, freedom, and law. How he loved the law! Until his infirmities overcame him, I believe he was a truly happy man. But I don't want to leave him in his bed, at the end — a bed that never knew the print of his body in the daytime until he was over ninety-three. I want to go back in time about ninety years. It's five o'clock in the morning, and a skinny, undernourished little newsboy is pushing a paper at you: "All about the death... Getcher paper here, mister! All about the death of Charles Stewart *Par*nell!"

All the best to you and the Study Club,

Carolyn

Horseback

for Raymond Carver

Never afraid of those huge creatures,
I sat sky-high in my western saddle
As we roared through the woods of skinny pine;
The *clump clump* of his great delicate hooves
Stirring plumes of pine-needle-scented dust!
One casual hand on the pommel,
The other plunged in the red coarse hair of his mane.

I remember the day he stopped dead on the trail
Trembling all over. We smelt bear, then heard
The chattering song of the rattler.
My hypnotized bay couldn't move. Time stopped:
The burnt odor of sage, the smoky noon air
And the old old snake, as big around as my skinny wrist,
Rising up from his rock.

Then the screen goes blank, and next it's summer camp:
I've mastered a wild mare bareback, whipping one arm
In sky-wide circles like a movie cowboy,
Screaming with joy.
So now when a stubborn skittery horse runs away with me
I give him his head. But as he tries to skin me off,
Plunging under low branches, I grit, "Oh no you don't!"

I bury my face in his neck, hang on for dear life,
Furious, happy, as he turns to race for home.
We pound into the stable yard and I dismount,
But wonder at curious glances turned my way
Until I see myself in the tack-room mirror,

My face a solid mass of purple welts.
Then I begin to sneeze and sneeze. My allergies

Burst into bloom, and I am forced to quit,
And don't sit a mount again for twenty years
Until I get to Pakistan
And Brigadier Effendi puts me up
On his perfect white Arab mare.
My thighs tighten the old way as I marry a horse again...
I just wanted to tell you about it, Ray.

To an Unknown Poet

I haven't the heart to say
you are not welcome here.
Your clothes smell of poverty, illness,
and unswept closets.
You come unannounced to my door
with your wild-faced wife and your many children.
I tell you I am busy.
I have a dentist's appointment.
I have a terrible cold.
The children would run mad
through our living room, with its collected
bibelots and objects of art.
I'm not as young as I was.
I am terrified of breakage.

It's not that I won't help you.
I'd love to send you a box
of hand-milled soap;
perhaps a check,
though it won't be enough to help.
Keep in mind that I came to your reading:
Three of us in the audience,
your wife, myself, and the bookstore owner,
unless we count the children who played trains
over your wife's knees in their torn jeans
and had to be hushed and hushed.

Next month I am getting an award
from the American Academy
and Institute of Arts and Letters.

The invitation came on hand-laid paper
thick as clotted cream.

I will travel by taxi
to 156th Street, where the noble old building,
as pale as the Acropolis,
is awash in a sea of slums.
And you will be far away, on the other Coast,
as far from our thoughts as Rimbaud
with his boy's face and broken teeth,
while we eat and drink and congratulate one another
in this bastion of culture.

The Valley of the Fallen

In this Valley of the Fallen, one finds the soul of Spain, beautiful and severe. When the great bronze doors — eleven tons each — swing open for state ceremonies, ten thousand worshippers can assemble there at a time.... Only Franco and his intimates know the cost of this monument with its adjacent Benedictine monastery and its lavishly fitted center for social studies....

BENJAMIN WELLES

I.

My new friend, Maisie, who works where I work,
A big, pleasant woman, all elbows and peasant skirts,
Has a young child, and debts, and struggles on her own.
Not twenty-one, I am her confidante.
Gallant, intrepid, she soldiers on;
But in the ladies' restroom, or when we munch
Our sandwiches at our adjoining desks,
Her bitterness erupts: the bum! the bum
Who, when she was pregnant, knocked her down,
Stole money from her purse to spend on drink,
And still harasses her with drunken calls
In 1946.
One day I have to ask,

"Maisie, why did you ever marry him?"
Gazing into her large, pale-blue eyes
That brim with rue: "Well, you see,
He fought in the Abraham Lincoln Brigade."
"Oh," I say. I would have done it too.

II.

When I say I wouldn't go to Spain
Till Franco died, I've told a whole
Biography: my age, my politics,
My Red — and red-haired — mother whose green eyes
Sparked at the sins of tyrants anywhere;
My father, who was counsel for the poor
And radical, against the bigot and the hater,
Burnt up the courtroom with his tongue of flame
(McCarthy got around to us much later).
So Spain burst in while I was still a child:
My introduction to the world.

At seventeen, my first love, Frank,
Gave me some records, battered seventy-eights,
The off-key songs of the International Brigade.
I still sing them, remember all the words
In Spanish, French, German:
"The Peat-Bog Soldiers," accompanied by harmonica
In a Barcelona basement; *Freiheit!*" we sing
To a guitar. You can still hear
The thuds of the bombardment.
I sing and listen till the tears run down.
That's forty years of tears.

> Seven hundred men worked every day for ten years to dig this
> place, and many of them were political prisoners of the regime.
> Franco lies now in a tomb before the high altar, and all day long
> the monks, the nuns and soldiers file through....
>
> JAN MORRIS, 1979

III.

My husband and I shudder a bit and smile —
He's an architect, has seen photographs
Of Franco's grandiose memorial,
The Valley of the Fallen.
At first the thought appalled, but we've decided
It's part of architecture, part of history too,
So we drive the road from the Escorial,
Climb tiers and tiers of stairs,
Take in the view.

The whole vast place is virtually empty
Save for a handful of tourists like ourselves.
Down the long gloomy hall, not as grotesque
As we expected; muted lights;
Chisels score the vault so that we'll know
They tunneled through the mountain,
Franco's slave labor, some the very men
Who fought him.

But at least they buried him!

We reach the circular altar with its flame;
First, the grave of José Antonio,
Primo de Rivera, who fathered the Falange,
On it a huge ugly wreath
From the Italian Fascisti.
I wouldn't be surprised if asps crawled out
Beneath its leaves of artificial bronze,
But still — at my age — am surprised
That the old evil lives.

Behind this, the Caudillo's stone.
I say, "I'm going to spit upon his grave."
John tilts his head toward the honor guard,
Impassive, armed, white-gloved.
He knows me well enough
To know I just might do it. But instead,
I speak a curse: *Franco, I spit upon your grave.*

On the way out, we use the men's room
And the ladies' room, try to buy postcards
But it's closing time;
Then drive back to Madrid,
Where I read poems to the kids
At the University,
In a classroom scarred with revolutionary slogans
Eight years old, that no one's bothered to erase.
I sing of Lorca, Chile, and Neruda
And the wars we lose.

> The Valle de los Caidos can be included in your trip to the
> Escorial.... Like a modern-day Valhalla, the crypt is cut through
> 853 feet of living rock and surmounted by a 492 foot cross of
> reinforced concrete faced with stone (with an elevator to the top).
> Admission 75 pesetas with two in a car; 100 pesetas for more than
> two. Open 9–7:30.
>
> FODOR'S SPAIN, 1984

Ingathering

The poets are going home now,
After the years of exile,
After the northern climates
Where they worked, lectured, remembered,
Where they shivered at night
In an indifferent world.
Where God was the god of business,
And men would violate the poets' moon,
And even the heavens become zones of war.

The poets are going home
To the blood-haunted villages,
To the crumbling walls, still pocked
With a spray of bullets;
To the ravine, marked with a new cross,
Where their brother died.
No one knows the precise spot where they shot him,
But there is a place now to gather, to lay wreaths.
The poets will bring flowers.

The poets are coming home
To the cafés, to the life of the streets at twilight,
To slip among the crowds and greet their friends;
These young poets, old now, limping, who lean on a cane:
Or the arm of a grandchild, peer with opaque eyes
At the frightening city, the steel and concrete towers
Sprung up in their absence.
Yet from open doorways comes the odor of grapes
Fermented, of fish, of oil, of pimiento...

The poets have come home
To the melodious language
That settles in their heads like moths alighting,
This language for which they starved
In a world of gutturals,
Crude monosyllables barked by strangers.
Now their own language enfolds them
With its warm vocables.
The poets are home.

Yes, they have come back
To look up at the yellow moon,
Cousin of that cold orb that only reflected
Their isolation.
They have returned to the olives, the light,
The sage-scented meadows,
The whitewashed steps, the tubs of geraniums,
The sere plains, the riverbanks spread with laundry,
The poppies, the vineyards, the bones of mountains.

Yes, poets, welcome home
To your small country
Riven by its little war
(As the world measures these events),
A country that remembers heroes and tears;
Where, in your absence, souls kept themselves alive
By whispering your words.
Now you smile at everything, even the priests, the militia,
The patient earth that is waiting to receive you.

Election Day, 1984

Did you ever see someone coldcock a blind nun?
Well, I did. Two helpful idiots
Steered her across the tarmac to her plane
And led her smack into the wing.
She deplaned with two black eyes & a crooked wimple,
Bruised proof that the distinction is not simple
Between ineptitude and evil.
Today, with the President's red button playing
Such a prominent role,
Though I can't vote for it, I wonder
If evil could be safer, on the whole.

Final Meeting

for James Wright

Old friend, I dressed in my very best,
Wore the furs I never wear,
Hair done at Bloomingdale's,
Even a manicure; splashed on the good perfume
Before I rode the bus up Madison
To the rear entrance of the hospital;
Traversed for miles the corridors underground
Where orderlies in green wheeled metal carts
Piled with soiled linen, bottles, pans, and tubes.

Then, elevators found, I followed a colored line
To the proper nurses' station,
Embraced your wife: pale, having wept for weeks,
Worn out with your care.
She led me to your bedside. I swept in with an air,
Wrapped you in fur, censed you with my perfume.
Jaunty and thin, with the fine eyes and pursy lips
Of one of Holbein's Unknown Gentlemen,
You could not speak
Except for some unintelligible grunts
Through the hole they had made in your throat;
Impatient with your wife
Who, after years of understanding,
Could not understand.

Months of practice with my dying father
(Shamed by his memory lost, he refused to speak,
Like Ezra Pound at the last) taught me a monologue:

Of our days in Roethke's room so long ago
Far off across a continent in Seattle:

One day when the bell had rung
We stood by the stairs in shabby Parrington Hall
As the hordes rushed past us to their classes.
"Oh, Carolyn," you said in such a grieving tone,
"Beautiful women will never love me."
And I replied, "One day
You're going to be a famous poet,
And you'll be pursued by lovely women."
"There! Wasn't I right?" I now say,
And you look up sweetly at the lovely woman
Who stands on the other side of your bed.

Dear one, back then you were so plain!
A pudgy face, a button nose, with a little wen
Right at the tip.
But we all knew, from the moment you spoke
On the first day in class, you were our genius.
Now pain has made you beautiful.
And the black satin domino
To shade your eyes when you nap,
Pushed back on your head, looks like a mandarin's cap.
With your shapely thin gray beard
You are phenomenally like Li Po,
A poet you adored.

"Well, dear, there's no Ohio left — except in poems";
I keep up a stream of jokes and reminiscences.
You scribble notes on your yellow pad,
Nod your mandarin nod.
Grief is not permitted till it's over,

And I'm outside, stunned, standing on Fifth Avenue
In the fierce cold of January.
Here I say what I could not say upstairs in your room:
A last good-bye. And thank you for the poems
You wrote to me when we were young.

         Now go in peace, my friend,
Even as I go
Along the soiled pavement of the Avenue
Banked in the gutters with old snow.

THE NINETIES

Gerda

Down the long curving walk you trudge to the street,
Stoop-shouldered in defeat, a cardboard suitcase
In each hand. *Gerda, don't leave!* the child cries
From the porch, waving and weeping; her stony mother
Speaks again of the raise in salary
Denied. Gerda demands ten dollars more
Than the twenty-five a month she has been paid
To sew, cook, keep house, dress and undress the child,
Bathe the child with the rough scaly hands
She cleans in Clorox; sing to the child
In Swedish, teach her to pray, to count on her toes
In Swedish. Forty years on, the child still knows how,
Is a great hit with children under seven, in Sweden,
Singing a folk song, praying, counting toes.
For twenty-five dollars a month in 1933
Gerda makes for the child her favorite, *fattigmand,*
A mix of flour, milk, and eggs you cut in strips,
Then fry in fat, then dust with sugar
(The child helps Gerda cook so she knows that).
In Stockholm the child will inquire of *fattigmand,*
But like lost Gerda it does not exist.

Deep in the Depression, the child fears for her
As Gerda trudges down the walk, four blocks to the bus,
Then the train to Minneapolis. *What will she do?*

Gerda, trained as a nurse, found no work before
She came to us. Twenty-five dollars a month
To sew a quilt for the child, covered with fabulous
Animals, feather-stitched in blue and white;
Now after fifty years it hangs on the wall
Of the child's grandchild, in a Chicago house.
Then, when the child awoke, addled and drunk with nightmare,
She dragged the quilt from her cot,
Stumbled sniffling into Gerda's room,
To be taken into her bed, soothed back to sleep
By the rough, antiseptic hands.

The child wakes up to naked light.
Ageless Gerda's steel-gray bob shakes into place
(She owns no mirror);
Blind Gerda gropes for her steel-rimmed spectacles
As the child sees, with fascinated love,
The curd in the corner of each of Gerda's eyes.
It is a magic substance the child has improvised
On a favorite tale: Hans Christian Andersen's
"Snow Queen." She thinks of it as the good cream curd,
The reverse of the splinter in the eye
Of little Kay: everyone, like the brave child in the story,
Everyone like Gerda.

Modest Gerda dresses in the closet,
Then the two on tiptoe steal to the child's room
So the stout handsome mother will not waken.
Then Gerda bathes the child, scrubs her hard all over
With the loofah, dries her carefully on the big warm towel,
Pulls on her panties of white cotton, then the dress,
Smelling deliciously of Gerda's iron, the dress
Gerda smocked at night while the household slept,

Then the pastel sweater Gerda knitted her.
The child sits on the edge of the bed while Gerda
Brushes then twists the child's fair hair
Into two fat braids secured with rubber bands.

The child, so much fairer than her parents, nearly believes
She's Swedish; is pleased then, and forty years on,
To be taken for Scandinavian: Gerda's own.
Now Gerda pulls up the white anklets, fastens the sandals.
Down to the pantry! — where the child climbs into her chair.
Gerda sets three places, one for the child,
One for the child's imaginary playmate, one for her.
And they eat the lovely oatmeal Gerda cooked the night before.

Thirty years on, her father will remark,
Your mother was jealous
So we let her go. Of course I could have raised her wages,
Gerda ran the house! The child's throat fills with bile
As, casually, he continues: *I always let your mother*
Decide these matters. Smug, he often used that phrase
As if the abdication of his parenthood
Had been a sacrifice. What did he know
Of the child's needs or passions?
So Gerda left the house, the yard, the garden,
The child's home long torn down,
A place that no longer exists.
Thirty-five years on, the child stumbles along the weeds
In search of the path down which her Gerda walked
Or a trace of the porch where she once stood, bereft.

The child's eighth year, like Gerda, disappeared.
Hazy recall of illness:
Asthma, the wheeze, the struggle for breath,

And the louder, rhythmic wheeze of oxygen...
Of the weeks in bed, lying inert, nothing remains,
Only the pallid joys of recovery,
Jell-O and milk, ice cream three times a day
(Was this a bribe?);
Dreamily sucking a spoonful of melting vanilla:
Only these splinters of a vanished year.

It must have been then that the icehouse dream began,
Her first and last recurring dream:
The child stands in a little room of ice;
Outside a song begins, impossibly nostalgic,
Played on a concertina or harmonium.
As the dream goes on
Slowly, slowly the walls move in, the ceiling presses down
Till she is encased in a kind of upright coffin
Of milky iridescent ice. Entranced by a vision
Of green hills and pure blue skies without,
She conceives freedom and flight!
She must memorize the tune as the ice moves in
To touch her on every side and on her head.
As the last, haunting note is played
The child wakes up. Of course the tune is gone.
It is always gone.

For ten years the child nurtures a secret plan:
At last she boards a train for the East,
Waits for the layover in Minneapolis,
Hurries to a pay phone, armed with change,
Opens the directory,
Faints to see four columns, closely printed,
Of Gerda Johnsons. *How could there be more than one?*
Ranging her nickels on the metal counter.

She calls from the top
As the hands of the clock spin round.
Gerda! Gerda! Half a page
With answers none, or ancient whispery Norse voices
Down a tunnel of years, and oceans crossed
And cold home villages abandoned long ago.
Then she runs out of change and time. A train to catch.
She weeps at terminated hope, nourished for so long,
As the old filmstrip runs again:

Gerda, you trudge down the walk forever;
The child, no matter how she calls and cries,
Cannot catch up.
Now from another life she summons you
Out of the earth or ether, wherever you are,
Gerda, come back, to nurse your desolate child.

Pearl

Every Thursday Pearl arrived in her old Model A
with a satchel of lotions cremes and balms
        to make over Mother.
Fresh from her bath, Mother lay on her ample belly
as Pearl pummeled, rubbed, massaged
        the firm fleshy back of Mother
till it turned from sweaty peach to glistening crimson.

Then they move from her bed to the still-steamy bathroom,
        where
Mother bends over the basin as Pearl soaps her head;
        and the witness-child
stares at the face of her mother, upside-down
        between brown curtains of hair.
Pearl, busy as any nurse or minister,
        moves briskly from sink to chair,
applies the harsh-colored henna the child abhors.

Pearl seems to ignore the child's disapproving frown;
        the child can't catch her eye,
though Mother's, luminous and green, are transfixed with pity
as she attends to Pearl's inconsequent chatter;
        beneath it, Mother and child
hear the drone of the terrible dirge that is never over,
the song of a fatally wounded Columbine
        with her crazed painted smile:

Pearl, frantic with a croupy daughter,
        frightened of losing days

of work with Madame Patenaud, her termagant employer,
had forced her own little girl to swallow her medicine.
But what was hastily thrust between the child's burning lips
was Lysol. The little girl abandoned her.
                    Pearl is alone forever.

Now this child imagines Pearl as hollow,
                    a decorated funerary urn
set on an altar not to God but to Beauty.
Pearl paints Mother's toenails propped on the sink.
                    Why hadn't she died?
But perhaps she had — and it's a ghost of her
who pearls these fingers, toes; then later paces
the nightmares of the child. Desolation and desertion!
Pearl's ivory face averted as the child begs mercy
                    from the bleak desert of dream.

But now, swathed like a houri in a heavy towel,
                    Mother leans back in her chair
while Pearl stirs magic in a jar: brown sticky unguent.
Pearl's mentor, Madame Patenaud, in long-ago Los Angeles
was a genius with cremes and lotions; even today
                    Pearl's voice hushes with awe
as she applies the secret formula reeking of tar
(the child's nose never forgets), a potion which,
faithfully used, confers eternal youth.

She would be Ponce de León to Pearl's elixir,
eternally youthful Mama, fat and beautiful,
                    transfixed
as Time is cheated; Pearl swabs her face, dabs it with ice.
They study her reflection, Pearl nods
with satisfaction; only a tiny frown

as Pearl tweezes a single hair from Mother's arching brows:
        a Japanese master gardener
who plucks one needle from a famous pine.

The child senses the bond between these two,
the tragic and the laughing Muse — she, barefaced now,
an empty canvas on which Pearl plies her skills
except that it is a speaking canvas, critical
of its creator, who reinvents her look
        as the child is shut out.

She who grimaces hideously in the mirror,
puffing her cheeks or putting out her tongue,
is stuck, she fears forever, with this pudding oval
        which no hand molds.
Oh, she will cartoon herself with bloody lipstick
        stolen from Mama,
but scorns her own lack of skill — presses Mother and Pearl
        to be let in.

As we grow older, Mother, you close the distances
between us, with kisses, dresses, tiny conspiracies.
We cuddle beneath one comforter, serene and mild.
But Pearl, O Pearl, I would have been your heart's fulfillment.
I was your prodigy, your dream of life.
        I was your murdered child.

Reunion

For more than thirty years we hadn't met.
I remembered the bright query of your face,
That single-minded look, intense and stern,
Yet most important — how could I forget? —
Was what you taught me inadvertently
(Tutored by books and parents, even more
By my own awe at what was yet to learn):
The finest intellect can be a bore.

At this, perhaps our final interview,
Still luminous with your passion to instruct,
You speak to that recalcitrant pupil who
Inhaled the chalk-dust of your rhetoric.
I nod, I sip my wine, I praise your view,
Grateful, my dear, that I escaped from you.

An American Beauty

for Ann London

As you described your mastectomy in calm detail
and bared your chest so I might see
the puckered scar,
"They took a hatchet to your breast!" I said. "What an
Amazon you are."

When we were girls we climbed Mt. Tamalpais
chewing bay leaves we had plucked
along the way;
we got high all right, from animal pleasure in each other,
shouting to the sky.

On your houseboat we tried to ignore the impossible guy
you had married to enrage your family,
a typical ploy.
We were great fools let loose in the No Name bar
on Sausalito's bay.

In San Francisco we'd perch on a waterfront pier
chewing sourdough and cheese, swilling champagne,
kicking our heels;
crooning lewd songs, hooting like seagulls,
we bayed with the seals.

Then you married someone in Mexico,
broke up in two weeks, didn't bother to divorce,
claimed it didn't count.
You dumped number three, fled to Albany
to become a pedant.

Averse to domesticity, you read for your Ph.D.
Your four-year-old looked like a miniature
John Lennon.
You fed him peanut butter from the jar and raised him
on Beowulf and Grendel.

Much later in New York we reunited;
in an elevator at Saks a woman asked for
your autograph.
You glowed like a star, like Anouk Aimée
at forty, close enough.

Your pedantry found its place in the Women's Movement.
You rose fast, seen suddenly as the morning star;
wrote the ERA,
found the right man at last, a sensitive artist;
flying too high

not to crash. When the cancer caught you
you went on talk shows to say you had no fear
or faith.
In Baltimore we joked on your bed as you turned into
a witty wraith.

When you died I cleaned out your bureau drawers:
your usual disorder; an assortment of gorgeous wigs
and prosthetic breasts
tossed in garbage bags, to spare your gentle spouse.
Then the bequests

you had made to every friend you had!
For each of us, a necklace or a ring.

A snapshot for me:
We two, barefoot in chiffon, laughing amid blossoms
your last wedding day.

On a Line from Valéry

Tout le ciel vert se meurt
Le dernier arbre brûle.

The whole green sky is dying. The last tree flares
With a great burst of supernatural rose
Under a canopy of poisonous airs.

Could we imagine our return to prayers
To end in time before time's final throes,
The green sky dying as the last tree flares?

But we were young in judgment, old in years
Who could make peace: but it was war we chose,
To spread its canopy of poisoning airs.

Not all our children's pleas and women's fears
Could steer us from this hell. And now God knows
His whole green sky is dying as it flares.

Our crops of wheat have turned to fields of tares.
This dreadful century staggers to its close
And the sky dies for us, its poisoned heirs.

All rain was dust. Its granules were our tears.
Throats burst as universal winter rose
To kill the whole green sky, the last tree bare
Beneath its canopy of poisoned air.

the Gulf War

Suppressing the Evidence

Alaska oil spill, I edit you out.
You are too terrible to think about.
I *X*, I double-*X* you out.
The repeated floods in Bangladesh:
The starving poor who stare at us,
Stare with plaintive smiles,
Smiles without hope
As they clutch a bulbous-bellied child,
I erase your dark faces.
I edit you out.

From the dark windows of their limousines
The rich long since have waved their ringed hands,
Said Abracadabra, to disappear the poor.
Their streets are swept clear
So the homeless are sucked down the dirty drains.
Only their reflections in the tinted glass
Stare back in their complacent discontent:
The blind rich, in their blind car.

On Madison a young emaciated man
In a threadbare jacket shivers in the snow.
Help me. Please. I have no place to go.
I hold out a dollar bill between his face and mine
Like the fan of an old Japanese courtesan,
Then hurry past as his face turns to smoke.

I flee the city, back to my comfortable farm
In the valley of wine. I drink the wine.
I do not turn on the news.

I and the wine will blot it out.
And we erase more and more of the world's terrible map;
How may we bear witness, as we should?

I must hold in my mind one small dead otter pup.

Fearful Women

Arms and the girl I sing — O rare
arms that are braceleted and white and bare,

arms that were lovely Helen's, in whose name
Greek slaughtered Trojan. Helen was to blame.

Scape-nanny call her; wars for turf
and profit don't sound glamorous enough.

Mythologize your women! None escape.
Europe was named from an act of bestial rape:

Eponymous girl on bull-back, he intent
on scattering sperm across a continent.

Old Zeus refused to take the rap.
It's not *his* name in big print on the map.

But let's go back to the beginning
when sinners didn't know that they were sinning.

He, one rib short: she lived to rue it
when Adam said to God, "She made me do it."

Eve learned that learning was a dangerous thing
for her: no end of trouble it would bring.

An educated woman is a danger.
Lock up your mate! Keep a submissive stranger

like Darby's Joan, content with church and Kinder,
not like that sainted Joan, burnt to a cinder.

Whether we wield a scepter or a mop
It's clear you fear that we may get on top.

And if we do — I say it without animus —
It's not from you we learned to be magnanimous.

Halation

A phenomenon... which caused an ambiguous shimmering
brightness to appear on the print where sunlight and foliage
came into contiguity.

JANET MALCOLM

My dear, you moved so rapidly through my life
I see you as a ghostly blur;
You are the subject, I the ornament
Eternally crossing cobbles on some *rue*,
Where a covey of pearl umbrellas glistens
And ladies pause — courtesy of Caillebotte — though
This is of an era before we were born.
But the impression is emotionally true:
A sheen of rain, a gray noncommittal sky;
Limp banners cling to window frames (Monet);
And the bonnet, shovel-shaped with a crimson brim,
Casts a becoming glow over my face,
No longer young, ambiguous, shimmering.
A bunch of violets tucked at the waist, the figure
Navigates curb and puddle, assisted by
A gentleman in black, a courtly crook of arm:
Poseur and posed, the painter and the painted
Doubly exposed. Now I am reminded

Of a woodland picnic slightly earlier,
You almost fully dressed, I not quite naked;
You in the serge of your reserve
And I as bare as in those disturbing dreams
That reveal our vast uncertainties, including
Those of Giorgione and Manet.
Background figures (us, in fair disguises)

Haunt the middle distance, bosky, green,
Stand witness, even when reclining...
But I am no *Chérie* but *Liebchen. Liebchen.*
Our expeditions did not end in halcyon places.
Instead, all roads led to a sanitary fill
In full sunlight. Nothing ambiguous about that.
We raise champagne in paper cups, toast each other,
Perched on the tailgate of an ugly car.
But the shutter snaps, and we slip into art,
Its negative image: sister into brother.

Once a little coarse, a trifle epicene
(A little too Rouault, whom you admired),
You've silvered over through the passing years.
Now, like a platinum plate, imagination,
That elusive luster, may transform
A row of poplars to the filaments of desire;
An alley, lit by one gas lamp, the path
To Charon's boat, that ultimate black stream.
This fluid which develops and embalms
Beyond the possibility of alteration,
Is cropped by us, to suit perversities
Of taste and time. Your sinewy arm (Cézanne's)
Seemed to wrap twice around my waist.
Dreamer and dream, in close-up confrontation,
The pair emerged as Bonnard's moving blurs.

Touch now, O author of my authorhood,
Your peer at last in contiguity
Before we went our ways and broke the frame.
What happened to us, friend? You saw the light,
Not that of haloed streetlamps. Halogen
Impersonally scanned us, banishing

All subtle shadows, a trace of leaves at night.
The hallowed moon, astigmatized before,
Is glowing with a brighter face than ours,
Scored by the years, focused last, and free.

Mud Soup

1. Had the ham bone, had the lentils,
    Got to meat store for the salt pork,
    Got to grocery for the celery.
    Had the onions, had the garlic,
    Borrowed carrots from the neighbor.
    Had the spices, had the parsley.
    One big kettle I had not got;
    Borrowed pot and lid from the landlord.

2. Dice the pork and chop the celery,
    Chop the onions, chop the carrots,
    Chop the tender index finger.
    Put the kettle on the burner,
    Drop the lentils into kettle:
    Two quarts water, two cups lentils.
    Afternoon is wearing on.

3. Sauté pork and add the veggies,
    Add the garlic, cook ten minutes,
    Add to lentils, add to ham bone;
    Add the bay leaf, cloves in cheesecloth.
    Add the cayenne! Got no cayenne!
    Got paprika, salt, and pepper.
    Bring to boil, reduce heat, simmer.
    Did I say that this is summer?
    Simmer, summer, summer, simmer.
    Mop the floor and suck the finger.
    Mop the brow with old potholder.

4. Time is up! Discard the cheesecloth.
   Force the mixture through the foodmill
   (Having first discarded ham bone).
   Add the lean meat from the ham bone;
   Reheat soup and chop the parsley.
   Now that sweating night has fallen,
   Try at last the finished product:

5. Tastes like mud, the finished product.
   Looks like mud, the finished product.
   Consistency of mud the dinner.
   (Was it lentils, Claiborne, me?)
   Flush the dinner down disposal,
   Say to hell with ham bone, lentils,
   New York Times recipe.
   Purchase Campbell's. Just add water.
   Concentrate on poetry:
   By the shores of Gitche Gumee
   You can bet the banks were muddy,
   Not like Isle of Innisfree.

Twelve O'Clock

At seventeen I've come to read a poem
At Princeton. Now my young hosts inquire
If I would like to meet Professor Einstein.
But I'm too conscious I have nothing to say
To interest him, the genius fled from Germany just in time.
"Just tell me where I can look at him," I reply.

Mother had scientific training. I did not;
She loved that line of Meredith's about
The army of unalterable law.
God was made manifest to her in what she saw
As the supreme order of the skies.
We lay in the meadow side by side, long summer nights

As she named the stars with awe.
But I saw nothing that was rank on rank,
Heard nothing of the music of the spheres,
But in the bliss of meadow silences
Lying on insects we had mashed without intent,
Found overhead a beautiful and terrifying mess,

Especially in August, when the meteors whizzed and zoomed,
Echoed, in little, by the fireflies in the grass.
Although, small hypocrite, I was seeming to assent,
I was dead certain that uncertainty
Governed the universe and everything else,
Including Mother's temperament.

A few years earlier, when I was four,
Mother and Father hushed before the Atwater-Kent

As a small voice making ugly noises through the static
Spoke from the grille, church-window-shaped, to them:
"Listen, darling, and remember always;
It's Doctor Einstein broadcasting from Switzerland."

I said, "So what?" This was repeated as a witticism
By my doting parents. I was dumb and mortified.
So when I'm asked if I would like to speak to Einstein
I say I only want to look at him.
"Each day in the library, right at twelve,
Einstein comes out for lunch." So I am posted.

At the precise stroke of noon the sun sends one clear ray
Into the center aisle: He just appears,
Baggy-kneed, sockless, slippered, with
The famous raveling gray sweater;
Clutching a jumble of papers in one hand
And in the other his brown sack of sandwiches.

The ray haloes his head! Blake's vision of God,
Unmuscular, serene, except for the electric hair.
In that flicker of a second our smiles meet:
Vast genius and vast ignorance conjoined;
He fixed, I fluid, in a complicit yet
Impersonal interest. He dematerialized and I left, content.

It was December sixth, exactly when,
Just hours before the Japanese attack
The Office of Scientific R & D
Began "its hugely expanded program of research
Into nuclear weaponry" — racing Germans who, they feared,
Were far ahead. In fact, they weren't.

Next night, the coach to school; the train, *Express,*
Instead pulls into every hamlet: grim young men
Swarm the platforms, going to enlist.
I see their faces in the sallow light
As the train jolts, then starts up again,
Reaching Penn Station hours after midnight.

At dinner in New York in '44, I hear the name
Of Heisenberg: Someone remarked, "I wonder where he is,
The most dangerous man alive. I hope we get to him in time."
Heisenberg. I kept the name. Were the Germans, still,
Or the Russians, yet, a threat? Uncertainty…
But I felt a thrill of apprehension: Genius struck again.

It is the stroke of twelve — and I suppose
The ray that haloes Einstein haloes me:
White-blond hair to my waist, almost six feet tall,
In my best and only suit. Why cavil? — I am beautiful!
We smile — but it has taken all these years to realize
That when I looked at Einstein he saw me.

At last that May when Germany collapsed
The British kidnapped Heisenberg from France
Where he and colleagues sat in a special transit camp
Named "Dustbin," to save them from a threat they never knew:
A mad American general thought to solve
The postwar nuclear problem by having them all shot.

Some boys in pristine uniforms crowd the car
(West Pointers fleeing from a weekend dance?),
Youth's ambiguities resolved in a single action.

I still see their faces in the yellow light
As the train jolts, then starts up again,
So many destined never to be men.

In Cambridge the Germans visited old friends
Kept apart by war: Austrians, English, Danes,
"In a happy reunion at Farm Hall."
But then the giant fist struck—in the still
Center of chaos, noise unimaginable, we thought we heard
The awful cry of God.

Hiroshima. Heisenberg at first refused
To believe it, till the evening news confirmed
That their work had led to Hiroshima's 100,000 dead.
"Worst hit of us all," said Heisenberg, "was Otto Hahn,"
Who first discovered uranium fission. "Hahn withdrew to his room,
And we feared that he might do himself some harm."

It is exactly noon, and Doctor Einstein
Is an ancient drawing of the sun.
Simple as a saint emerging from his cell
Dazed by his own light. I think of Giotto, Chaucer,
All good and moral medieval men
In—yet removed from—their historic time.

The week before we heard of Heisenberg
My parents and I are chatting on the train
From Washington. A gray-haired handsome man
Listens with open interest, then inquires
If he might join us. We were such a fascinating family!
"Oh yes," we chorus, "sit with us!"

Penn Station near at hand, we asked his name.
E.O. Lawrence, he replied, and produced his card.
I'd never heard of him, but on an impulse asked,
"What is all this about harnessing
Of the sun's rays? Should we be frightened?"
He smiled, "My dear, there's nothing in it,"

So reassured, we said good-byes,
And spoke of him in coming years, that lovely man.
Of course we found out who he was and what he did,
At least as much as we could comprehend.
Now I am living in the Berkeley hills,
In walking distance of the Lawrence Lab.

Here where Doctor Lawrence built the cyclotron,
It's noon: the anniversary of Hiroshima:
Everywhere, all over Japan
And Germany, people are lighting candles.
It's dark in Germany and Japan, on different days,
But here in Berkeley, it is twelve o'clock.

I stand in the center of the library
And he appears. Are we witnesses or actors?
The old man and the girl, smiling at each other,
He fixed by fame, she fluid, still without identity.
An instant which changes nothing.
And everything, forever, everything is changed.

Parents' Pantoum

for Maxine Kumin

Where did these enormous children come from,
More ladylike than we have ever been?
Some of ours look older than we feel.
How did they appear in their long dresses

More ladylike than we have ever been?
But they moan about their aging more than we do,
In their fragile heels and long black dresses.
Then say they admire our youthful spontaneity.

They moan about their aging more than we do,
A somber group — why don't they brighten up?
Though they say they admire our youthful spontaneity
They beg us to be dignified like them

As they ignore our pleas to brighten up.
Someday perhaps we'll capture their attention,
Then we won't try to be dignified like them
Nor they to be so gently patronizing.

Someday perhaps we'll capture their attention.
Don't they know that we're supposed to be the stars?
Instead they are so gently patronizing.
It makes us feel like children — second-childish?

Perhaps we're too accustomed to be stars,
The famous flowers glowing in the garden,
So now we pout like children. Second-childish?
Quaint fragments of forgotten history?

Our daughters stroll together in the garden,
Chatting of news we've chosen to ignore,
Pausing to toss us morsels of their history,
Not questions to which only we know answers.

Eyes closed to news we've chosen to ignore,
We'd rather excavate old memories,
Disdaining age, ignoring pain, avoiding mirrors.
Why do they never listen to our stories?

Because they hate to excavate old memories
They don't believe our stories have an end.
They don't ask questions because they dread the answers.
They don't see that we've become their mirrors,

We offspring of our enormous children.

Arthur's Party

I came with some trepidation to your vernissage
Knowing your palette: bellicose neon rainbows
Staining the white walls of our old garage.
But who looked at paintings? Elbow nudging elbow,
Your friends and I were exchanging persiflage.

One of Mother's favorite words was "persiflage,"
So I swore one day I'd put it in a poem. Here,
Mom! Many and many's the Village vernissage
We attended, she and I, exchanging badinage —
Another good one! we said, sewing togas in our garage.

I put on plays for the neighborhood in that garage:
Hamlet — its end a stageful of limp doll's bodies;
Then Comedy Time: my improv, my leaden persiflage.
(What a tedious child I was!) You painted sets with brio.
But now is now: we return to your vernissage.

Your friends grab wine from trays at the vernissage
Where color strangles color — rude, avenging rainbows!
As badinage grows more vulgar, more blurry the persiflage.
But you'll succeed one day. Be patient. (Ha!) My mother
Fingered you young, as we played in our garage.

In Hell with Virg and Dan

"Yo, Dan, just give a look at this repulsive creature
Called Fraud, the wall-buster; He's the prime polluter.
The poison in his tail's an added feature."
Then Virgil gave the high sign to that stink
Of rottenness, to make a three-point landing on the shore.
But he told it not too near that awesome brink.
It sunk its head and chest but not its tail.
10 Its face was mellow, friendly-like, and human,
But like a great big ugly snake its torso;
Hair to its armpits like a hippie, only more so.
Its front and back were covered with some weird design
Tattooed with knots and circles to the hip, he
Shone like a rainbow or embroidery, just so fine
No third-world Turk or Tartar stitched it better
18 Or the Spider Woman spun a thinner line.
Then like a boat half-beached and half in water,
Or when they're home, gross Germans overeat
22 Or a beaver waits for prey (*but Dan, it was an otter*),
That squalid monster lay where shore and water meet.
Its poisoned tail was quivering in the empty air.
Now my leader told me, "Just direct your feet
To where you're closer to that crouching Geryon."
No way to duck my fate. I had to carry on.
Though, man, I was terrified, not paranoid.
We stuck to the right, took ten steps round the bend,
Trying to dodge the sand and fire — but then I saw
36 Some ways on, a bunch of dudes that sat like in a spell.
Then Virg says, "Go check out those moneylenders
So you'll learn the score about this ring of Hell.

And while you're rapping with them, I'll cajole
Old Geryon, to see if it will lift us
Out of here on its humongous shoulders.
But make it quick. This is no place to stick around."
So all on my own I crept along the strand
Of the Seventh Circle where those sad jerks hung out,

46   Weeping cascades, lifting their butts off the burning ground.
They slapped at the flames or at the red-hot sand
Like dogs in summer, with their paws and snouts
Trying to fend off gnats or fleas or flies.
I stared like hard at all their fire-scorched faces
And I didn't recognize a single man.

55   But I saw a purse that was hung round every neck,
Each one with a fancy color and design,
That all those wretched creeps were grooving on
As if each pouch was good enough to chew.
One yellow purse was stamped with a turquoise lion;
Then I saw on another chest a bag all bloody red
That showed a goose pale as oleo or sweet butter.
A guy with a white purse showing a pregnant sow

65   Turned on me with a ferocious mutter:
"Get the hell out of Hell, and do it now!
Ditch this ditch — but since you're alive I'll tell you
My old pal, Vitaliano, will pretty soon be dead;
He'll sit on my left. Meanwhile these fucking Florentines
— And me a Paduan! — keep screaming in my ear,

72   'Let's hear it for that awesome cavalier
Who wears a purse with three goats printed on it.' "
He twisted his ugly lips, stuck out his tongue at them
Like an ox that licks its nose. I thought I'd better split
Before my peerless leader chewed me out.
And Virg had climbed aboard. "Don't let your nerve fail.

82   We gotta go down this scary flight of stairs.

Hop on in front, away from that vicious tail."
I'm shaking like a guy who croaks from fever,
His fingernails already turned blue-white,
At the thought of a place where there's no sunlight ever.
From Virgil's words I'm so panicked I'm passing out.
Because he's so gutsy though, I'm struggling to be brave
90 Like a junior camper facing an Eagle Scout.
So I climbed on and clung to those scaly shoulders
And tried to say — but the words wouldn't come out right —
"I'm begging, Virgil baby, hold me tight!"
I knew I could count on Virg when things got scary;
He'd saved my ass a few times before this.
He hugs me close, goes, "Get a move on, Gery!
Sail in wide circles, retract your landing gear
As we sink with this new load you have to carry."
It slipped, inch by inch, off the edge of the abyss
100 Like a big ship sliding from its moorings;
And when it had backed enough to feel in the clear,
Geryon took off, went spinning in a circle
Till its chest was where its tail had been before,
Stretched out that eely tail, using it to steer,
Gathered up the air in its huge paws.
No one had ever been more scared than I was,
Not even Phaëthon when he let go the sun-car's reins
And scorched the sky — the scars still seen in the Milky Way;
Not even Icarus, wings falling off as he neared the sun
110 When the wax that held them on had begun to melt,
And his old man yelled, "You've gone too far!" That's how I felt.
Nothing but air around me, nothing to be seen
Except for horrible Gery, swimming, swimming down,
And me so petrified I've turned from white to green.
Geryon wheels, starts to descend, but all I know
Is the wind that slams my face, and I hear the horrible roar

Of a giant whirlpool — like an idiot I look down:
Then I get one heavy case of acrophobia,
Sweating as I hang on even tighter than before.
But landing is worse than flying: I see fire and I hear sobs.
124 That whirlpool is boiling blood, like old Khomeini's fountain.
Gery spirals for a touchdown. Around us screeching mobs
Of pain and terror: evil coming nearer, nearer, nearer...
Like an exhausted raptor, a falcon that won't quit
Though all day it hasn't spotted anything to capture
Until its trainer cries, "Come down!" — releasing it
To fall from the sky; but the big bird won't go near
Its master: weary, sulking, perched far off on a jagged stone:
That's how horrible Geryon acts as it sets us down.

And, man, when it unloads, it's outta there, like gone.

NOTES:

Numbering: I've numbered according to Dante's lines, but if you're a compulsive counter you'll notice that some of the numbers are missing. That's because occasionally I've conflated two lines into one. Dante gets a bit long-winded from time to time, while I am noted for my concision.

Line 22: Dante messed up here. He should have said an *otter*. So I threw in an editorial comment in parentheses. Dan thought these animals fished with their tails, which nicely expands his metaphor even though it isn't true.

Line 46: *Nobody else* (poets, that is) has translated that phrase about the usurers raising their rear ends from the burning sands. (See Singleton's notes.) Tsk.

Lines 55–68: Who cares about a bunch of corrupt dudes who lived 700 years ago? Oh all right, so they're the Gianfigliazzi, the Obriachi, the Scrovegni — and the Umbriago (just kidding).

Line 72: This is (sigh) Giovanni Buiamonte dei Becchi. Dante is going in for some heavy irony here: the Florentines heaping honors on this piece of scum.

Line 124: I couldn't resist referring to the late Ayatollah's attractive Fountain of Blood in Tehran's cemetery. An old failing of mine. Sorry about that.

Lost in Translation

for Lu Xing'er

"Why wouldn't she entertain her nephew?
There has to be a reason in the story."
Mr. Chuck, who translates, wouldn't translate
Or couldn't. He says the brilliant Chinese novelist
Seems to say the nephew doesn't matter.

"There has to be a reason for the nephew."
I don't think that Mr. Chuck is trying.
"She denies there is a lesbian component
In this story of a friendship between women."
I grow impatient. "That's really not the issue.

"A friendship between two such different women,
One older, lonely, the other kind, gregarious —"
I challenge Mr. Chuck to translate *that* —
"Seems to founder on the issue of the nephew."
He says she says the nephew's not important.

"But when the nephew asks if he may visit,
And the older woman doesn't want to bother,
Though the other urges her to be adventurous,
Reach out! befriend the young! — that's not important?"
"There is nothing homosexual in the story."

"I didn't say there was!" I'm getting cranky.
As the novelist talks more, he translates less.
(What kind of crazy Chinese name is Chuck?)
"Isn't the cooling of the women's friendship
Due to their differing views about the nephew?"

The friendship ends because the older woman
Learns that her friend has had a married lover
When she had thought they were celibate together.
"There is nothing homosexual about it."
"But, Goddammit, what about the nephew?

"A writer doesn't just throw in a nephew
For no good reason. He must advance the story.
Are you saying that Lacan *et cie* are right,
That the author doesn't know what she is doing
Until the critic condescends to tell us?"

The brilliant Chinese novelist is famous
Especially for "One on One," this story.
Mr. Chuck is just an old-time Chinese journalist
Who smiles opaquely at the two articulate women
Snagged on the barbed wire of the language barrier.

He doesn't care. It's only a couple of women
Trying to discuss another pair of women.
His part is to neuter this conversation.
No sex! Especially no homosexuality.
He, not the nephew, is just an old Red herring.

Cultural Evolution

after Pope

When from his cave, young Mao in his youthful mind
A work to renew old China first designed,
Then he alone interpreted the law,
And from traditional fountains scorned to draw:
But when to examine every part he came,
Marx and Confucius turned out much the same.

Medicine II

for John Murray

When the nurses, interns, doctors came running full tilt down
                                                    the hall,
Dragging the crash-cart with shrieking wheels and flagless IV pole,
And that squat box, the defibrillator, made to jolt the heart;

Then we next-of-kin, pasted against the walls, ran after them
To your room, Mother-in-Law, where they hammered hard on
                                                    your chest,
Forcing you back to life in which you had no further interest.

For the third time they pressed like lovers on your frail bones
To restart the beat. They cheered! Marked you alive on your chart,
Then left you, cold, incontinent, forlorn.

When the man loved by you and me appealed to your doctor
To know why you couldn't have your way and be let go,
He said, "I couldn't just stand there and watch her die."

Later, when it was over, we spoke to a physician
Grown gray and wise with experience, our warm friend,
But ice when he considers the rigors of his profession,

And repeated to him your young death-doctor's reply,
We heard the stern verdict no lesser person could question:
But that was his job: to just stand there and watch her die.

Poem for Your Birthday

for Barbara Thompson

This year both our birthdays end in zero,
Symbol, perhaps, of the nothing we'll become
Except as the reflections of our children —
Your boys, my girls — in the next millennium
Now so near. Who thought we'd see it come?

Let us reflect awhile on us, my dear:
Born fortunate, two creatures petted and well-fed
With milk and vitamins, thus our good teeth and skin;
Curled hair and handmade clothes and patent slippers,
This side of the moat from the desperate unemployed.

Ah yes! — and hasn't that come round again!
We circle back to the fascinating question:
How did we get from there to where we are?
We've perched on the edge of revolution, war,
I, in China, you, in Pakistan.

We both knew children who have died by fire.
We're yoked in sympathy for all that's human,
Having loved those of every tone of skin,
Having lived the loss of extraordinary men.

And the poems we've read aloud to each other!
You wave your arms in a wide arc of rapture,
Moved by the Muse and another glass of wine.
I cherish that characteristic gesture
As you must smile at some oddity of mine.

Truly to relish trivia in flower,
Woman-talk of recipes and clothes,
One must be aware of that high discourse
On art and life we could deal with if we chose.

"The flow of soul," as Pope extravagantly called it,
Unstopped, though years of parting intervene,
Though illness, duties, children interrupt,
We know we'll go on talking to the end

Or after, when we still reach out in thought,
Or waking, sense the living person near.
The password at the boundary is *Friend*.

Marriage Song

with commentary

We begin with the osprey who cries, "Clang, clang!"
Which is the sound of the door of marriage slamming.
Our metaphor sits on a nest, surrounded
By blooming succulents; ospreys, like swans, mate once.
For form's sake they appear in public together;
Because she and her spouse play separate roles
They will forgo connubial bliss if necessary
To save their feathered souls.

Complementary image: young, pale, scared,
Has menstruated once, sequestered in a cave,
Miss Chou Dynasty, under lock and key
Thus to preserve her sacred chastity,
Knows that someday her Prince will come.
But this occurs between stanzas two and three.
Thus far she is only a dream in his questing eye.
He doesn't come, he just breathes heavily.

The principal commentaries differ here:
Mao-fang believes the lady tossed from side to side
In bed with long long thoughts of separation.
A respected version claims that the aging bride
Dutifully tried to recruit the limberest dames
For her still-randy spouse, states earnestly
That she worried about the good ones getting away
— Or so the followers of Confucius say.

But what, Students, was the intention of the Poem
Before the moral scholiasts worked it over?

The text obscure: was it maid or matron here?
Did not our Princess roll from side to side
Alone with long long thoughts of her absent lover,
Reluctant, yes, to pick out next year's successor
Yet feeling perhaps it was better to marry *and* burn
Than to stay yearning in that cave forever.

Now cry desire, shake silver tambourines
To cue the strings of gypsy violins
As the Fisher-Prince mates with his fluttering Bride.
O her chaste joy! She will hold him in her bosom
(Suckle her spouse in dream), then toss and turn...
The girls glide out of reach like water-lilies
Slipping along the current of the stream.
Though Pound and Waley speak of zither and gong
In truth our modest heroine breaks into song:

"Alone, I become virginal again.
I know the cave, I learn the cave within.
And you, my Lord, are somewhere out of reach.
I hear your breathy sigh: the aging man
Tuning his lute in our remotest room.
Beside myself at last, I think and think
Of ospreys on their island, dark of wing,
Snow-breasted, and transfixed in abstract love."

Index, a Mountain

part of the Cascade Range, Washington State

I.

Early one day a mountain uprose, all cased in silver
Where morning fog caught in the tips of cedars
And a moon-colored sun polished virgin timber.

As Red Freddie, our old new Studebaker
Steams over the Cascades, Mother says to Father,
"I wanted to bring you here on our honeymoon;
First growth. Never cut over." In my fifth year,
Carsick on hairpin turns, bribed not to chatter
A penny a mile; the black-timbered Inn at the summit
Where I roll out and under the bed at night,
Awake, screaming with claustrophobia,
Clawing the bedsprings, having dreamed
Me in my coffin.

Motoring on at dawn, to Index then we came:
A cut muscle. A smoking cinder.

An old bald lumberman had cut God's finger,
Himself missing a limb. (As usual, Retribution
Didn't know when to quit, took the whole arm.)
One day he'll appear on sixteen-millimeter film,
Bracing his brassie between one stump
And a tough left arm.
The drive sails down the fairway, hooking slightly.
He gloats; a ghostly hand pinned to his shoulder.

Twenty years have passed, and I, all unknowing,
Have married the grandson of this predator.

O friends and our descendants, what remains?
Banquets of sawdust, hazy leisure bought
From the swink of loggers and the stink of pulp;
Victorian mansions ugly as the mills
Bulldozed for malls, car stalls defined
By rows and rows of scruffy little trees.

Preserve nothing! The simple motto of our frontier
Because men choked on green, were suffocated
By a press of trees, fire was their liberator.
Fire went too far, like Retribution,
Like any Revolution. Revenge has a long finger.

O Pioneers, who stripped the earth so fast,
Who toiled so hard Imagination failed.
How could you dream of the later Marxist
Trailblazers, enshrining worker-heroes
On their plinths of crumbling concrete,
Giant fingers that pierced the ancient ceiling
Scarred with the junk of her astronauts and ours?
Our icons: Lenin, Bunyan: Peter and Paul
Like Barnum pointing, "This way to the Egress,"
To be saved from our follies by fleeing to the stars.

II.

Ours is a world full of finger-worship
As the holy Roman bone-collectors knew:
Keepers of femur and tibia, toenail sniffers
Their artisans formed silver reliquaries,

Cool tubes, like those that encase a good cigar,
To hold erect the dust of an index finger.

Now, for history, we drive a car
From the empty summit (the old inn long burned down)
Past Troublesome Creek to Goldbar, a mining camp
Where a few Chinese were saved from an early riot
By shipping them out-of-town in slapped-up coffins,
To Sultan, where they lit the lamps at three
In the afternoon, woods were so dense.
Lilacs were as large as fruit trees once;
Houses of pioneers, with weathered siding,
Looked like birds' nests fallen among the cedars,
Such great dark brooding trees they were!

The barren shade of the high Cascades ends here.
It's all burned-over, pocked with stumps that look
Like the old man's arm. The view, as we descend,
Blending to smooth pasture, pastoral landscape
Dotted with cows, gives way to golf-course lawns,
A strident green, bobbed willows, men on carts.
While just outside the gates a sign proclaims,
"The Wages of Sin is Death!" A finger aimed at *you.*

This West! full of crank religions, bleeding atoners,
Raw, shapeless women, stringy men with tracts
On your porch at dawn, wanting to play you a record.
The pulp they press on us with bony fingers
Conceiving us in Sin, had its own conception
In the sawmill's sweet dust — pressed from our trees!

O Index, naked mountain, with your scarred flanks
Still your raw summit points to heaven.
Serve as God's tombstone. Have no green mercy on us.

A Song for Muriel

No one explains me because
There is nothing to explain.
It's all right here
Very clear.
O for my reputation's sake
To be difficult, and opaque!

No one explains me because
Though myopic, I see plain.
I just put it down
With a leer and a frown...
Why does it make you sweat?
Is this the thanks I get?

No one explains me because
There are tears in my bawdy song.
Once I am dead
Something will be said.
How nice I won't be here
To see how they get it wrong.

Anniversaries: Claremont Avenue, from 1945

I'm sitting on a bench at One Hundred and Fifteenth
and Riverside Drive, with my books beside me,
early for my lesson in Chinese
at Twenty-one Claremont, right around the corner.
Two little girls pass in front of me
wheeling a doll carriage, fussing
with the doll and the doll blanket: then casually
one of them says, "the President is dead,"
pulling the coverlet over the doll's head.
The other replies in a flat little voice, "Yes,
the President is dead." I think, "Strange children
who toy with the notion of mortality!"

Wind sweeps from the Hudson. Chill. It's time to go.
In the lobby I press the button for the elevator;
at last it clanks to a stop, the doors slide open
and I confront the seamed black face of Joe
runneled with tears. So I know it's true:
The President is dead. We rise in silence
past the floor where a lonely boy may play
those holidays when he's freed from boarding school.
Thirty years later almost to the day
I'll marry him, in a church eight blocks away.

The elevator groans to the fifth floor.
Bliss, the gentle Chinese wife, opens the door,
her smile faint in the lotus of her face.
My teacher, Chen, expressionless. We start the lesson
as if nothing unusual has occurred,
then fall silent. Bliss brings the balm of tea,

exquisite Bliss who, ten years further on,
will hang herself in their pale-blue bedroom
with one of Chen's ties.
Before our tea is cool my mother comes
smiling and weeping. Though the President and she
are of an age, like Bliss and me
she has lost the father
who'd almost seen us through a war.

When Mother and I take the Seventh Avenue subway
the cars are stuffed with people black and white;
strangers murmur to strangers, strangers crying
as they clutch their papers, headlines black on white.
There's comfort here, but it's cold as we straggle out
in the dark, to Sheridan Square.
Later my first sister-in-law will tell me
that at Vassar, girls were dancing on the tables
cheering the news — an alien breed of stranger.
I'm glad I wasn't there
but with the bereaved on Seventh Avenue.

In the eighties we go to stay with my husband's mother,
this cultivated student of art history
and liturgical music. She is a baseball nut
comparing notes with Joe as they watch TV.
Chen, who is friends with no one, reappears
in the Claremont lobby, after thirty years,
and invites us for a drink.
As the elevator labors up I am suffused
with memories of Bliss: Bliss and her taste:
celadon walls, peach-blossom silk embroidery,
jade objects on the tables, jade

on her wrists, a flower at her throat,
that porcelain throat...
Bliss and your incense, your pleading tremulous heart.

At six, Chen answers the bell
and we step into a cavern grim as hell:
bare boards, a cot with dirty sheets,
card table, metal folding chair — and that is all.
In great gray swags, wallpaper peels from the walls,
a stack of *Wall Street Journals* in the corner.
Where are the carpets, the bibelots, the scrolls?
All gone, sold or destroyed. A bottle of whiskey
and three tumblers sit on the rickety table.
Miserable, we stand awkwardly and drink
while Chen tells us he's gambled it all away;
matter-of-factly says what we don't care to hear:
how in their final years Bliss and he
could only masturbate each other.
I bless my husband's upright stone-faced Mother.

It's 1985: in pain, my mother-in-law has died.
Appraisers from Doyle pick through her possessions:
old furniture blistered by sun and central heat.
Twenty-one Claremont is no longer ours.
Recollections are blistered and faded too:
My husband's boyhood toys, my fragments of Chinese.
Mothers have disappeared. Wars come and go.
The past is present: what we choose to keep
by a process none of us can ever know.

Now those little girls are grandmothers
who must remember, after fifty years,
the doll, the chill, the tears.
Greatness felled at a blow.
Memory fractured. Black and white apart.
No sense of direction, we Americans.
No place to go.

Fin-de-Siècle Blues

I.

At seventeen I'm told to write a paper
on "My Philosophy": unconscious Emersonian
clone, courtesy of my father,
"There is no evil," that's what I say,
"merely the absence of good." I read the papers.
Where was my head? (In the clouds, like Father
and the senior William James.) I must have known
some of the bad news. No evil, eh?
Ho, Ho, Ho, Holocaust! Tell it to the Jews.

I wrote another paper, worrying
about the fate of historic monuments,
Art, not people, during World War II.
Give me that tired query from Ethics 101
concerning the old lady and a Rembrandt etching
in a sinking rowboat: which one would I save?
Now that I *am* one, still I have serious doubts
about saving the old lady.
Rembrandt would have won.
And if they could have been crammed into the rowboat
so would the French cathedrals and the Parthenon.
(There was some kind of screaming aesthete
naked within my transparent ethical overcoat.)

But now, take Sarajevo: Old ladies, buildings,
children, art; all perish together
along with honor and philosophy;

the hypothetical rowboat long since sunk
in the polluted Mediterranean Sea.
The century suffers entropy — and so do I.

II.

Well, it's been one hell of a century:
Endless lists of victims, Armenians, Jews,
Gypsies, Russians, Vietnamese,
the Bosnians, the Somalians,
torture and rape of the dissidents all over
the map; and as Time winds down
the music slows,
grows scratchier, plays off-key,
America chimes in with its own obbligatos:
what we did to the Nicaraguans, the Salvadorians,
diminuendos with Granadans, Panamanians —
and we're still hassling poor old Castro.

Whole continents go on living under tyrannies
till tyrannies give way
to chaos and criminality.
Is it the horror, or that we know
about the horror — this evening's blood
on the screen?
Yugoslavia, before our eyes, is Balkanized
to death; but today, brave us,
today we recognized Macedonia.
(Vasco is dead, thank God,
and how are you faring, dear Bogomil?)

Then we have AIDS...
Maurice, Tom, Tony, Gordon, Jim, Peter, Bill,

bitterly I mourn you
and wait for the next beloved name.
The redneck senators who would starve the Arts
are a less efficient scourge.
We who are merely witnesses
to all this grief
also pay a price.
NOT AN ORIGINAL THOUGHT
(that's part of the price).

Horror numbs.
Violence, whether fictional or true,
is socially addictive.
NOT AN ORIGINAL THOUGHT
Serious satire undermined
by sexual and political
grotesquerie.
NOT AN ORIGINAL THOUGHT
So why go on? I'm blue. Boo-hoo.
Got those End-of-the-Century blues.

III.

Now to personalize and trivialize the topic,
as writers, what are we to do?
We gag on scandal, our lives are gossip fodder.
In our marginal way, we are becoming stars.
Never mind the work. Who cares for that?
Did the man who reinvented the sonnet
urinate in his bed one night when drunk?
Did our great fat nature poet
throw up in his hat?

Forget the revolution they created
with their raw confessional poetry;
it's the suicides of two women
which fascinate,
not their way of working
but their way of death.

O you serious men and women
who wrote your poems, met your classes,
counseled your students, kept your friends
and sent magic letters home,
your lives are pillaged and rearranged
by avid biographers who boast that they tell all,
so it seems you always reeled in a mad whirl
of alcohol, abandonment, and sexual betrayal.
(I sorrow for the stain on your memory,
Anne, Randall, Ted, Elizabeth,
Delmore, John, and Cal.)

As writers, what are we to do?
Our roles as witnesses ignored,
our fine antennae blunted
by horror piled on horror,
our private matters open
to the scrutiny of voyeurs.
If we have wit and learning
it's met with the apathy
of the ever-more-ignorant young.
How do we hope to carry on
in the last gasp of the millennium?

Much as we always have: writing for one another,
for the friends we tried to impress in school

(like Tonio Kröger), for the dead father or mother,
for our first mentor, compassionate and cool,
for the dead authors who watch over us.
We'll write when bored in strange hotel rooms,
we'll write when the conscience pricks,
we'll write from passion, present or reviving,
making copy of our pains or perverse kicks.
We'll write if a cookie dipped in tea
transports us to the fields of memory.

But first of all we'll do it for ourselves,
selfish and narcissistic and obsessed as ever,
invading the privacy of those who care for us,
spilling sad secrets confided by a lover.
We take note of the café where Valéry took notes,
van Gogh's yellow chair, the monastery
where Murasaki wrote, as Petrarch did,
in a room eight feet by three;
name-and-place-dropping, grooming our fur,
fanning and shaking our peacock tails
(dry sticks rattling in the wind),
always, always ourselves our own mirrors.

The burden of our song: good luck to the young!
Let's drink (for we drink) to a better world
for them, if they should live so long.
As my father the optimist used to say,
"It's the unexpected that happens."
There is little point in being fatalistic;
whatever occurs will be different from
what we anticipate,
which, to be frank, is universal doom.

Everyone who reads this is older than Mozart,
than Masaccio, than Keats, much older than Chatterton.
We're taller, handsomer, healthier than they.
So let's just count these years we've lived as velvet
as Carver said at the end — sweet Ray.
I'm blessed by parents, children, husband, friends
for now... Nothing can take that away.

NOT AN ORIGINAL THOUGHT

Call up Voltaire. Tend the garden.
Seize the day.

NEW POEMS

Trio

Some say sorrow fades.
I shall carry my sorrow forever
After I smile farewell
To those who led me here.
Only joy endures.
Joy remains in the mind
As do those who made us glad
In a moment of light forever.

My mother, my early lovers,
One tall and fair — a friend;
One fearful, swart, and tired,
Antagonist to the end.
My mother, tall and fair,
Embracing death and weather,
Fearful and glad together!
What silence shakes the mind
Now it has lost your way,
Your full consoling laughter?

Now that your light has gone
A long long light remains.
I weather into age
Mourning the brave and kind.
I pace the days along,
Three shadows follow after:
Two who were tall and fair
Are caroling behind,
And a third, who had no song.

In the Night

There are spirit presences
Around my bed
Waiting for me to die.
They are in no great hurry
Nor am I.

Do not fear death,
I whisper to my keepers.
Fear life if it goes on too long.
For the lost losers
Make winners weepers.

It's so quiet tonight
I can hear the angels breathing.
Our hands are transparent,
As veined as autumn leaves.
I rest in their arms
And sense the mist rising.

Shalimar Gardens

In the garden of earth a square of water;
In the garden of waters a spirit stone.

Here music rises: Barbelo! Barbelo!
Marble pavilions border the water.

Marble petals of lotus bevel
The edge of the pool.

All about us a green benediction!
God's breath a germination, a viridescence.

From you the heavens move, the clouds rain,
The stones sweat dew, the earth gives greenness.

We shiver like peacocks' tails
In the mist of a thousand colored fountains,

Miraculous water, God's emissary,
Lighting our spring once more!

Here spirit is married to matter.
We are the holy hunger of matter for form.

Kizer, you enter into the dark world forever
To die again, into the living stone.

Second Time Around

You're entangled with someone more famous than you
Who happens to vanish.
You marry again in haste, perhaps to a nurse
Or your late wife's good friend,
Someone whose name will never appear in print
Except, perhaps, in your entry for *Who's Who;*
Someone obliging and neutral, not too good looking,
To whom you say, "Darling, the supper was excellent."
Free, now, of that brilliant aura, that physical dazzle
That you always acknowledged, insisting
You relished her fame, believing you meant it,
And love her you did, but you're so relieved she's gone.

How sweet to embrace the mundane, endorse the ordinary,
In its starchy smock or its ruffled apron,
Saying, "Bronwyn — or Carole, or Elsie —
Suits me down to the ground." The ground.
There's no more celestial navigation;
It's the end of smart missives, of aerial bombardment.
One can relax, and slump into being human.

Sometimes you sift through her papers
When you're bereft of ideas,
Though of course ideas are not what stimulates art:
It's snapshots of people in old-fashioned bathing suits,
The man she saw by the road with the three-legged dog,
That week in Venice when it never stopped raining, the odor
Of freshly washed hair when she dried it in the sunlight...
Something she lightly sketched in that needs fleshing out;
Could you? Should you? You put it to one side.

With a minor effort of will you stop thinking about her,
And decide instead to update your vita,
Or work some more on that old piece
On Descartes that has always given you trouble.
And Bronwyn, or Elsie, or Carole
Comes tiptoeing into your study with a nice cup of coffee.

Days of 1986

He was believed by his peers to be an important poet,
But his erotic obsession, condemned and strictly forbidden,
Compromised his standing, and led to his ruin.

The objects of his attention grew younger and younger.
Over sixty, and a father many times over,
He tried to corrupt the sons of his dearest friends;

He pressed on them drinks and drugs,
And of course he was caught and publicly shamed.
Was his death a suicide? No one is sure.

But that's not the whole story; it's too sordid to tell.
Besides, the memory of his poems deserves better.
Though we were unable to look at them for a time,

His poems survive his death.
There he appears as his finest self:
Attractive, scholarly, dedicated to love.

At last we can read him again, putting aside
The brute facts of his outer life,
And rejoice at the inner voice, so lofty and pure.

The Oration

after Cavafy

The boldest thing I ever did was to save a savior.
I reached heights of eloquence never achieved before
Or since. My speech turned the mob around!
They lifted the rood from his back, they dropped to the ground
Their nails and flails. But the whole time I spoke
(It's a wonder it didn't throw me off my stride)
The prophet or seer or savior, whatever you care to call him,
Kept groaning and muttering, telling me to be silent.
He was mad of course, so I simply ignored him. Poor fellow,
The beating they had given him must have turned his wits.

Every ounce of persuasion it took to convince the crowd
In the powerful sun, including the priest and his followers,
Exhausted me utterly. When I was sure he was safe —
The ungrateful fellow! — I took my way home and collapsed
On my cushions with chilled wine. Then, I heard later,
The savior harangued the mob with outrageous statements
That roused them to fury anew: he denounced the priesthood
As corrupt; he pronounced himself king of the world;
He said God was his father. So they strung him up again.

A violent thunderstorm woke me to a sky full of lightning
So I rushed out in the rain, forgetting my cloak,
And found him dead and alone except for a handful of women
Weeping and carrying on. Well, it taught me a lesson,
To mind my own business —
Why, the crowd might have turned on me!
Still, I have to be proud of my eloquence.
                                    It was the speech of my life.

Eleutheria

She was named Eleutheria,
Which means "freedom" in both ancient and modern Greek.
In translating it, she altered the meaning.
Freedom was not in her vocabulary.
Hers was a jealous nature; she didn't care
For the poets who were her husband's friends.

"Aren't you afraid to visit them," she mocked,
"Afraid you'll track in shit on their fine rugs?
You leave me alone in this wretched shack
With your bawling brats
While you flee to the elegant homes
Of your stuck-up friends, to recite your poems."

Once he confessed to us that he had married her
Because he believed he couldn't do better,
Being plain and provincial, a shy, awkward man,
Except on paper, where he was as light-footed
As the elusive muse who danced in his mind.

He worked so hard he was always tired,
Hoping a drink or two might give him relief.
It must be admitted
That sometimes he beat his little sons
Whom he adored, pleading for quiet
So he would have freedom to write.

One morning as he left to teach his first class
Of unruly students — far too many
For the pittance he was paid —

Eleutheria followed him out of the door
As he stepped, all nerves, into the snowy street,
Clutching his shabby coat that had lost its buttons
And the ancient briefcase with a broken clasp.
She leaned close, as if to kiss him,
But instead she whispered, "You're not a man."

She was no fool; she knew he wanted freedom,
So she began to threaten: "If you leave me,
You'll never see your boys again."
So he hung on, but at last, pushed to the wall,
He left her.
And it was as she had predicted:
He didn't see his boys till they were grown.

He moved; and he was lost to us for years,
Though we saw his face in the literary journals
Whenever he had won another prize.
We read the praise of each new book
That he faithfully sent us, tenderly inscribed.
Sometimes his poems and letters would begin,
"When I lost my sons…"

If we ran into him, he was as loving as ever,
And when we could, we resumed those old evenings
Of poetry, ours and his, and the writers we admired.
We knew when he was getting truly drunk:
He would slip from word-for-word quotations
Of Samuel Johnson, to poetry in German:
Rilke and Trakl; we didn't know the language
So, brilliantly, he improvised the translations,
As we were enthralled by that amber voice
Full of passion and tears.

Famous and lonely, he went on like this for years...
But this poem began with Eleutheria,
And will close with our last encounter
At a poetry reading by one of her sons:
I said to a man who knew both of us,
"I have nothing to say to her,"
And I looked right through her.
At once she moved from the seat next to mine
While I sat stunned by my own behavior.

Of course by then our friend was dead,
Prematurely, a victim of his hard life
And that hard woman,
Who had given him his freedom.
I discovered later that Eleutheria
Had become a marriage counselor.
A marriage counselor!
Do we thank God for irony, or curse it
When it comes too close?
We are free to choose. Eleutheria.

Union of Women

At a literary gathering in Santa Monica
I encounter a bearded lady wearing a union button.
We engage each other in friendly conversation:
When I was a little girl in Spokane, Washington,
I took enormous satisfaction in the label
Sewn to my clothes by the Ladies Garment Workers Union.
I was contributing to the Wealth of Women
As I chose my dresses. O Solidarity! O Feminism!
Much later I met a Ladies Garment Workers Union
Leader who told me that she was the only woman
Who'd ever been an official in that union,
Always ignored, outvoted. I felt retrospectively cheated.
Now my new friend, the one with the white beard (she
Won't mind if I mention it, she wrote a cinquain about it)
Says that her Local 814 (mostly women) engages in struggle
With the terrible Sheraton, its unfair labor practices
Concerning the ladies who change the beds and mop the bathrooms,
And fold the ends of the toilet paper
Into those stupid triangles, and put the mints on the pillow.
Of course they're all blacks (I mean African Americans)
Or Mexicans who hardly speak English and fear deportation.
It's clear my bearded friend though old and lame is a fighter;
And she writes excellent cinquains; she just sent me a bunch.
(You know what a cinquain is? A nifty form in five lines
Adapted by Crapsey from the medieval French.)
She, as the current jargon has it, made my day.
So here's to Solidarity, cinquains, brave bearded ladies — Hooray!

The Silent Man

In your first book of poems, printed
When you'd been dead for forty years,
As if it were an advertising flyer:
Apt symbols of your fate, where, page by page
Your life has fallen to the dust.

Good poets are almost never fortunate;
You were less fortunate than most:
Born in Prague, catastrophe came early:
Your only sister died at age nineteen.
You saw your parents last in 1938.
You went abroad. And then the Germans came.

In England news arrived that cracked your heart:
Your parents perished in Treblinka.
You wandered Egypt, Palestine, and Greece;
Then Oxford, where you weren't allowed to teach
Because you lacked a British doctorate —
So you stayed a student all your life.

You never felt at home in England
Or anywhere. Hundreds of poems
You left behind in Prague were lost.
Of your later poems, only twenty-six
Were printed, but never in a book.
So for the rest of your brief life
You called yourself "the silent man."

The subject of your doctorate was slavery.
Years of research, your notes and references

Were packed into a suitcase that was stolen
On a train from Paddington to Oxford.
Laboriously reassembled, page by page,
It got your doctorate at last in '49,
Three pain-filled years before you died.

On April Fool's Day, 1950, someone
Played a heartless joke on you,
Phoning to say your poems had been published.
Brief joy! But of course it wasn't true.
You swore to your friends the broken life-line
In your left palm had mended.

You had three pieces of good fortune:
Canetti was your loyal friend;
Your lover was a famous novelist
(She lost her memory, including you);
Your English translator was devoted.
But you were dead at forty-three.

How can I name or praise you
In one small stab at restitution?
Who am I to tamper with your fate?
Isn't that up to God, whom you never mention?
Isn't that true, Herr X?
                    But you are silent.

The Ashes

for William Gass

This elderly poet, unpublished for five decades,
Said that one day in her village a young girl
Came screaming down the road,
"The Red Guards are coming! The Red Guards
Are Coming!" At once the poet
Ran into her house and stuffed the manuscript
Of her poems into the stove. The only copy.
When the guards arrived they took her into the yard
For interrogation. As they spoke
The poet's mother tried to hang herself in the kitchen.
That's all I know about the Red Guard.
It is enough.

The elderly poet is bitter — and why not?
She earned her Ph.D. at an Ivy League school
And returned to China in 1948. Bad timing.
She is bitter with me
Because I've chosen to translate a younger poet,
Young enough to be her child or mine.
The truth is, her poems are forced,
But not flowering. The good work died in the stove.
She knows this. She wants me to recompose them
From the ashes. She wants the noose
Around her mother's neck untied by me.
She wants — oh, she wants! — to have her whole life over:

Not to leave America in 1948;
To know me when we are both young promising poets.
Her rusty English is now flawless,

My Mandarin, so long unused, is fluent.
No dictionaries needed. A perfect confidence
Flowing between us. And the Red Guard,
Except as the red sword-lilies
That invigilate the garden,
Unimagined by us both:
I, who believe the Reds are agrarian reformers,
She, who believes she will be an honored poet,
Her name known to everyone, safe in her fame.

The Erotic Philosophers

Part Five of "Pro Femina"

It's a spring morning; sun pours in the window
As I sit here drinking coffee, reading Augustine.
And finding him, as always, newly minted
From when I first encountered him in school.
Today I'm overcome with astonishment
At the way we girls denied all that was mean
In those revered philosophers we studied;
Who found us loathsome, loathsomely seductive;
Irrelevant, at best, to noble discourse
Among the sex, the only sex that counted.
Wounded, we pretended not to mind it
And wore tight sweaters to tease our shy professor.

We sat in autumn sunshine "as the clouds arose
From slimy desires of the flesh, and from
Youth's seething spring." Thank you, Augustine.
Attempting to seem blasé, our cheeks on fire,
It didn't occur to us to rush from the room.
Instead we brushed aside "the briars of unclean desire"
And struggled on through mires of misogyny
Till we arrived at Kierkegaard, and began to see
That though Saint A. and Søren had much in common
Including fear and trembling before women,
The Saint scared himself, while Søren was scared of *us*.
Had we, poor girls, been flattered by their thralldom?

Yes, it was always us, the rejected feminine
From whom temptation came. It was our flesh
With its deadly sweetness that led them on.

Yet how could we not treasure Augustine,
"Stuck fast in the bird-lime of pleasure"?
That roomful of adolescent poets manqué
Assuaged, bemused by music, let the meaning go.
Swept by those psalmic cadences, we were seduced!
Some of us tried for a while to be well-trained souls
And pious seekers, enmeshed in the Saint's dialectic:
Responsible for our actions, yet utterly helpless.
A sensible girl would have barked like a dog before God.

We students, children still, were shocked to learn
The children these men desired were younger than we!
Augustine fancied a girl about eleven,
The age of Adeodatus, Augustine's son.
Søren, like Poe, eyed his girl before she was sixteen,
To impose his will on a malleable child, when
She was not equipped to withstand or understand him.
Ah, the Pygmalion instinct! Mold the clay!
Create the compliant doll that can only obey,
Expecting to be abandoned, minute by minute.
It was then I abandoned philosophy,
A minor loss, although I majored in it.

But we were a group of sunny innocents.
I don't believe we knew what evil meant.
Now I live with a well-trained soul who deals with evil,
Including error, material or spiritual,
Easily, like changing a lock on the kitchen door.
He prays at set times and in chosen places
(At meals, in church), while I
Pray without thinking how or when to pray,
In a low mumble, several times a day,
Like running a continuous low fever;

The sexual impulse for the most part being over.
Believing I believe. Not banking on it ever.

It's afternoon. I sit here drinking kir
And reading Kierkegaard: "All sin begins with fear."
(True. We lie first from terror of our parents.)
In, I believe, an oblique crack at Augustine,
Søren said by denying the erotic
It was brought to the attention of the world.
The rainbow curtain rises on the sensual:
Christians must admit it before they can deny it.
He reflected on his father's fierce repression
Of the sexual, which had bent him out of shape;
Yet he had to pay obeisance to that power:
He chose his father when he broke with his Regina.

Søren said by denying the erotic
It is brought to the attention of the world.
You must admit it before you can deny it.
So much for "Repetition" — another theory
Which some assume evolved from his belief
He could replay his courtship of Regina
With a happy ending. Meanwhile she'd wait for him,
Eternally faithful, eternally seventeen.
Instead, within two years, the bitch got married.
In truth, he couldn't wait till he got rid of her,
To create from recollection, not from living;
To use the material, not the material girl.

I sip my kir, thinking of *Either/Or,*
Especially *Either,* starring poor Elvira.
He must have seen *Giovanni* a score of times,
And Søren knew the score.
He took Regina to the opera only once,

And as soon as Mozart's overture was over,
Kierkegaard stood up and said, "Now we are leaving.
You have heard the best: the expectation of pleasure."
In his interminable aria on the subject
S.K. insisted the performance *was* the play.
Was the overture then the foreplay? Poor Regina
Should have known she'd be left waiting in the lurch.

Though he chose a disguise in which to rhapsodize,
It was his voice too: Elvira's beauty
Would perish soon; the deflowered quickly fade:
A night-blooming cereus after Juan's one-night stand.
Søren, eyes clouded by romantic mist,
Portrayed Elvira always sweet sixteen.
S.K.'s interpretation seems naive.
He didn't seem to realize that innocent sopranos
Who are ready to sing Elvira, don't exist.
His diva may have had it off with Leporello
Just before curtain time, believing it freed her voice
(So backstage legend has it), and weakened his.

I saw La Stupenda sing Elvira once.
Her cloak was larger than an army tent.
Would Giovanni be engulfed when she inhaled?
Would the boards shiver when she stamped her foot?
Her voice of course was great. Innocent it was not.
Søren, long since, would have fallen in a faint.
When he, or his doppelgänger, wrote
That best-seller, "The Diary of a Seducer,"
He showed how little he knew of true Don Juans:
Those turgid letters, machinations, and excursions,
Those tedious conversations with dull aunts,
Those convoluted efforts to get the girl!

Think of the worldly European readers
Who took Søren seriously, did not see
His was the cynicism of the timid virgin.
Once in my youth I knew a real Don Juan
Or he knew me. He didn't need to try,
The characteristic of a true seducer.
He seems vulnerable, shy; he hardly speaks.
Somehow, you know he will never speak of you.
You trust him — and you thrust yourself at him.
He responds with an almost absentminded grace.
Even before the consummation he's looking past you
For the next bright yearning pretty face.

Relieved at last of anxieties and tensions
When your terrible efforts to capture him are over,
You overflow with happy/unhappy languor.
But S.K.'s alter-ego believes the truly terrible
Is for you to be consoled by the love of another.
We women, deserted to a woman, have a duty
To rapidly lose our looks, decline, and die,
Our only chance of achieving romantic beauty.
So Augustine was sure, when Monica, his mother,
Made him put aside his nameless concubine
She'd get her to a nunnery, and pine.
He chose his mother when he broke with his beloved.

In Søren's long replay of his wrecked romance,
"Guilty/Not Guilty," he says he must tear himself away
From earthly love, and suffer to love God.
Augustine thought better: love, human therefore flawed,
Is the way to the love of God. To deny this truth
Is to be "left outside, breathing into the dust,
Filling the eyes with earth." We women,

Outside, breathing dust, are still the Other.
The evening sun goes down; time to fix dinner.
"You women have no major philosophers." We know.
But we remain philosophic, and say with the Saint,
"Let me enter my chamber and sing my songs of love."

CARRYING OVER

Poems from the Chinese, Yiddish, Urdu,
Macedonian, French African,
German & Romanian

Introduction

Unlike my distinguished friends Mike Keley, Donald Keene, and William Merwin, I am only an occasional and amateur translator. Though I retain a few phrases of kitchen and tourist French, Urdu, and Chinese, I speak only enough Macedonian to order plum brandy. I know those useful words of Yiddish employed by many American gentiles of my generation who were raised by radio, by Jack Benny in particular, and further educated by Norman Rosten — words and phrases that have no equivalent in English. Furthermore, I have not, as my friends have, translated the entire body of work of a given period or a given author.

Prompted by Donald Keene and assisted by Cyril Birch, I have "translated" more poems from the T'ang Dynasty, particularly those of Tu Fu, than from any other source. My interest in Chinese poetry is passionate, and of long standing. Mother read me the translations of Arthur Waley beginning when I was around eight; in due course, I wrote my college thesis on the influence of Chinese poetry in translation on the Imagists (and, by reference, me). Upon graduating from Sarah Lawrence, I took up a Chinese Cultural Fellowship in Comparative Literature at Columbia University, interrupted by the chance to go to China, where my father was administering United Nations relief. Most of the Chinese I learned from dear Professor Carrington Goodrich at Columbia and spoke in Peking afterward has slipped away. For years, I flattered myself that I could still use Mathews's great *Chinese-English Dictionary*, but now I read it only for pleasure and enlightenment.

The two poems translated from the Yiddish of Rachel Korn were commissioned by Irving Howe who, with Eliezer Greenberg, edited *A Treasury of Yiddish Poetry* (Holt, Rinehart & Winston). Mr. Howe sent me a tape of her poems in Yiddish, along with a prose crib;

then my versions were carefully checked by the editors. I later had the great pleasure of reading with Rachel Korn at the YMHA in New York, along with other Yiddish poets and their translators. After the terrible background of the Holocaust from which these few emerged, I expected to see a group of crumbling and broken men and women. I "dressed down" for the occasion, as they say. What joy, then, to be instantly eclipsed by Ms. Korn, an erect and handsome woman in a glittering gold dress with sable cuffs!

I spent the academic year 1964–1965 in Pakistan, where I became acquainted with a number of poets, and returned for a meeting of the M.L.A. in 1969. Before I left in 1964, I met the late N.M. Rashid, then Pakistan's Ambassador to the United Nations, and translated the poem included here with him. My late friend James Wright has translated a number of Rashid's poems. I met Faiz Ahmad Faiz in Pakistan — Faiz, the greatest Urdu poet of the subcontinent (now ably and extensively translated by my friend Naomi Lazard). More about Faiz is included in the "Journal" that is printed here. An early draft of Faiz's poem "If I Were Certain" was composed with the help of Mohammad Sarfaraz, of the Pakistani United Nations delegation, in New York, and later gone over with the author, as were the other poems by Faiz included here. Faiz died in Lahore in the autumn of 1984, making this a sadly mortuary paragraph.

My "Pakistan Journal" appears in this volume because it sheds some light on the background from which these poems spring, and because I think it is still amusing to read. Little has changed in the eighteen years since it was written, and nothing has changed for the better, an opinion reinforced by friends who live there now or have visited recently. Would I go back again, despite wars, dictators, refugees, the oppression of women, the wistfulness of men? Like a shot.

I have been to Macedonian Yugoslavia a number of times to attend the Struga Festival, and early on formed a fast friendship with the poet and playwright Bogomil Gjuzel. Our translations of his work are a collaboration, as are those of the poets Mateja Matevski and Radovan Pavlovski. (Anté Popovski's poem was translated from the French with the help of my husband, John Woodbridge.) There exists a hilarious tape of Bogomil and me, translating. Excerpt: Bogomil: You understand what I mean by erection? Upright pennies? Me: Upright *pennies?* You mean like when we were children and put them on the railroad track so the train would flatten them? Bogomil (total consternation)!!! Me (total lack of communication)??? Bogomil: No, fool! *Pennies!* cock!

Versions of Macedonian poems were originally solicited by Milne Holton and Graham W. Reid for their anthology of Modern Macedonian poems, *Reading the Ashes* (Pittsburgh).

I wrote the poem "Race Relations" for my courageous South African friend, the exiled Dennis Brutus. At a poetry festival in Rotterdam one year, we poets wrote poems to each other and stuck them in one another's mailboxes at the hotel: this poem was one of those, as is the prose-poem to Lars Gustafsson at the beginning of the Macedonian section. What a lovely time.

The Edouard Maunick poem was translated with the author on a memorable visit of his to Washington, D.C. When not translating he cooked, magnificently. (I've been trying to duplicate a sort of ratatouille with chicken that he made, ever since.) I especially remember one translation session around a friend's swimming pool beginning about ten in the morning. Suddenly I noticed we were both shivering. Night had fallen.

To quote from Ellen Kennedy in her book, *The Negritude Poets* (Viking), "Edouard Maunick comes from a volcanic dot 720 miles square that lies west of Madagascar, midway between Africa and India": Mauritius. He is a mixture of French, African, and Irish blood. Mrs. Kennedy goes on to say that "Miss Kizer accomplishes the difficult technical feat of duplicating the seven-syllable lines with which Maunick composed his poem. His powerful imagery is intact, along with the challenging syntax." "Seven Sides and Seven Syllables" was translated for Mrs. Kennedy's book but appeared first in *Poetry* magazine.

Shu Ting, by far the youngest of the poets included here, younger, in fact, than my youngest child (an odd feeling for the translator!), was born in 1952. When the Cultural Revolution swept China in 1966, she was a school-girl of fourteen; nevertheless, she was rusticated, and in a mountain village far from her home she lived as a peasant. Under these difficult circumstances, reflected by implication in many of her poems, she began to write. None of her poems was allowed in print until 1978, although they circulated from hand to hand; what the Russians call *samizdat*, the Chinese call *di xia wen xue*. When the well-known Peking Spring arrived, she attracted enormous attention, and only a year after her first published poem she won the National Award for Poetry. I've had the pleasure of touring with her and giving bilingual readings. Her charm and dry wit shine right through the language barrier. For example, at a gathering in Santa Cruz, to which all the local writers were invited — many of whom looked as if they had emerged, blinking, from the woods, after two decades of hippiedom — she was asked what influence Zen Buddhism had had on her poetry. Her answer was that she had been more influenced by Christianity. I wish you could have seen their faces. I was introduced to her work by Y.H. Zhao, then earning his graduate degree at Berkeley. He wanted to do an anthology of contemporary Chinese women poets, an idea that attracted me very much. However, I found that only Shu Ting really appealed to me. So Mr. Zhao and I went to work, with the results you find here.

The tone of this introduction — up to this point where I allow Mrs. Kennedy to pat me on the back — has been pretty self-deprecating. Why then, you may well ask, with these shaky credentials, do I have the nerve to put this collection together? Partly it's the instinct I share with the bowerbird: to pile along my path a heap of glittering objects that have attracted me. Partly it's the herding instinct of a sheepdog: to round up a number of my friends in a tight circle. Partly, it's because some people have admired one piece or another and complained because they were hard to get hold of. But mostly because this potpourri of white Slav and black African, Chinese, Muslim, and Jew, is a kind of paradigm of our world as I wish it were, of the United Nations as I pray it might become: all of us, with sharply individual voices, but together — an orchestra!

Berkeley, 1988

Classical Chinese

Tu Fu to Li Po

My lord, how beautifully you write!
May I sleep with you tonight?
Till I flag, or when thou wilt,
We'll roll up drunken in one quilt.

In our poems, we forbear
To write of kleenex or long hair*
And how the one may fuck the other.
We're serious artists, aren't we, brother?

In our poems, oceans heave
Like our stomachs, when we leave
Late at night the fourteenth bar,
I, your meteor, you, my star.

When autumn comes, like thistledown,
We'll still be floating through the town,
Wildly singing in the haze,
I, past saving, you, past praise.

*literally: fine paper and hairpins, i.e., trivia

My Home Town

When I go home, the old are older.
The aspens quiver, the winds blow colder.
I find that I am mildly celebrated:
My father, not my verse, is venerated.
And I fear daily that I shan't survive
This noble ancestor of ninety-five...

For the Prince in Exile

Li Chin, AD 750

Peerless and solitary
You allow me to stay
Our first meeting night:
The height of autumn,
The air crisp-clear.

      But the mists come soon,
      Then the rain,
      Then, toward morning,
      The milky moon.

          Then the thunder,
          Then the flood,
          Then your stoic sleep,
          While I drop tears
          You scorn to weep.

Déjeuner sur l'herbe

I.

It's pleasant to board the ferry in the sunscape
As the late light slants into afternoon;
The faint wind ruffles the river, rimmed with foam.
We move through the aisles of bamboo
Toward the cool water-lilies.

The young dandies drop ice into the drinks,
While the girls slice the succulent lotus root.
Above us, a patch of cloud spreads, darkening
Like a water-stain on silk.

Write this down quickly, before the rain!

II.

Don't sit there! The cushions were soaked by the shower.
Already the girls have drenched their crimson skirts.
Beauties, their powder streaked with mascara, lament their
ruined faces.

The wind batters our boat, the mooring line
Has rubbed a wound in the willow bark.
The edges of the curtains are embroidered by river foam.
Like a knife in a melon, Autumn slices Summer.

It will be cold, going back.

TU FU (AD 712–770)

Lo Yu Park

freely adapted

An opulent park: serene, we chose the heights.
       Here the horizon fades
              And the bright grass goes on forever...

Our hosts move consciously, aware they create the view,
       themselves the foreground.
Aristocratic, darkly groomed: forms disposed on emerald lawns.
Distant rivers, flat and shiny as freshly painted landscape flow
       into the ladies' shoulders,
Emerge like scarves the other side.
Sport with the women! Open the lavish hampers!
Guzzle the wine, gleaming and wet as rivers...

Later, half-drunk, slung into saddles,
We are the slaves of horses that gallop away.
Passing the Princess' Pond, we lean over fondly,
Find Spring's young green reflection sobering.
Then, battered by drums from the covered passageway,
We move on.

      The sun is free to enter the Palace yard.
The gate spreads wide, lured open by the sun.
There, where the river curls, we meet the chariots
Sun-plated in silver, moons below the sky.

Blinded by polished gleam, we are distracted
By dancers: their long sleeves dip toward the water.
Courting the water, their skirts tease.
Distracted, distracted: focus our concentration

On a song:

> *the singer's voice a thin wire spiraling*
> *To the clouds...*

I always get drunk this time of year.
Spring and her melancholy — but now it's too long
Until the wine takes hold. I become so morose!
One doesn't achieve the pleasure any more,
Just the stupidity.
                    I query a half-draped girl:
Who could want this poor pedant with thin hair?
Not the Court, surely. God alone feeds me.
She is tawny from the sun, she is half turned away.
Other bodies recumbent: "Who cares for you?"
I don't mind how drunk I get. I'll take every dare,
Every forfeit. But I can't see beyond the party's end!
Stand alone in the landscape, a sanguine figure.

You, poet, make a song by yourself. Be lost in your song.

TU FU (AD 712–770)

The Meandering River Poems

RAIN THERE

Spring clouds rest on the walls of the Royal Park.
Dusk mutes the passionate coloring of blossoms.
Enclosed by the forest, in the River Pavilion,
I look at painted petals, dark from rain.

The wind has extended the waterweeds
Into long, writhing forms:
Like girdles of pale jade, they are curling,
Uncurling on the surface of the stream.

Incense burns in the Hibiscus Hall,
The scent faint, to no purpose.
Where, then, is the irresistible chariot
Guarded by dragons and Imperial tigers?

O King, return! Be liberal with your money!
Revive those elegant Royal entertainments
So I may doze, my old head tilted back
Against a tipsy old brocaded wall

While suave, accomplished ladies
Pluck at my sleeve, as they touch painted lutes.
Or let the prettiest ones
Coax me half-awake...

DRINKING WITH FRIENDS

Tall marsh fowl stalk through the shallows
As little birds nag at the willow buds;

A few wild ducks: puce patterns on gold ground.
Sand on the riverbank is dry and bright

Like our eyes, dry and bright
My friends, our dry, white years!

Eternal yellow sand and sparse white hair,
I ask you what they have to do with Spring?

They come together in the wine-jar, where
We worship all that blooms, all that smells sweet.

Our families? We are bonded to the Court.
The Emperor is our wife, our work, our home.

Ah, we are dry and brilliant, old but strong!
Could *you* learn to seed a furrow, and be free?

DRINKING THERE ALONE

I perch on the riverbank, forgetting to go back,
Gaze down at the lucent palaces as they slip their moorings.
Another pleasant blur — peach-blossoms, redolent
Of bees and heat, compete with willow blooms:
Which will faint first?
                              Birds, white and tawny,
Stripe their migrations, warp
And weft of one another's flight.

Abandon me! But leave me a single swallow
And another. And one more. Dear wine, I don't care!
Abandon me, all of you. This world does not suit;
Not a court regular, unfitted for routine…
Well, well, I am demoted, and my dreams also.
I may no longer look forward to Paradise:
The immortal pleasure of being left alone!
For I summoned, too late, my lost young self
When decision was obsolete.

SPRING GOES

Petal by petal, the Spring dissolves.
A small wind carries the rest away.
All nature conspires to sadden me,
But gross, unrepentant, I will be gay.

I devour the flowers that yet remain.
I shall not stint myself on wine.
A cock, red-throated, a green-winged hen:
The kingfishers nest in the ruined vine.

The River Pavilion lists in decay.
Beyond these boundaries I see
A grave stone unicorn, adamant;
He leans on a tomb, stares far away.

You natural laws! I take your measure;
Forgetting rank, work, weary days.
I find my nature made for pleasure,
And drink and linger, all at ease.

I GO TOO

Each day when Court is over, I skip to the pawnshop,
My nice Spring wardrobe underneath my arm.
Bit by bit, I am drinking up my clothes!
At night I return from the riverbank, quite soused.

Trying not to glance in the taverns — I owe them all —
Slipping past, I reflect on the shortness of life
Especially mine. I'll never see seventy now.
Well, not many do. Who wants to, anyhow?

Saffron butterflies browse deep in flowers;
Dragonflies dint the placid water now and then.
Soothe me, Spring wind! Keep me gentle forever!
Never cross-grained, as Light and Time pass over.

Thwarted

Thwarted, old friend! Here we are, balked again!
We live at opposite ends of the same lane
But we haven't seen each other for ten whole days.

I returned my Official Horse to the local authorities;
And this road is rotten, like a deliberate plot,
An obstacle race! Now, thanks to my lack of credit

I can't even rent a conveyance, though I still have shoes.
But what if my department-heads caught me afoot?
Taking such risks with protocol, face, future!
You know I'd walk through brambles to get to you.

By morning the rain is furious. I'm resigned.
The Spring wind raves as I do, in my sleep.
But I'm deaf to the ring-bell and the bang-drum,
The summons to Court. Next door a lame donkey grazes.

A complaisant neighbor owns him, lends him. Ho!
But I daren't ride the beast in the slick mud,
Not to that slippery Palace! Let them mark me absent.
Life is one long, fragmented, murky episode.

I hate getting through the day without a word;
When you hum your heavenly poems I brim with awe,
Nostalgia at the thought of your sweet cadence.

Magnolia petals fall when they have bloomed,
But you and I are overripe, my friend!
How many times have we two not complained

At the high cost of drinking! Even the corner vendor
Puts too high a price on our Illumination.
We can't steep ourselves in Oblivion any more.

High-sounding, isn't it? Come quickly, then,
To my place, for now it just so happens
I've saved enough small change to buy a gallon.

TU FU (AD 712–770)

Adviser to the Court

EAST OF THE PALACE GATES: WORKING LATE

By the water clock it's past dawn as the day watch sounds.
Spring banners are being unfurled for the morning procession.

Officials march back and forth from the Emperor's audience;
Coming away, we break ranks, to wander among the blossoms.

I turn back toward my office: willow fronds brush my face
As if to veil my yawns. Eyes blurred in the morning mist.

The city walls are moist from snow that has melted
From the high spires. Oh, the fresh odor of wet stone!

Clouds drift among the towers. Alone again,
I burn the draft of another memorandum.

The next time I lift my head I see twilight outside,
Dawn and dusk identical. Time for home, I suppose.

As I amble along on my horse, I hear sleepy cluckings,
The rustle of hay. The chickens are settling down.

TO A BROTHER OFFICIAL

Sound of the fifth watch! Dawn hastens to obey
The water clock. Officially, day has begun.
Peach blossoms, bibulous and blushing
From spring wine; on the banners
The embroidery dragons move uneasily
As if warmed into life by the new sun.

High above the Palace, swallows dip
In the light breeze. As you hurry from the audience
The odor of incense lingers in your sleeves.
Oh, your crystalline mind, my friend!
You move as lyrically, as rapidly
As you write poems.

Because we honor two talented generations,
Your father and you, we call your offices
West of the Palace Gate, the Phoenix Pond.

WORKING ALL NIGHT IN SPRINGTIME

When day begins to darken,
Flowers along the wall
Merge into the shadows.
Skyward, the birds chirp softly,
Searching for a roost.

Ten thousand common households
Are illumined by the stars,
But the firmament of Heaven
Is soaking up the moonlight
Of this most brilliant night.

So quiet! I hear keys turning
In gold locks of the Palace doors.
The wind a faint jingle, sounding
Like the horses of importuners,
As they shake their pendants of jade.

I must present a memorial
To the Throne-room, in the morning.

Sleepless here, whether I work or not,
All night I measure the hours
Of all night, in my mind...

END OF AN AUDIENCE

Their sleeves like purple orchids,
Two ladies of the court stand by the inner door
Of the Throne-room, ushering courtiers from the chamber.
Incense whirls in the hallways — the Spring wind!
Sun sparks on the flowered robes of a thousand officials.

The water clock in the tower shows the hour.
I stand close enough to the Prince to see his expression:
His Majesty looks brilliant with joy today!
When I leave the Palace, I collect my colleagues,
Then we pay our respects to the Ministers of State.

REPLY TO A FRIEND'S ADVICE

Leaving the audience by the quiet corridors,
Stately and beautiful, we pass through the Palace gates,

Turning in different directions: you go to the West
With the Ministers of State; I, otherwise.

On my side, the willow-twigs are fragile, greening.
You are struck by scarlet flowers over there.

Our separate ways! You write so well, so kindly,
To caution, in vain, a garrulous old man.

ON THE WAY OUT

Last year I rejoined the Emperor by this road
When the barbarians swarmed over the Western suburbs.
I'm so far from having recovered from my fear
That shreds of my soul still dangle in the air.

Dangling and wandering, as I am now,
Loyal to the Throne, yet driven away
To a vast, distant province! — surely his Majesty
Could not have intended this. I have been betrayed.

Ruin! As my talent fails, and I grow old.
My steadfastness in trying times has aged me.
I pull on my horse's reins, and, pausing,
Gaze for a final time on the Palace walls.

TU FU (AD 712-770)

Banishment

TOO MUCH HEAT, TOO MUCH WORK

It's the fourteenth of August, and I'm too hot
To endure food, or bed. Steam and the fear of scorpions
Keep me awake. I'm told the heat won't fade with Autumn.

Swarms of flies arrive. I'm roped into my clothes.
In another moment I'll scream down the office
As the paper mountains rise higher on my desk.

Oh, those real mountains to the south of here!
I gaze at the ravines kept cool by pines.
If I could walk on ice, with my feet bare!

REUNION

Joy in this meeting grieves our two white heads
Knowing they greet each other a final time.
We nod through the long night watches, still resenting
The speed with which the candle shrinks and pales.

I dread the hour the Milky Way dries up forever.
Let us fill our cups and drain them, over and over
While we can, before the world returns with dawn
When we blot our eyes, and turn our backs on each other.

A Visit in Winter

to the Temple of His Mystical Majesty (formerly
known as The Grand Infinitesimal Palace)

Polestar and northern capital: equal as scepter and orb.
Fences march up the hill like troops protecting the city.
The officer-priests are severe, the guards grim and cautious.

The sky of early winter, celadon, not ice-blue,
Matches the roof-tiles which repel the cold.
Sound of a slap! War between tiles and the weather.

All things come together: In the yard, the gilded tower
Celebrates oneness. Doors, painted with mountains and rivers,
Merge with the true landscape, which supports them.

Artifice! To concoct realities, reorder the minute universe,
These roof-beams carved with infinite skill
So that the sun and moon revolve around this place.

The deathless plum-tree has tenacious roots,
Strong as the scent of orchids, sturdy as dynasties.
The victim of history, our emperor, master of virtue.

When we toll the names of great painters, begin with Wu
Who moved whole countrysides into this room,
Nourished to gleaming life, in a hothouse for Heaven and Earth.

Five learnèd men, in procession like elephants,
Heavy, gray, never breaking their close-linked chain;
Then an orderly flight of geese: a thousand pale officials

Follow them, tame civil servants in dragon robes.
The tassels on their ceremonial headgear
Toss like flames; wind whips the triangular banners.

Great cedars cast their shadows across the temple grounds
In dark diagonals. Pears, early gold, blush now from the frost.
Hidden by shadows, jade wind-bells move in the eaves:

Their music. The naked, frozen windlass on the well;
Like the silver emperor of Han, immobilized
For a while. The spirit thaws as the old beliefs are revived.

But is the spirit of man hollow as the note of wind-bells,
Or as a great tree, ripe for felling? Indeed, if we are deathless,
Where then is randomness, Art's impulse, true disorder?

Testament

100 lines from Tu Fu

I come from Tu Ling, an unimportant man,
Only more vulnerable as the years wear on.
To serve my country! I've clung to this mad dream
Without avail, as better men have done.

I bow to hardship whitening my hair,
Old, already spent at forty, I don't care.
When they slam my coffin lid I shall stay down.
Till then, I will persist, I will endure!

I mourn for my poor people, laboring,
Starving all seasons — I rail against their wrongs.
Though my cloistered fellow-scholars laugh at me
I shall go on pouring out my passionate songs.

I must cleave to the center of life, not the edge of a dream,
Stay with my brilliant Prince, deep in the living stream.
How could one such as I say good-bye to life forever?
Architects, all we need to build a world is here!

I have cherished dreams of living by the river;
Spindrift days in sun, without a care.
As clover and sunflower lean toward the source of light
I exult in selfhood, assent to my own spirit.

Any infinitesimal ant wants its own burrow.
Why try to be a whale, prey to great waves or the undertow?

Though I learn my own limitations, I can't learn to obey!
Leave me here on earth, to fail again tomorrow.

When I am silent dust, I will persevere.
To emulate the hermit in his cell,
Relinquishing all! I envy his self-control
And drink uncontrollably to celebrate his call.

I will endure, then thud to earth like a bird
Stricken, to the eternal dust. I will persevere!
So I soothe myself by pouring out the wine
And pouring out my grieved and passionate song.

I find the grasses dying with the year.
Wind rips open the hedgerows; the thoroughfare
From the capital is black when I start out,
Midnight at my back — I, perpetual traveler!

I cannot tie my coat, the frost is so severe;
Intractable buckles, and fingers stiff with hoar.
The icy sun arises. Troops on the chill frontier
Gather their spears and banners against the invader.

Armies have trampled this ground so many times
Crags are worn smooth; but music fills the ravines!
I arrive at the Mountains of Li with the morning watch.
Beside the sulfur springs is the Emperor's coach.

A gust of steam smokes in the frigid air.
Echoes of bells and drums and resonant cries!
Soaking voluptuously in the opaque jasper waters,
The Imperial ministers loll here, take their ease.

The humble and poor are excluded, all their ilk,
Though they are permitted to weave the pure white silk
For the Imperial harem; women full of fear,
Their husbands flogged by greedy courtiers

To extort their exorbitant taxes. Yes, collect the skins
Of miserable men! That's how you serve your King.
Benevolent talents, beware! You will be done in.
It isn't enough simply to love your fellow man.

What happened to the gold plate on which we used to dine?
Now it decks the boards of the Emperor's rich hangers-on.
But women like goddesses move through the corridors,
Borne on a perfumed wave and swathed in furs.

Incense! You will hear the pensive harp and lute,
Sup on camel-pad broth and nibble rare winter fruit:
Frosty oranges, and little pungent tangerines,
They glow in the hand against warm sable sheens.

When you've gorged, let the wine sour, food to carrion rot!
Fling the meat and drink out of the lacquered gates!
Outside, only steps from plenty, men lie down
To starve, the courtyards littered with their bones.

The span of a woman's arm separates the gilded pillars
Of the Palace from old posts rotten with wind and rain.
On the wild roads the sons of Han lie frozen,
And I, the courtier, freeze with unappeasable pain.

So my traces turn to the North, where two streams meet.
I find the ferryboat moored at another spot.
The western skies dumped lakes upon the land;
Floodwaters rise to meet my outstretched hand.

Is this wet retribution? Will Heaven's Pillars crack?
A myriad river bridges have swept to rack.
One creaking span remains. We travelers crawl across,
Hand clutching hand. Wide river, hear our curse!

In an evil time, I left my wife in a strange house
Remote from the Court. Now I rejoin my spouse.
I'd rather starve at home than feast at Court.
My Beloveds, I have come to share your fate.

I open my door to wailing. In anguish and anger
My cries join theirs: my infant son has died of hunger.
Even the casual neighbors weep, why not a father?
His guardian, useless and broken, ashamed forever.

My own little child has starved, while I wasn't aware
That our fine autumn harvest had made no difference here.
Dear family, we belong to the privileged class.
How then do the poor endure, starved and harassed,

Their property seized, themselves dragged off in bonds
To guard a garrison thousands of miles from home?
What of my life, who have never paid a tax,
Hefted a spear, manned a frontier, beaten a drum?

Our land in flood, and my own heart in flood,
These frantic thoughts are rising like the waters
To flow toward you, wounded, oppressed, bereaved,
In desperate love, China, your sons and daughters.

A Present for Tu Fu from Li Po

Last time we met
on the mountaintop
in the noonday sun,
you in the shade of
your preposterous hat

you were much plumper
than you are now.
Perhaps you were
pregnant with poems?

HSÜEH T'AO (AD 768–831)

Spring-Gazing Songs

I.

Blossoms crowd the branches, too beautiful to endure.
Thinking of you, I break into bloom again.
One morning soon, my tears will mist the mirror.
I see the future, and I will not see.

II.

We cannot glow as one when petals open;
We cannot grieve as one when petals fall.
Dare I ask where we may meet in mutual love?
A secret time of opening and closing:
Blossoms that separately bloom and die as one.

Weaving Love-Knots

I.

Daily the wind-flowers age, and so do I.
Happiness, long-deferred, is deferred again.
Of sand and ocean, the horizon line
Lies in the middle distance of a dream.
Because our lives cannot be woven together
My fingers plait the same grasses, over and over.

II.

Two hearts: two blades of grass I braid together.
He is gone who knew the music of my soul.
Autumn in the heart, as the links are broken.

Now he is gone, I break my lute.
But Spring hums everywhere: the nesting birds
Are stammering out their sympathy for me.

Yiddish

RACHEL H. KORN

Keep Hidden from Me

Keep from me all that I might comprehend!
O God, I ripen toward you in my unknowing.

The barely burgeoning leaf on the roadside tree
Limns innocence: here endeth the first lesson.

Keep from me, God, all forms of certainty:
The steady tread that paces off the self

And forms it, seamless, ignorant of doubt
Or failure, hell-bent for fulfillment.

To know myself: Is that not the supreme disaster?
To know Thee, one must sink on trembling knees.

To hear Thee, only the terrified heart may truly listen;
To see Thee, only the gaze half-blind with dread.

Though the day darken, preserve my memory
From Your bright oblivion. Erase not my faulty traces.

If I aspire again to make four poor walls my house,
Let me pillow myself on the book of my peregrinations.

God, grant me strength to give over false happiness,
And the sense that suffering has earned us Your regard.

Elohim! Though sorrow fill me to the brim,
Let me carefully bear the cup of myself to Thee.

RACHEL H. KORN

Generations

for my daughter

Loving another, yet she married my father.
That other portrait faded with the years.
From her album paged in musty velvet
Glimmered forth his paling, yellowing smile.

To watch her embroider a towel or tablecloth:
She pricked the vivid silk with her nostalgia.
The stitches flowed like narrow streams of blood.
The seams were silvered with her silent tears.

And my grandmother — how little I knew of her life! —
Only her hands' tremor, and the blue seam of her lips.
How can I imagine my grandfather's love of her?
I must will myself to believe in her suffering.

No letter remains, no, not a scrap of paper
Did she leave us; only old pots in the attic
Crudely patched: tangible maimed witnesses
To a dead life: the young widow, the mother of five.

So she planted a luxuriant garden
That would embrace the newly barren house
And her new barrenness. So the trees grew,
Obedient to her will, in perfect rows.

Now my daughter is just sixteen
As I was on that quiet day in May
When I became pregnant of a single word
Scented with lilac, the remote song of a bird.

A few letters, and what is called "a slender volume":
These are the relicts of my life. I lacked perspective
On happiness, so I ran ever faster
To escape the happy boundaries of my fate.

Listen, my daughter, never go in pursuit!
It all lies *there,* in the woven strands of blood.
How the straight trees whisper in my grandmother's garden!
Only listen! These dim echoes in my poem…

But what can sixteen years conceive of sorrow?
And pensiveness? The tremor of old lives?
For her, only the eternal beginnings.

Where she goes, old shadows kiss her footprints.
Somewhere, in white lilac, the nightingale
Gasps out his fragile song

Which ends always with the note of eternal beginning.

Pakistan Journal
&
Poems from Urdu

Pakistan Journal

As we leave Lebanon behind us, to span the mountains and oceans of dust, and salty lake-beds, and dead cities between us and our destination, I feel excited joy at returning to Pakistan after four years. In America, particularly among those of my acquaintances who have spent time in India, these feelings are met with some incredulity. But such a reaction is rare among those who know Pakistan, and have fallen under its peculiar spell.

During the time that I lived there — from September, 1964 to April, 1965 — I thought that I was maintaining a wholly detached attitude toward the place and the people, right up till the end of my visit. Then, when I went to the Lahore Airport about six in the morning, I was startled to find a contingent of about a dozen Americans and a dozen Pakistanis who had come to see me off. Decked out in the chains with silver pendants and the wreaths of jasmine or marigolds which are customary gifts to the dear departing, I climbed on the plane. My emotions were focused on getting home and seeing my family again. Then I looked out of the plane window and saw the struggling mass of my friends alternately waving their handkerchiefs and dabbing at their eyes, and thought, how extraordinary.

"I don't feel a thing," I said to myself. The waving continued at a more frantic pace as the plane taxied off, and suddenly there was a rush of tears to my eyes, and I was beating on the plane's window and shouting — although of course they couldn't hear me — "I'll be back! I'll be back!"

As the plane took off, and turned in a great half-circle toward the south, I sat there numb: "So I'm hooked," I thought. "I am well and truly hooked, like those old relics of the British Raj you find teaching school in the Sind or managing hotels in Peshawar, or sitting in their rockers on the porches of cottages in the Murree Hills. They never belonged, and they never will belong, but they're stuck, and so am I." By the time you realize it's happened to you, it's too late to escape. It was unnerving then, and it still is, as I return.

Later: With the exception of a Pakistani intellectual from London, I seem to be the only person on this chartered plane-load of delegates to a scholarly conference who has been there before. As I listen to myself answering questions from every side, I feel that I am making noises like an Old — or at least Middle-Aged — Pakistani Hand. And I lived there just long enough to know how little I knew. But, by golly, I was a Lahore-wallah, and this feels more like coming home than it would to, say, Seattle, Washington, where I spent fifteen years of my life feeling like a transient.

LAHORE, SEPTEMBER 13, 3 AM

It's 11 PM, London time. The temperature is about 90°, and the humidity goes right along with it. We're sitting numbly in the — thank God — air-conditioned transit lounge, waiting for a mass clearance of immigration and customs.... Later: The Intercontinental Hotel was just a hole in the ground when I left. It's opposite Faletti's, that gloomy old caravanserai surrounded by huge dark trees decked with colored lights. Louis MacNiece wrote a poem on his fortieth birthday in Faletti's, his first visit since Partition. Fortunately, I have with me the diary I kept five years ago, and I look at the poem again:

> Along and back the creamed arcade
> The tall scared Sikh had paced and paced,
> Beyond the asylum of the hotel
> The Five Rivers had run to waste
> With rivers of men's blood as well,
> While on the lawn the colored lights
> And tawdry band jollied the nights
> A little along, a little back.
>
> "So long! Come back!" So back I came
> To find Lahore a matter of course,

400

At peace, and dull...
Town of the Moghuls, town of fear,
Where is your cyclist with the spear
Who lurked so long, who looked so back?

Along and back, along and round:
Maybe the cyclist killed the Sikh,
Maybe Jahangir in his tomb,
Though slow and dead, inspired the quick
To gems of fury, flowers of doom.
No matter: this remains Lahore,
Oxcarts and tongas, as before,
Jingling along or lumbering back.

I spent my fortieth birthday here too, and wrote my poem about it. Now Louis is dead, and Faletti's is superseded by this monster hotel, where I stand looking at the arcades across the way, faintly silver in the rain and dawn, and the little colored lights that burn all night. Lahore remains Lahore....

Later: I rise at noon, and go down to the lobby. I woke at nine and debated: Shall I go to Anarkali Bazaar, where the writer Intezar Husain took me, shortly after I arrived, to show me "the real Pakistan"? We ate fresh, chopped fruit mixed with nuts (damn, I forget what it's called), and *ferni* (a kind of smooth custard made with rice flour and flavored with pistachio nuts, in little, disposable pottery bowls), outside the great Wazir Khan Mosque presiding majestically over its slums; I took my first tonga ride, and little boys ran out of the side streets and began beating on my legs with sticks because my skirt exposed my legs from the knees down. We went to the Pak Tea House, where the writers hang out all day and half the night, getting as high as talkers in an Irish pub, on coffee and the Kashmir dispute.

Or shall I take a taxi to the Bad Shahi Mosque, my favorite structure in the world — it, and the Lahore Fort, and Jahangir's tomb, two miles out of town, make the Taj Mahal look carved out of Ivory Soap, to my taste. Then I could salaam in the direction of Iqbals's tomb, to the left of the entrance. After all, today is the twenty-first anniversary of the death of Mohammed Ali Jinnah, and one should pay at least token obeisance to the poet who invented "Pakistan" for him.

First, though, a quick swim. Five years ago I didn't see a swimming pool in all Pakistan, though perhaps there were some tucked away in back yards in some of the fancier establishments in Gulberg. One step onto my balcony kills that idea. The air is as wet as the pool. I picked up the *Pakistan Times* which had been shoved under the door. O blessed oblivion, conferred by a highly selective memory! I had forgotten the true quality of that gruesome journal, where English syntax has suffered such fatty degeneration that you can read the same paragraph four times over and not have the least idea what it is trying to convey. I read the headlines with one eye shut, breaking myself in gently: FLU EPIDEMIC RAGES IN LAHORE. With a shudder, I read the weather report. I went back to bed. Now it is raining, raining, raining, great horizontal sweeps and curves across the entire sky. The scholars are milling around the lobby waiting to have their passports returned to them. Strange how many Americans, particularly inexperienced travelers like most of these, suffer from passport panic. The man in charge on arrival practically had to pry their fingers loose from their little blue-gray security symbols.

Easily I've slipped back into the old, patient rhythms. We may be here half the day. I gaze placidly out of the French doors toward the new swimming pool, cracked and empty except for rain and leaves; and an embryonic golf course stretches back to a mud village, not fifty yards from the hotel. A mud village just like the one beside my old house on Sikandar Road (named for Alexander the Great, no doubt), where the tinny, amplified voice of the muezzin calling the faithful to prayer used to punctuate my days. Now, I am told, the live muezzin in his minaret has been replaced by a recording. "The Progress of Reaction" might be a pretty good title for a piece on the Muslim world.

Now a hotel functionary is dealing out passports like a quick game of poker. No one knows enough to be in the least grateful for the favor done them: On my arrival, last time, I waited interminably at the pleasure of the Lahore fuzz. I remember the sight of great, rust-colored splashes on the walls of the stairway leading to Police Headquarters, shuddering at the thought they might be bloodstains of prisoners being dragged to and from interrogation. They were, of course, the stains made from spitting out chewed betel nut.

Evening, Islamabad: The rain had much abated by the time we took to plane for Rawalpindi. So all that I saw of my lovely old Lahore was the great stretch of the Upper Mall lined with massive plane trees. Lahore looked fresh and clean, whether because the rains had laid her habitual red-brown dust and swept clear her avenues, or because the city has tidied itself up in recent times. I missed the camels, scooters, mendicants, holy men dabbled with dust and chalk and kohl stretched out beside the road, the cricket swarms of children, the gaudy dilapidated tongas, the saggy taxis, donkeys, bicycles laden with tottering towers of fodder or boards, the burquas of the women providing black accents to a dusty scene. I had seen a sign announcing that the zoo is being remodeled at the cost of a couple of lakhs of rupees. Having seen the poor people of Lahore, I never had the courage to visit the zoo....

The skies were clear over 'Pindi airport, which also serves Islamabad, the brand-new capital. The bus drove through an ugly part of 'Pindi, unfamiliar to me. I think of it as a gracious town with broad avenues, trees that rustle incessantly in the slight wind, and at night the soft — yes, soft — cawing of crows among the leaves. (Against this, the nightmare in broad daylight of a human spider scuttling across the avenue, ubiquitous figure out of Kafka — undoubtedly kidnapped as a child, its limbs broken and forced into this black parable of man become insect.)

From the sky, Islamabad looks as geometrical as a chessboard, defying the undulating Rawalpindi landscape, which resembles

Urdu script. Approaching by car, Islamabad is indeed square, but our hotel is set apart in lots of green space, with the breathtaking Margala foothills as a backdrop.

Hundreds of cups of tea are lined up in rows awaiting us, as we fall gratefully through the door into the air-conditioned lobby. I've been thirsting for Pakistani chai for four long years. After several gulps of non-ambrosial liquid, I notice the tell-tale cardboard squares hanging over the sides of the pot. Lipton's, by God! And I curse as I formulate Kizer's Law of Emerging Nations: when air-conditioning comes in the window (which is promptly sealed forever), an old amenity flies out the door. When I return, five years hence, *Insha'allah,* the buses will be air-conditioned and we will be served Diet Pepsi.

Before I retire to my room, after the usual, interminable wait, I am introduced to Ralph Russell, the distinguished Urdu and Persian scholar from London University. He is small and prematurely white-haired, and full of ebullient charm. His eyes are bright as a bird's, and he talks entrancingly of Ghalib. I feel slightly better about having muffed all my chances to meet Arthur Waley....

SEPTEMBER 14

My old friend, B., has arrived, and we have a beer and chat in the late morning. I have many questions to ask him, based on a close reading of the English-language papers. I can't ask most Pakistanis, because they simply tell me that the English-language press is no good, and I should read the Urdu papers. Yes, well, I know *that,* but I don't know Urdu. I mention the increased frankness of the press since Ayub Khan's regime, citing an article on the two dozen families who control the Pakistan economy, for example. B. says he is worried about the polarization between the students, the intellectual and professional classes, and much of the working class on one side, and the *ulema* (right-wing religious leaders) on the other, backed by much of the illiterate peasantry. These religious fanatics are more dangerous, in the long run, than the wealthy and privileged, who may even have a fragmentary idea or two about social progress inasmuch as it relates to their self-interest and survival. But the *ulema* and their supporters want to drag Pakistan even farther back into a distant and partly imaginary past: total theocracy is their aim and game — all power to the pulpit! There are disturbing indications that some of the more progressive politicians, who know better, are paying increased lip-service to this, to garner votes for next year's elections.

Ayub Khan, when he took over Pakistan, was a tough military man, and considered incorruptible at that time. Like General Eisenhower, he had the approval of most of his people, and his spiritual life concerned him about as much as it did Eisenhower. However, Billy Graham is about the worst we have to offer in the way of organized hypocrisy, relatively harmless by comparison to the political ambitions of the *ulema*, who are determined to own and operate the state. Ayub continually catered to the official Islamic pieties, thereby encouraging the recrudescence of religious fanaticism. Although in a strong position, at the beginning, to bring about reform along the lines of Kemal Ataturk, curtailing the power of the *ulema*, and doing away with purdah and the veil (he might well have been less abrupt than Ataturk, and, like the present leaders of Afghanistan and Iran, liberated young girls from the portable jail of the burqua, while allowing the older women — like old prison lags who can't endure the reality of freedom — peaceably to wear their shrouds into the grave), Ayub did very little. The tragedy of Islam: Fanaticism, all too prone to break through the membrane of gentleness, natural courtesy and spontaneous friendliness of this people, has been encouraged rather than otherwise. And it is entirely possible that our children, or the children of our children, will die horribly because of this single fact. One of every five members of the human race is a Muslim.

SEPTEMBER 15

Although the newspapers no longer resemble government press handouts, I notice an ominous pattern in the headlines now: constant references to "anti-Islamic activities." This must make some of my liberal Pakistani friends shudder all over, the way it would affect anybody who lived in the America of the fifties. On the lighter side, one article quotes from a booklet called, "The Islamic Constitution," published by the Khatib of a Lahore mosque and signed by ten *ulema;* I am particularly infatuated by their proposed Article II: "No films will be shown in cinema houses, except those which have an all-male caste [sic]." They also advocate the abolition of banks and insurance companies (they must own stock in a mattress monopoly), and the reinstitution of slavery. They want an unpaid army which will live off booty, and "each soldier will acquire the property of the enemy whom he kills in battle." (How would they arrange this with India and Afghanistan? Through the U.N.?) This is a nut group; but history has taught us not to disregard nut groups, or we may find ourselves laughing all the way to the morgue.

SEPTEMBER 16

Yesterday, everyone went off to Taxila, but I preferred to stay here and talk to various Pakistanis. It stormed violently all morning, and I congratulated myself on not squelching through the glutinous red mud of that impressive memorial to Gandharan civilization. My most vivid memory of an earlier visit is peripheral to the site itself: we were invited to tea by a farm family living in a tiny cluster of mud huts on the edge of the ruins. We sat on a charpoy while my friend Tony practiced his tea-table Urdu. When asked if I wanted milk in my chai, I nodded (sideways, in Urdu), and the man of my house took my filled tea-cup into the yard and held it under a water buffalo. Squirt! The rich milk poured from udder to cup while a baby buffalo looked on with a certain amount of resentment. That is my favorite cup of tea for all time. Sanitary too, unless the buffalo had tuberculosis (a disease that, I am told, has now been brought almost entirely under control).

Later: I have been writing through most of the night, and now, at five, I hear the ringing of bells, and the discreet taps of the bearers on my neighbors' doors, rousing the group for an early morning flight to Peshawar (where I am going next week, so again I abstain). It is raining again, with furious lightning bursts, as it was when I first took plane for Peshawar five years ago, and the skies black at midday. I hadn't been well all day. My only intestinal ailment in Pakistan occurred after staying at the A.I.D. Staff House in 'Pindi, which was sterilized till it squeaked, thus illustrating another of Kizer's Laws of Emerging Nations: Eat everything in moderation, so that the local bacteria don't feel rejected and wreak their revenge. It was a terribly rough flight; finally I sidled off the plane in the bitter darkness, and crouched beside a fence, where I vomited onto the tarmac. Then I threw back my head, mouth open into the strong black rain which cleansed me. I nipped back onto the plane, made up hastily, and exited ceremonially right into the arms of my reception committee, which had just pulled up. I spent that evening lying in front of a hospitable fire while various people recited poetry in Pushtu, and the Head of the English Department at Peshawar (who was also a Head in current usage) smiled opaquely and gently crossed his eyes....

SEPTEMBER 17

Ralph Russell made a sign in Urdu for me to prop on my typewriter. I asked him to write, "Do not touch the papers," but Ralph said that would be baffling in Urdu. After some thought he wrote, "Do not move the papers from one place to another." Through this, I have acquired great prestige with all the bearers on the floor, who believe that I wrote it. I have no intention of disabusing them unless trapped.

I show Ralph a sample sentence from a "Teach Yourself Urdu"

book that I had picked up in the lobby: "The British have the biggest navel in the world." "Now I know the basis for that British air of superiority," I tell him.

I spent the better part of yesterday in 'Pindi with B. We told our driver that we wanted to get some Urdu books (recent poetry, fiction) so, quite sensibly, he took us to the Urdu textbook bazaar, a long, long, book-lined alley in an old part of the city. Neither B. nor I have been in the 'Pindi bazaars before, although he comes here on business at least twice a month. I love so much these crowded alleys, the streets of silk, the streets of brass and copper, streets for glass bangles, and bedspreads, and children's toys, and tea in bulk, and persimmons, and tailors (though I have to avert my eyes in the meat street, I confess) — the whole, desperate, vivid, earth-clawing life of the very poor — that I utterly fail to comprehend the overheard remarks of some scholarly delegates: "*Don't* waste your time at the bazaar here. There's nothing to buy, and it's dirty, and smelly and awful..."

Our driver gamely tries again, and we find ourselves in the technical book bazaar. (To the driver, I suspect, as with the majority of Pakistan, literature is not something written down, but something you have in your *head* — the tales of the storytellers in the bazaars, the hundreds of lines of Persian and Urdu poetry that thousands and thousands of illiterate people have by heart, the songs one hears on the street and in the tea and coffee houses — no religious prejudice in *music:* Ragas are much beloved — popular music may be set to lyrics composed by the greatest poets living and dead: as if we had Crashaw and Keats and Yeats and Berryman pouring out of our jukeboxes and Muzak.)

We ask the driver to take us downtown, and from there we walk to a wonderful bookshop next to Shezan's restaurant, owned by a local poet. B. buys a copy of a magazine run by the Maudoodi crowd (Maulana Abul Aala Maudoodi, head of Jamaat-i-Islam, a right-wing group of religious reactionaries), widely believed to be supported by the CIA. B. says to the intelligent bookstore owner, "They talk too much about Islam." "Doesn't everybody?" I remark automatically, and raise a general laugh that I hadn't expected.

We go to Shezan's for tea. At once we are encumbered with waiters, who take our order promptly and disappear for half an hour. B. finally collars the manager. As usual, B., a brave, wise, amusing man, makes unpleasant truths palatable. He asks the manager to join him in prayer. The bewildered manager asks why. "*Tea*, for the love of Allah!" He points out that I have waited four years for a decent cup of tea, and asks if the manager is trying for five. We are then overwhelmed by a flurry of service. I have not only tea but pomegranate juice, lavender and lovely. Surely if there is a paradisial liquid, it is here, it is here, it is here.

SEPTEMBER 18

A marvelous expedition to the Murree Hills yesterday: up, up through the mountains, on our right shadowy stands of giant pine, and rock outcropping that convinced one that God is a Japanese gardener; on the left, saffron-colored valleys surrounded by terraced slopes. Lots of corn growing. Lots of melons. What great vineyards could be here! A girl in a flame-red kurta and dark green trousers stands by the door of an orange barn in the middle distance, the glowing fields at her back. I think again, resentfully, how this country has needed great artists, and how great artists need *her*. (Who can paint Rome, or the bridge at Avignon, again?) But with the old Muslim proscription against anything but decorative design, and the modern prohibitive duty on art materials of all kinds, the artists of Pakistan are either mediocre representationalists of tourist-shop quality (unless they live in Paris) or Abstract Expressionist (as they would have it) daubers, who've not had the opportunity of seeing the stream of great world painting except through the most inferior of reproductions. Yet the light, the landscape, the dramatic power of the isolated human figure, cry out for a Manet or a Corot. The trouble is — I think I'm about to promulgate another of Kizer's Laws — if an Emerging Nation happens to skip a few centuries in the rush to modernize, it can't go back and pick them up later on. The higher we climb, the more prosperous the people. And the desperate poignancy of the children's faces down below — great glittering black eyes above the thin triangles of their cheeks — is here plumped out by cleanliness, fresh air and adequate food; the latent beauty of the Muslim people flowers, far above the hell-heat of the lowlands, where the uncounted millions of the subcontinent wear out their lives.

The first stop is Lawrence College. The Principal and all his staff are on hand to greet us, dressed in academic robes. We are ushered into the great hall for the Principal's welcoming address, in English so poor that one wonders how it can be the medium of instruction here. (But he is a lava flow of eloquence compared to his staff, who fail to understand our simplest queries.) I pass the time by reading wall plaques. One of them lists the principals since the school's founding, in 1890, as a home for British orphans whose fathers died serving the army of occupation. The first principal was the Reverend H.W. Tabernacle. And so goes the parade of English divines, M.A. Ox., until 1958 when, in larger letters and brighter gold appears the name Muinuddin, B.A. Dip. Ed. The school was co-educational until Partition, when of course the first move was to throw out the girls and install them in some outbuildings down the road.

The archaic British syllabus, inculcating vast amounts of irrelevant rubbish by rote (which presumably prepared little boys for future military service, and little girls to be housemaids and seamstresses) is still in force. The Principal speaks wistfully of the time when the switch to instruction in Urdu can take place.

Outside there is a huge memorial to dead graduates who took part in the Pakistan-Bharat War of 1965: three names. The one Indian member of our group, a sour soul at best, passes by it, muttering.

I try to sit through some demonstration classes, but the spectacle of these bright-eyed little boys being yoked like the buffalo to an endless treadmill is more than I can bear. I escape to the sunlight, and spot a chapel at the top of the hill. I ask the Principal about it. The dear man is under the impression that it had been a Roman-Catholic cathedral. It is locked and bolted. He asks solicitously if I would like to have it unlocked so that I might go in and pray. I say yes. So I am admitted to the Chapel of the Holy Innocents, long abandoned to the dust. It's evident that at some point the chancery was closed off from the pews, and used for instructing the primary grades in the laws of living creatures. A few glass cases stand about: in one is a pickled python; in another a stuffed squirrel who starved to death, two ravens, and a parrot, none of them labeled. In another case, grandly, is a large, iridescent bird of fierce and splendid mien. He is labeled *Mirgh-I-Zarreen*. I stare for a long time and work it out. He is the Golden Cockerel.

I climb the stairs to the choir loft. What a sight to behold! An advanced director or playwright would weep to transport the whole thing intact, back to off-off-off-off Broadway. The old oak pews are piled with hemp, great untidy loops and heaps of red-orange hemp, layered with dust, sliced with light from gothic windows. I run down and outside to find somebody to share this with, and seize on Northrop Frye, who is contemplating a Rose of Sharon bush in full bloom.

Later, we wander through the chapel, savoring, not without nostalgia mixed with pity and despair for men, the long and pointless life of the British Raj. I sound a few notes on the organ, and the ghosts wheeze faintly, "We have done those things which we ought not to have done, and there is no health in us. But Thou, O Lord, have mercy upon us, miserable offenders...." I examine the Bible on the lectern, and decide to play Bible Roulette before departing. I close my eyes, flip the pages, and stab my finger right on 1 Kings VIII: "I have surely built then an house to dwell in, a settled place for thee to abide in forever." Dr. Frye and I exchange a long look, and walk out of the chapel and down the hill, forever.

Later: We pile on the bus for Murree, and there walk up from the

Bazaar to the circular road around the summit. Once there, Kashmir, Russia, all Asia lies piled up before our eyes.

On the way down, we collapse on the grass of the kitchen garden of the British High Commissioner, and contemplate an organized fantasy of turnip beds surmounted by a single shock of corn (did Sir James Fraser plant it, perhaps?) which looks like Louis XIV, with his attendant turnips. Some shy and beautiful children approach us. I ask them about a plant that borders the turnip court. With cries of "Muli-muli! Muli-muli!" they pull up a long, sallow dour parsnip. It looks like Malvolio, cross-garters and all. Clearly, the altitude has gone to my head.

Departing, we have nearly reached the top of a long flight of stone steps leading back to the road when I am halted by clear bird-cries. Some distance away, the littlest girl, the loveliest of them all, is running pell-mell after me, with a bunch of marigolds. I want my life to stop, right now, right here.

Still Later: On the bus ride back, past opalescent mountains, through smoke, dust, and moonlight, I transfer the marigolds from a heap on the floor to my capacious coat pocket. Then I proceed to sit on them. Though they look hopelessly defunct, I would as lief throw them away as the plays of Shakespeare. In my room, after they drink water for an hour or so, they are quite resurrected, glorious, gold.

SEPTEMBER 19

Up until 4 AM with C. who arrived last night, in time for dinner. One of the most emotional and devastating evenings I can remember. After four years during which we haven't seen each other, or even kept track of each other since the Indo-Pakistan War, nothing has changed with him. It's a passion rather like that of a medieval troubadour for a woman briefly glimpsed and fantasized about forever. But we must begin by replaying every syllable, every gesture we can recall of that time four and five years back. And his memory is fanatical, precise and complete, as only the inheritor of 4,000 years of oral poetry could possess. Then we must lay every musical note of our separation.... In one way, all this is manna to my woman's ravenous heart; in another way I realize that to him I'm not anyone that I might even imperfectly recognize — almost wholly symbolic. Intently as he listens, he doesn't really listen. And what does he see?

His words flow endlessly; he cocks his head as I reply. But it is the motion of his own feelings which prompts his responses. Perhaps the suppleness of the Urdu tongue lends itself to the diminution of the distinction between language and emotion.

My marigolds, a little middle-aged, are the symbols of eternal life. I am both ruined and restored.

Later: The conference opens officially tomorrow, and today the Pakistani delegates are streaming in — poets from Lahore and Karachi and 'Pindi, journalists who are literary men, and literary men who have abdicated in favor of journalism (although like literary men everywhere, they don't admit it), teachers from everywhere. For political reasons, East Pakistanis have absented themselves, leaving dangerous holes in the agenda.* Frantic attempts are made to patch it up. Here is D., once a poet, from Lahore, dramatically attired in native dress, with a huge Kashmir shawl thrown across his shoulder like Julius Caesar. He recoils violently when I start to hug him. It had slipped my mind that his anti-Americanism, never feeble, had come to a boil and stayed there at the time of the war with India, when he finally abjured poetry for polemic. Unlike E., a far finer poet, who is just as outspoken in his Communism, he is a rancorous man, although trimming his sails in public, except for oblique remarks in his column which often pass unnoticed, owing to the opacity of his style in English. E. on the other hand, manages to be amiable, in a detached way, to everyone, while maintaining a far tougher position. And then, being a genius, he has

---

* I did not realize that the troubles which led to the hideous war between East and West Pakistan, which led to the founding of Bangladesh, were coming to the crisis.

really transcended ideology (although for various reasons he doesn't care to say so, particularly to avoid confusing the uneducated, whose tutor he is).

D. is the only Pakistani who cold-shoulders me. I am moved by the warmth with which I am greeted and embraced by old acquaintances. The great poet, Faiz Ahmad Faiz, gives me a cordial squeeze, and spirits me off to the bar. My friend Margaret Harbottle from Peshawar, who combines the finest qualities of Margaret Rutherford and Jane Austen, is here — alas, with bad news about ailing friends on the Frontier, who are in political hot water as usual, although much of the old fuss about the Pathan separatist movement seems to have calmed down; I would suppose that the customary bravery of the Pathans during the outbreak with India has had a lot to do with it.

Margaret is so great an example of what the British could have been to India that she ought to be permanently preserved after death, like Lenin. The British should have some kind of memento of their presence on this great subcontinent for a hundred years. Why not, "Margaret Harbottle Was Here"? Although she is one who became hooked on the Northwest Provinces, she is no wan relict of the past. She is a vigorous teacher, revered by the Pathans, despite race, sex, and national origin. I envy her that. And in her cottage garden in Peshawar, with its ethereal, almost inhuman cranes stalking about, and the cats purring within, she is at home.

SEPTEMBER 20

Last night I had a long fantasy about becoming C.'s second wife (in addition to — not by elimination of — the first Mrs. C., who is as nice as can be). The fact that I could consider such a thing, and without jealous pangs about the present incumbent or other ladies visible or invisible, makes me realize what a long way I have come — a long way toward sympathizing with certain attitudes fundamental to this society. I never thought I'd make it. (Also, a good man is hard to find.)

Later: The conference opened officially this morning, with a brilliant address by Northrop Frye. He spoke of the unexpected and astonishing rebirth of the oral tradition in modern Western literature, and how it has invalidated some aspects of the old New Criticism. The speech was a superb bridge between the preoccupations of the Eastern and Western literary worlds represented here: "All change takes the form of the recovery of some neglected aspect of tradition." "Myths are culturally rooted, while folk tales are nomadic." "Where myth exists, a magic circle is drawn around society." "Literature is born of a specific culture and a specific locale." Each one of these themes would serve for meditation on the present and future direction of Asian literature. One of the major problems for the Asian writer is how to remain within the stream of his ancient literary traditions without becoming swamped. Another is how to deal with the ancient carapaces of literary form. I suspect that the way you come to terms with your literary tradition is *not* to accept it in its nineteenth-century manifestations, but to tackle it deeper down and further back, and not get stuck along the way in some mode of literary antiquarianism.

As to traditional forms, such as the Urdu *ghazal* (a subject which Ralph Russell discussed in dazzling fashion), the older poets tend to keep to the form but have cracked the shell of traditional content: roses, nightingales, the Beloved, etc. — although unrequited love will always be an important strand of poetry in a society which officially disbelieves in personal love, and does a great deal to repress and punish it. So the *ghazal* may last another lifetime, or longer, but it is clear that the fragmenting of old forms is taking place here as it is everywhere else.

SEPTEMBER 21

The conference has been invited to use the swimming pool of the Islamabad Club, a mile or so from the hotel. It is patronized for the most part by families of the diplomatic missions here in the new capital. It's the finest swimming pool I have ever seen. Someone has said that it is metaphorically possible (and physically too, for that matter) in many parts of Asia to span the centuries in the course of a short walk. I think of this daily, as I walk from our modern hotel to this luxurious pool, through a landscape and past a people unchanged for a thousand years. Encapsulated culture-shock produces a pervasive sense of unreality: Someone at the pool remarks casually, "I see a unicorn over there." Ah yes, a unicorn. I look up, quite unsurprised. There is a man dressed like a Brigadier.

Listening to the idle talk around the pool, I am amused by the way many of the scholars generalize about the culture here, on the flimsiest evidence. How indignantly they would review a book based on such superficial research and such subjective reactions! Yet here they are, wrapping up a whole society in a catch phrase or two.

I attract a certain amount of attention because I wear twenty-four glass bangles in swimming. (Too much trouble to take them off. Anyhow you have to be a little drunk in order to make your hand flexible as a porpoise. Otherwise the bangle snaps, and you sustain a nasty cut in the fleshy part of the thumb.) Bangles... I remember when Miss Altaf Fatima, the short, pudgy, heroic novelist (who lived next to the movie theatre, where the multiple-features accompanied her thoughts most of the night), in the cheapest of cotton saris, took me to Anarkali to buy me bangles. They cost only a few annas apiece. Another Welcome to Pakistan gesture. Bangles, like the poor, have lives that are brief and fragile, and like the poor they are expendable. Bangle Time: day by day by day, they snap, and fall away, leaving your arm naked again: existential time. Bangles bestowing grace: my arm dips in the water as I swim and lifts in a graceful arc — all because of bangles glinting in the light, shedding a thousand drops of water in crystal cascades. It is well known that in a sari (or even a burqua, God forfend!) your walk becomes undulant and sexy. Add a lot of tinkling jewelry to the rustle of silk. Easy. More difficult: add a head of long, oiled, perfumed silken hair that falls down your spine to the back of your knees in a braided coil as thick as your arm. Grace incarnate. (Sour postscript: Then waste 98% of your femininity in the company of other women, mainly relatives, where almost the sole topic of conversation is where you obtained your finery and how much it cost — while the men are off having what they think is a good time. I love to recall the remark made by a woman friend of mine in — I am happy to say — the American diplomatic service, at a typical party consisting of around forty men and the two of us. Fed up at last, she said, "When I first came to this country I was sorry for the women. Now I'm sorry for *you*. You don't know what you're missing.")

I bought the bangles in the Murree bazaar. For so long I've been yearning for bangles and *pan* — the collection of mild narcotics bound up in betel leaf and folded like a diaper. Two bangles broken so far. (The bangle-wallah had given me two baker's dozen.) My aging marigolds, still bright, and my bright bangles: Eternity versus existential time.

Later: I went with B. and his wife, just arrived, to a reception in 'Pindi given by the Minister of Education and a clutch of Cabinet members and big shots, and their good ladies. The B's are living proof that even this system can produce a happy marriage. Although I persist in believing that there are more actively unhappy marriages here than in the West — or perhaps it would be more accurate to say more marriages where, in the words of my friend, they don't know what they're missing.

At the reception, with that old-time hypocrisy which irritates me so intensely, they served only orange drink and the local cola. If all the men didn't drink their heads off in the privacy of their own homes, as the phrase has it, I wouldn't mind so much. As it is, it's like the Catholic Church trying to ban contraception for the rest of us. Or perhaps they just don't want to suffer watching us drink while they abstain. I was annoyed enough to lead a rump group into the hotel bar, after checking with a couple of Pakistani pals to see if that would constitute Impossible Behaviour. Not at all, they said wistfully.

I came back to the dining-room just in time for Faiz to lead me over to a table where it was wall-to-wall poets, including D., who proceeded to make rude remarks about me in Urdu. I was tempted to regale the group with stories about how he used to show up at my house in Lahore at all hours, in his Pakistani drag, go through a series of ritual courtship motions much like those of a trumpeter swan, and then sit back and wait for me to drop dead from joy. After I left Pakistan he gave up, and married his mother, or somebody. Now I restrained myself, in memory of his early, lovely poems.

I spent most of the evening being told stories by Faiz, an enchanting talker, both at dinner and back at the bar later on. I remember the first time I saw Faiz, sitting quietly on the platform at a *mushira* (a large, group outdoor poetry-reading, under a canopy) waiting his turn to read. Even before he spoke — and of course I couldn't understand when he did — I knew without hesitation that he was a great man. How?

SEPTEMBER 22

For days the letters column of the paper has been taken up with a subject both ominous and encouraging: ominous that it happened, encouraging that people are making a fuss, and that the papers print their letters. When I was here before, probably the ablest Pakistani professor of English in the country was Eric Cyprian of Islamia College. He required, and produced, a high standard of English prose and poetry. Recently he was abruptly discharged from his post for (1) anti-Islamic activities, and (2) lack of funds to pay his salary. He was within months of retiring with a pension. Now he doesn't even get severance pay. He will be utterly destitute, as the salary scale for professors allows them to accumulate nothing but debts.

The letter-writer's standard line of defense of Professor Cyprian probably wouldn't make a good impression on either the A.C.L.U. or the A.A.U.P. A sample, under the running head, "A Sordid Affair" (I should say that the word "sordid" seems very popular among Pakistani intellectuals and journalists): "Sir, Every pupil of Mr. Cyprian must have been shocked to hear of his dismissal... I beg to cite just one incident: It was the month of Ramadan. We were having a meeting of The Young Writers. One young man lit a cigarette. Nobody took any notice of him except Mr. Cyprian. He made the smoker put out his cigarette, saying, 'You must respect the month of Ramadan.' As for the second objection, I say that no salary is too high for a kind, devoted, and sincere teacher such as Mr. Cyprian. Yours, etc."

I used to visit Cyprian's classes, to talk about American poetry, and to read the students' work, and comment on it. The subject matter of much of their writing was obsessed with the cataclysm of blood, fire, and brimstone, which was their earliest memory: Partition. This was a time when, at two or three years old, you were dug from the bottom layer of bodies by frantic hands, barely breathing, often wounded yourself, in a railway car in Lahore station, where every adult in that car had been slaughtered. Your parents had flung themselves protectively on you, in their last moments. If they died without being disemboweled or mutilated in ways too horrible to mention, by the Sikhs of Srinagar, as the train passed through the station, they were the fortunate dead. Can this be written of in the stately couplets and intricate rhymes of the *ghazal?*

But, not long before my stay in Pakistan, Allen Ginsberg had penetrated the sub-continent. (This is an over-simplification, but even so, the tremendous *positive* impact of his visit, in contrast to the scandalous impact which most people know about vaguely, can hardly be overestimated.) Through the influence of Ginsberg and his large and immediate following, free verse did more than liberate form; it liberated consciousness. Through it, the students discovered the instrument of their catharsis.

When asked to "criticize" such work, Cyprian and I tended to throw up our hands. How do you criticize a volcanic eruption?

Never mind. As we have seen with our own writers who happen to be black, the shouts of pain and rage, or grievance and horror, precede the ability to create a controlled work of art. Liberation now, literature later.

But it is precisely at this point, when young writers need to make new accommodations between their traditions and their immediate experience (post-catharsis), that the help of teachers like Eric Cyprian is urgently required if they are to become artists, or even self-comprehending men and women. That is why I am so gloomy that he — and no doubt others like him — has been driven from his post. And I, as an American, am in absolutely no position to do anything to help. I confirm this with B. later, who says to stay out of it. I: "What about money?" B. (severely): "We will see that he is cared for." Bless B. I'd like to give many examples of his goodness and courage, but they would identify him too clearly, in these uncertain times.

SEPTEMBER 23, 6 AM

I am to give my paper this morning, and then depart at once for Peshawar by car, to catch up with a party of people going to Swat, then to Afghanistan and Iran. I've always wanted to go to Swat, "because of Babe Ruth," I tell my Pakistani friends. Even if I explained it, I wouldn't explain anything. But that helps make up for all the jokes in Urdu that I don't get.

Yesterday, various emissaries from the group going to Swat came by this hotel to look for me. Everyone to whom they spoke, from manager to busboy, assured them that I was in conference, they didn't know where, and could under no circumstances be disturbed, even if they did know. The hotel people were perfectly aware that I was in the bar with Faiz all afternoon, drinking gin and going over translations. They damned well weren't going to interrupt us. They know how to treat poets in this country.

Saidu-Sharif, Swat, 8 PM: My speech went over reasonably well.

I closed by reading a poem of Faiz. He graciously came forward and recited it in Urdu before I read my English version. We brought down the house with that, although I could see some Pakistanis looking peevish at the translation — it is a very famous poem. But for the most part they were the kind who believe you can't translate *anything* without losing *everything;* and people of this sort are the principal reason why the bulk of Urdu literature is so little known in the West. As I used to say to my Pakistani friends when I lived here, "Would you rather have a door open a crack into a beautiful garden, or would you prefer to keep it locked and bolted?"

Here is the poem, much improved by yesterday's session in the bar:

IF I WERE CERTAIN

If I were certain, O my dear companion,
If I were certain that your muffled pulse,
Grief in your eyes, heart in your breast afire
Could be relieved by my devoted care,
If sympathetic phrases were a cure
To lift the sterile shadows from your brain,
To wipe the stain of insult from your brow,
And to restore your failing youth again;
If I were certain, O my dear companion,
I would nurse you day and night without repose.
How I would croon you tender, moving songs,
Tunes of cascades, of spring, and orchard blossoms,
Morning's commencement, the traveling moon and planets,
How I would spin you long, romantic tales!
Tales of proud girls whose stiff, unyielding bodies
Melt beneath the urgent warmth of hands,
How the features, learned by heart, of a single face,
Alter at once, and bloom before your eyes,
How the marmoreal pallor of her skin
Warms, of a sudden, with a glow like wine.
How roses bend meek stems that you may pluck them,
And how the imperial night bursts into fragrance.
Then I would sing, sing endlessly for you,

Weaving my songs, kneel endlessly beside you.
No song of mine can be a panacea
For suffering, though it may soothe your grief.
My song is not a lancet but a salve
Anointing the long anguish of your life.
Only a knife can end your agony,
Killing, redeeming. I cannot fulfill you
Nor any breathing being on this earth
Except yourself, except yourself, except yourself.

FAIZ AHMAD FAIZ

SEPTEMBER 24

I split for Swat, right on schedule — good to make a fast getaway, and avoid prolonged and painful farewells. The driver made fine time out of Islamabad, and soon we swung onto the Grand Trunk Road. The world's greatest road. The road between Europe and Asia, between India and Greece, the route of Alexander, Tamburlaine, and Genghis Khan, the road built by the greatest man of all, to my mind, the first Moghul Emperor, Akbar, who created more than he destroyed, who created much that still lives today. Road of traders, and armies, and nomads and fierce tribesmen, and bandits, of thousands upon thousands of caravans, camels, donkeys, horsemen, and peasants transporting their produce or fleeing their oppressors, measuring off the miles with two bare feet — road mercifully and blessedly unchanged.

As the driver tore along, I hung my head out of the car window, singing over and over, "Oh the Grand Trunk Road is a grand trunk road," exhilarated as all hell, and mad to see everything once more. At the same time I was holding back tears at having to leave my friends, and C. For another half a decade, I suppose. Well, never mind. Age cannot wither me in those eyes. And custom is damned well not going to stale my infinite variety, worse luck.

I held myself in suspense, not wanting to miss the first glimpse of a place I love: Attock Fort, at the confluence of the great Kabul and Indus Rivers. First, a couple of small, ruined caravanserais (built by Akbar, I bet); then the graveyard, and a bare, ruined mosque; then around the curve, and Attock Fort! Built by Akbar, its massive walls swoop down the hills to the river in waves of scalloped stone. (I have about eighty-five photographs of it at home, none of them any good.) Then we go down past the village which separates the fort from the road, to the famous suspension bridge built by the British. After the bridge, the road wanders along the river for a while, then gives itself a shake and takes off in a straight line, on a dead run, for the Frontier. At Nowshera, an old army town just this side of Peshawar, I see some soldiers making the only sensible use I can imagine of a couple of armored tanks: grading a road. Let us beat our tanks into road-graders....

We roll up to Dean's Hotel, in Peshawar, with about eleven minutes to spare.

The car broke down five times on the way to Swat, so we missed a visit to a Buddha carved in rock which has lost much of its frontage, according to my fellow-travelers. But, being tardy, we hit the Swat Valley at just the right time, late afternoon: Low sun nearing the mountain's rim, but still gleaming on green-yellow fields that give off an unearthly glow. The fields divide for a pure blue river, gliding along its broad bed. It took me quite a while to realize that the rich green crop we saw was *rice*. I'm familiar with Chinese rice fields: peasants sloshing through icy mud to harvest puny stalks no higher than your hand. This glorious stuff must be waist-high. Oceans of chartreuse rice! And melons, huge mounds of melons, like orange balloons. And nomads: stunning women, striding along with erect backs, looking you dead in the eye. (What a contrast to the burqua-bundling and scarf-grabbing and sideways shuffling apprehension down below!) They are dressed in a profusion of clashing prints and jangling jewels that would send Vuillard and Bonnard into fits.

The hotel is a superb old place, with ample lawns and huge trees, formerly the Wali's guest house. Our timing is not all that it might be. Today the Government put the Wali, and the heads of the other Frontier states, out of business. Their principalities are now Districts. The Wali, poor Wali, was supposed to receive us. Olly, olly, oxenfree, Wali! But the Wali is lurking, and skulking, and sulking, deep within his walls. He is weeping at the bitter ingratitude of men and states. He sends a Cabinet Minister (as of yesterday) in his place, who makes sad, polite noises to us, and we make sleepy polite noises back. And then we go tumble into our beds, by the light of the huge full moon. All goodly report of Swat is right: Paradise lives!

SEPTEMBER 25, KABUL, AFGHANISTAN

Swat left me speechless. Anyway, the less people know about the splendors of Swat, the better. The whole place ought to be Classified Information, or all sorts of unworthy types will be wanting to go there and spoil it. Wednesday a day of desultory sightseeing and mooning around. We drove back to Peshawar on Thursday. Wandered about in the bazaar for a while, everything permeated by the lovely, smoky, sandalwood-sweet odor of hashish. You can get high just walking around. An evening of "ethnic dancing" on the lawn of Dean's Hotel, the only amusing part of it the way other Western guests went into raptures about the two dancing girls, who were boys. Typical Pathan tarts they were, too, tough as nails, throwing in a bump here, a grind there, and batting their eyes at the guests in a parody of lust.

This morning we climbed on buses and headed for the Khyber Pass. When I was here before, I got myself adjudged a suspicious character in the eyes of the authorities because I spent too much time with the Pathan poets, some of whom were suspected of being involved with the Red Shirts, or Pathan separatist movement. When I wasn't avoiding a bumbling oaf from the CIA (in those innocent days I thought the Pakistanis were paranoid about the CIA

424

— now, of course, I know better), for fear I might be thought a colleague or pal of his, I was trying to avoid well-meaning officials of both governments, who tried to dissuade me from staying near Charsadda Village with friends of mine, an experience I wasn't about to miss. My host was perhaps the best poet writing in Pushtu; at any rate his poems were once used in school and college textbooks, before he got in too much political trouble. He is the son of the illustrious Abdul Ghaffar Khan, known as "the Gandhi of the Frontier," now an ancient man who is forced to live exiled in Kabul, but still a potent symbol to his followers and to his enemies. Why the Pakistani authorities worried about his son Ghani is more than I can understand. Years of prison (mostly under the British), drink, drugs, failing health and spiritual dishevelment would seem a more than effective bar to his leading a tribal uprising. Furthermore, no man as totally obsessed with art and poetry as Ghani has time for politics. But the story of my friendship and love for Ghani, and Roshan, his wife, is a book that I am not going to open now. All this was by way of explaining why I didn't get to the Khyber Pass in 1965. One good feint toward Afghanistan, and I probably would have been declared *persona non grata*, and pushed out of the country.

It is a fine, clear morning as we roll toward the border. The entrance to the pass is not impressive, and we are held up the usual length of time while passports are inspected. I run into the weedy son and heir of the Meer of Hunza, who was a child when I met him last in Lahore, in the hall of the Customs and Immigration Building. I suppose the poor old Meer is out of a job, too. It is amusing to introduce "the Crown Prince," wearing an ancient sweater, sneakers, and jeans, to a couple of impressionable people in our party, who barely refrain from dropping him a curtsey.

At last we're off. The mountains begin to draw closer, but I am craning my neck to stare back at the Pakistan border — a wooden gate, a cluster of shacks and parked cars, a couple of wooden conning towers, and a lot of troops — for as long as I can. But I can't really see very well. I seem to be crying again. Good-bye, Pakistan! So long! I'll be back! I'll be back!

Bangla Desh: 1

The festival of massacre: how make it vivid?
How entertain you with the mourning of my blood?
My emaciated body is nearly drained of blood:
Not enough to light the lamps.
Not enough to fill the goblets;
Nor to light any fires,
Nor to slake any thirst.
My lacerated body is nearly drained of blood.
But every vein brims with a fatal poison;
Every drop is the fury of a cobra,
Distilled from the anguish and pain of centuries,
Enflamed with the passionate fury of decades.
Beware of my body! It is a river of poison.

Beware of my body. It is a charred log in the wilderness.
If you attempt to burn it in your garden compound,
Instead of the jasmine and the rose,
The thorns of my bones will flower.
If you scatter my body over the hills and valleys,
Instead of the perfume of the morning breeze,
You will fling away the dust of my anguished soul.
So beware. Because my heart is thirsting for blood.

FAIZ AHMAD FAIZ

Bangla Desh: II

THE BLOOD IN MY EYES

Layer by layer, the dust of bitterness
Silts up my heart till it reaches my eyes.
There is nothing for it; I must obey my healer:
Rinse my eyes with blood.
Now my blood-filled eyes see red:
The sun that was gold is blood.
The silver moon is blood.
Each tree is a pillar of blood;
Each flower an eye dipped in blood;
Each gaze is spun on a thread of blood.
Every image is smeared with blood.

The bloodstream flows with the brilliant crimson of anger,
Of suffering, of the passion of martyrdom.
When the blood clots, turns black,
It vanishes in darkest night, in death,
Where all color strangles and drowns.
Don't let this happen, my healer!
Send me a river of tears,
The baptismal waters.
Then, bathed in that river,
Perhaps my eyes, my heavy, dust-laden eyes,
Will be cleansed of blood forever.

Bangla Desh: III

revisited after the Holocaust, 1973

GHAZAL

We who are strangers now, after our years of easy friendship;
How many times must we meet, before we are reacquainted?

How can we reclaim that old camaraderie?
When shall the eye see once more that spring of spotless green?

How many monsoons are required
To wash away the stains of blood?

Merciless, merciless was the moment when love ended.
Cruel, cruel were the mornings, after the nights of tenderness.

As heartbreak gave no respite, the heart yearned
To quarrel as friends once more, after the prayers for forgiveness.

But the word I had come here to speak,
With the offering of my life as sacrifice,

That reconciling word remained unspoken
After everything else had been said.

Elegy for Hassan Nasir

killed by torture in the Lahore Fort, 1959

Today, all at once, when the thread of my vision snapped,
The sun and moon were smashed to bits in the skies.

Like my heart, no trace of the road of faith remains.
Now, where I stand, there is neither light nor dark.

Now, let someone else tend the garden of sorrow!
Because, friends, in my heart the nourishing dew has dried.

The riot of madness has subsided.
The rain of stones has ended.

And, in the path of the Beloved,
The banner of my blood has been unfurled.

The dust of the road stained red as the mouth of the Beloved;
Let me see who is willing to take my place when I am gone.

"Who else can drain the murderous wine of love?"
The cry heard again on the lips of the Saqi, when I am gone.

Izhab-O-Rasai
(*Expression and Reach*)

Paintbrush and lute-string or new modeling clay
Are ways of saying what we want to say.
But we, who wrote once of lovers coming together,
How can we speak, now, of the whole world's weather?
What we would reach is always out of reach.
The end of art is not the end of speech.

Within each heap of ashes gleams a spark
Of pained and random passion in the dark,
Driven without volition by the heat
Within its breast, to move on drunken, dancing feet
To where creation bursts like song, deranged,
But from itself perpetually estranged.
Yet here conjoined are colors, curves, and lines:
Divinity rules the meaning it divines.

A single ray of this impulsive gleam
May whirl the months and years into a dream,
Twitching the limbs of any drowsing dancer,
To an old potter at his wheel, revealing answer:
Poetry! Fashioning the bricks without the clay,
Dark tenements suffused with deathless day.

To whom shall I address my artful speech
When you are lost, eternally out of reach?
Two lovers now become our whole estate.
But I am lost, my muse, its burdensome weight
That I long to lay down with my life, to share
With you, apathetic reader. But you don't care.

Elegy

In the May breeze
        the water-lily sways
        on a wave of water.
In the May breeze
        my heart sways
        on a wave of ardor.
In the May breeze
        my branch of jasmine,
        you went to sleep
In the May breeze
        under the earth
        just a year ago.

Macedonian

Translation

for Lars Gustafsson

I am now utterly translated into Macedonian, after two days and nights, nonstop in Skopje. Never has anyone been so well and truly translated. I feel that I, myself, have been translated. Henceforth, I shall write *only* to be translated. All complexities have been eliminated. All polysyllables. All ambiguities. All multiple meanings. All humor. My new poetry is of such a transparency that it virtually has no identity at all. It is a glass vessel, waiting to be filled with the colorful liquid which is translation. In creation, now, the only question is, "Yes, but how will it sound in Macedonian?" I will greet you, hug you, and hand you this, on the morrow — hand you this wordlessly, because, alas, you do not speak Macedonian. Perhaps you can pick up a few words if you try, for we must have a common language, if only to hug in.

Professional Poet

The last word, the hasty swallow

you get up from the table, after your working day
and catch the first bus to the kitchen
you tear off a hunk of bread, inhale the good oven odors.
Your body, leaden with weariness, the mold
you cram with rich food.
Switch on the set
                      and inspect the backyard
through another screen
                         with a wet finger
you flip the pages of the sky.

Nothing will come of nothing.
                          Clematis tendrils
float in the void… "THEY MUST BE TRAINED ON A TRELLIS"
your daughter brings you a chair
The table is set, your wife calls
through the window of a parallel world.

After dinner, you walk in your garden
alone in your pressurized space-suit,
                        stars all around you
even beneath you. Your antennae must be redirected.
The pear tree, newly pruned, requires manure.

Back to the module:
                    Daddy, what does it mean
to be a monster?

Suddenly, the chain of command dissolves
bits of paper whirling in free fall
around the table:
                    untouched paper
and your pencil, ominous as a revolver.

Flood at the International Writer's Workshop

Since the sky started crying
I haven't been out-of-doors for thirty-one days:
By now the earth must be a pair of pliers
With tatters of human flesh stuck to its jaws.

I imagine myself on a seesaw, balanced so lightly
That if even an atom fell on it (let alone a bomb)
I would be hurled like a stone from a catapult
Straight back into the trap of Macedonia.

My people, are we God's voracious eye
Suspended in the air like a traffic-light
Which, as it blinks, directs the flow of nations?
Right now I'm only that greedy eye of legend
Which, on my side of the scale, outweighs the world.

In the Ark, our elevators work erratically:
Every deck is bursting with trapped livestock!
On the first floor, insects have turned into neurons
Without any owners:
On the second, saurians form a mythic chain
To swallow one another so they will all disappear,
But too feeble to achieve total consummation;
On the third floor, the mad vegetarians
Roaring with hunger, lay waste the Frigidaires;
On the fourth, the carnivorous flowers
Make plans to devour God;
On the fifth floor, this lone Macedonian
Mangles their languages, recreating Babel.

And every line that occurs to me sinks like a plummet
When it should splash about like a happy dog
And, like a dolphin, jump through its trainer's hoop.
But I'm dense when it comes to featherweight words!
The verb should be in a state of constant erection,
In equal readiness to strike, or stroke;
The adjectives stick to the noun
                                        like a lizard catching flies;
And the noun should swing both ways,
While the conjunctive is a universal passkey.

So the sky sobs on, like a hysterical child,
Like the she-dragons of my legends.
The gutters gurgle, and gargle.
The drainpipes are subterranean Mississippis.

The words refuse to swallow us any longer
Now we have set them to quarreling among themselves:
Trying to strangle one another, they bite off their tongues.
They have burned to tell us everything they know,
But, being dumb now, drooling idiots,

Speechlessly, they copulate with rainbows.

My Sister's Letter

Your letter wrecked my day.
I read and re-read it, till
          the words blurred into gibberish.
How can I be expected to go on writing
When you refuse to explain what happens at home?
We are separated by thousands of miles of silence.
Here, too, I'm imprisoned in ignorance.

I'm expected to put my ear to this alien earth
— As we used to do as children, listening
          for the tremor of unseen trains.
Haven't you learned by now
That even the ground has learned how to dissemble?
No train arrives — only a false vibration.
The land has learned to hold its breath, play dead.

Thanks very much for your silence.
          Now I'm utterly dismayed.
You go on spinning sentences out of emptiness...
          Are you trying to be the poet
Instead of me?
Somehow I managed to survive the day.
I've had practice staying alive;
          What choice do we have?
Deep into sleep, swamped by a sea of nightmares
A voice I thought was yours awakened me:
          screaming, "Help! help!"
Having fallen on the bed without undressing,
I could have rushed downstairs into the lobby,
          aroused the desk-clerk

To call the police.

        But who would have believed me,

Phantom victim of a phantom cry?

"Help!" once again

        and then the voice broke off...

Thoughtfully, I put on my pajamas.

        What does any of it matter?

Even the dead still cry out in their sleep,

Protest injustice, screaming from the grave

        for vindication,

Still persecuted by the living

        survivors who defame them,

Who conspire to pretend we are all deaf to the dead.

But at least they don't send me empty letters

So that I tremble with all they fail to say.

When I Came Back

When I came back
from discovering America
unfinished phrases drifted in the wind
samara for commas

and the wind tied my reed flute
into a knot.

My old clothes were returned to me
re-cut in my absence
to fit the image you had of me.

When I put them on
they split at the seams.

On the Way Back

London

When we speak of freedom
our breathing is as casual
as flight for birds,

when it should be hard labor
which tires us out,
so tired
that we may not show up for work.

Only this effort
not automatic, achieved by an act of will,
could give back breath to the dead.

Prostitution

Provocatively, our epoch swings her breasts.
Who will suck at her tits?
— Who won't?
As she passes my window, I get a whiff
of her randy scent.

At night, when I'm stretched on my back,
the whole world turns on my axis.

After a while
an old crone will come by,
slightly touched in the head,

who will try to pay me
for my favors.

Climate and Lyre

Where is the sky born?
Or will my triumph be recorded
Only in my sad eyes which face Olympus?
O my soul, the seasons change the climate
Like gamblers dealing cards.
Why do you echo in my ear
This random note of sorrow?

I don't know if my country really needs me
But I give myself to her with words
As if I were an unknown warrior.
Suddenly, color invades the void;
With a bronze resonance, a poplar leaf
Drops from its stem.

A harsh word breaks my lyre in two.
Sky, where are your lightnings?
The tree, in its grief for the bird,
Begins to resemble the bird.

MATEJA MATEVSKI

from *Equinox*

This is an hour of calm, a quiet hour,
an idyll of days and nights like a folding of hands
the sky soft on the stretched body of the plain
Now is the hour when nothing happens
as if the world didn't breathe, as if the rain didn't pour
a dream enclosed in the dark of a hazelnut
a stone forgotten under the body of a hill
Now is the instant when wheat is harvested
when the chimney doesn't smoke nor the road resound
Man lies beneath the body of the sun
distilled into nothing by its shadows
This is the total moment: the balance of black and white.

ANTÉ POPOVSKI

from *Samuel*

from part one of a five-part dramatic poem

There was nothing left for man:
The lava rose over the horror,
Overflowing the gulfs,
Leveled the chasms.
The rivers were effaced
By the rock,
        Hard, black rock.

The moon no longer set
Over the axis of the plains.
Grain was no longer seen on the threshing floors.
The trees bore rock instead of fruit,
And the peasants took it in their hands like bread.
And instead of children, the pregnant women
Brought forth rock:
        Hard, black rock.

The wild animals howled through the forests.
The last she-wolf died on a dry outcropping.
She will no longer give birth to wolves.

And the wide winds, driven mad,
Blew enormous ashes
And heaped them on one another,
And, higher than centuries, pushed the rock,
The bare rock, the black rock.

Nothing, nothing left for man.
It rose up over the horror,

And the gulfs overflowed,
The chasms leveled,
The rivers effaced
By the rock,
The bare rock, the black rock.

French African

EDOUARD MAUNICK

Seven Sides and Seven Syllables

for Aimé Césaire and Pierre Emmanuel

I.

happen you come on your own
to this contradicted place
re-celebrate ebony
the original metal

> happen you essay the dream
> before you outlive yourself
> before the blood surges back
> before your father expires

this land once was a mirror
which was silvered by the sea
in the sweat of oars, islands
with keys girded up their loins

> good fortune surrounded us
> in no way surprising us
> if we wager on the sea
> for the last possible time

but what can be the last time
for the deracinated?
again, for those who oppose him
share the flesh of the poet

unaware, he keeps going
not heeding all the mad ways
all countries merge dizzily
in this country of his own

II.

my love is improbable
let the saliva well up
neutrality, its token
skimming the garden of birth

here the roses are roses
sword-lilies prohibited
a man who speaks standing up
has his eyes bandaged with rain

we all take powerful root
on assassination day
with the garden's iron pickets
stained bright by the equinox

here a man who speaks standing
is submerged in the symbol:
I say rose and it means hope
but who will live by this game?

who will take up sword-lilies
in their form of machetes
to knot up with blood once more
what survives as a mongrel?

the whole world I name garden
I leave no place unbaptized
who will plant garden fences
if not I, or my kinfolk?

I, the child of all races
soul of India, Europe,
my identity branded
in the cry of Mozambique

III.

thus I am anonymous
while holding the heritage
of your ancestral truncheons
and your black man's evasions

I could accept your labels
and stay unidentified
be tattooed by your numbers
while remaining uncounted

command all your battlements
cloak myself in your panic
recognizing the thunder
and recognizing the wind

know the substance of exile:
on the sea, wind, and thunder
recognizing all the roots
of the tree that rejects me

recognizing all the roots
tongue-ties me with bereavement
on the shore of denial
I will choose to be Negro

I've read Senghor and Césaire
and Guillèn and Richard Wright
but Lorca and St. John Perse
Dylan Thomas and Cadou

Paul Éluard, vertical
all reinvent memory
you step out of the mirror
to marry morning with night

IV.

rising in me, the promise
my mouth will spit bitterness
to crack the rejecting rock
at the end of all stanzas

utterance moves toward a place
where snow, thunder cohabit
of words fouled by long weeping
of visions seared on the skin

with desires pure and bitter
tumultuous silences
I here spell out my poem
releasing my love of you

withholding what must be said
dividing my blood from blood
inhabiting somewhere else
than the habitable space

exile is no easy thing
despite obscure boundaries
open doors and living hands
no, it is never easy!

to accept is to refuse
refusal reveals anger
fling open your registers!
bring your mortal crucifix!

I swear to understand flesh
transparent as lake water
I shall murder ancient seas
set fire to their slave cargoes

v.

but CHRIST, this odor of chains
and this rattling of metal
against the defeated bones
these quincunxes of ropes!

I can force my eyes to see
but the sight is too tragic:
dogs trained to attack the blacks
and their spirituals stabbed

yes, to watch the capsizing
of women and child voices
whose offense is vertical
because they refuse to crawl

is this Christmas and manger?
are these our poems pure white?
are these our poems deep black?
this the summation of poems?

VI.

what right have I to denounce
while shooting with your own guns?
or healing with your own hands?
I freeze and starve for us all

If I could find a kingdom
between midday and midnight
I would go forth and proclaim
my mixed blood to the core

for I choose the you-in-me
without color or passport
they say we all long for God
and we are all forgiven

VII.

happen you come on your own
to this contradicted place
to embrace the bitter dream
of the solar boundaries

discover the point of light
which is the true equator
having no need of the sea
to conceal your departures

happen you come without wrath
to this place of denial
open your eyes to the rain
lave the body till it splits

at last, for a final time
adjust your steps to the steps
of the sole presence in you:
a man the size of a man

my love may only exist
when endorsed by your absence
I no longer need the past
to stand up in the present

the carousels of the sea
are not mad carousels now
I had to silence my fate
with this, my derisive voice.

German

Maryam

From whom did you inherit your dark hair
And the almond sound of your sweet name?
It isn't youth that makes you gleam of dawn.
From an Eastern land for a thousand years you came.

Promise us Jericho; waken above the Psalter,
The source of the River Jordan in your hand.
Startle the murderers when you stone them,
And, in a moment, see your second land!

Every stony breast you touch, a miracle;
Every teardrop slipping down the stone.
Be self-baptized with the steaming water.
Stay alien till we are alien to our own.

Often, snow will fall into your cradle,
Beneath its rockers the groan of ice in thaw.
Sleep deep enough, the world will be your captive.
The waters of the Red Sea will withdraw!

INGEBORG BACHMANN

What Is True

Truth kicks no sand into your eyes,
Truth required of you by death and sleep
As if carved in flesh, prompted by agonies,
Truth rolls back the boulder from your tomb.

Truth — so subterranean and faded
In leaf and kernel, in your tongue's lazy bed
A year, another year, year after year —
Truth does not make Time, it leaves it dead.

Truth parts the earth, combs out the dreaming,
Combs out the braided wreath and all the leavings,
It twirls its comb, knocks into you
The ripened crops, drains you completely.

Truth's never quelled till it is looted,
Which is perhaps for you the crucial way.
Where wounds appear, you are its booty;
It overtakes you only to betray.

Here comes the moon with sour tankards.
Drink up! In the fall of bitter night
Not a single twig is rescued,
Foam flakes the dove into a feathered flight.

Loaded with chains, the world is your encumbrance
But truth is driving cracks into the wall.
As you grow you search the dark for what is righteous,
Facing the obscure exit of your cell.

Romanian

NINA CASSIAN

Tirade for the Next-to-Last Act

I'm leaving you, I won't touch you anymore.
I've run out of things I have to prove to you,
so there's no reason to postpone the drowning
of molecules called hands or eyes or mouth
in the patient earth which waits — but not for me.
Earth knows it owns me, right to horizon-zero.
I've told you almost everything I know;
even the lie I told was a pious lie
because it leapt to life, came into being
embodied as a leaf, or as a rabbit,
and I cannot reject a living creature.
Also, I leave you because I am so weary
of the way the century melts into the one before
as if the milk the child sucks from its mother
went back into her breast — or worse than that,
as if the brow of a philosopher
kept sloping back till it rejoined a species
long extinct, and hirsute, and prehensile.

I've picked up information on my way
but none of it from scholarly pursuits
or from the established canon of great books;
mostly from heat and cold, from birth and death,
all that comes past us only once, alas,
so it's no guide for what will happen next.
I remain as vulnerable as ever,
knowing a thousand objects by their names,
a thousand states of mind I cannot name.
I don't see their utter metamorphoses,
I didn't notice when they took their leave,

abandoning me to confusion,
as if dropped into a pool of blood.
So I'm leaving; I won't touch you anymore.
You've said so many times you can't abide me
though I drew my portrait for you with such care,
relying on the way you had sketched it out.
But I'm incapable of imitation,
or so it seems. I lack the talent
to resemble you — much less, myself.

My smiles are always misconstrued as grins.
And when I laugh, all heads are turned away
as if I had committed some indecency.
I pick the wrong occasions for my tears:
when the crowd cheers a city holiday.
When I sculpt a statue, everyone screams,
"He has made himself into a graven image!"
When I shrivel with a serious illness,
I'm not believed: it's the devious way
my sad body causes an obscure epidemic...
So I'm leaving you, good-bye. I'm gone. Good-bye.

Modern Chinese

The Singing Flower

> Thanks to your shining
> my agony has a faint halo.

I.

I am already a singing flower
Upon your breast
Stirred by the breeze of your breath
As the moonlit fields are stirred

Cover me, please
With your wide palm
For the time being

II.

Now permit me to dream:
Snow. Huge forest.
Ancient wind-bell. Slanting tower.
May I ask for a genuine Christmas tree?
Ice-skates on its branches,
Fairy tales, magic flutes,
Fireworks vaunting their ardent fountains.
May I rush through the streets laughing loudly?

III.

What has become of my little basket
Heaped with weeds from my Bumper Crop Allotment?
What has become of my old army canteen?
Oh, those thirsty naps under the scaffolding!
The barrettes I never had a chance to wear.

My English exercises: I LOVE YOU LOVE YOU*
My shadow, stretched or shortened under the streetlamp
And my tears
             that flowed so many times, so many times choked back.
And more
And more

Don't ask me
When I toss lightly in my dreams.
The past, like a cricket in the corner
Whines in its low, persistent voice.

        IV.

Permit me a calm dream
Don't leave me alone
That short street — so short!
We have been walking for years

Permit me a quiet dream
Don't disturb me
Those wheeling crows that pester us —
Pay no attention if your eyes are clear

Permit me a dream of absurdity
Don't laugh at me
Each day, newly green, I walk into your poem
Each evening I return to you, bright rose

Let me have an indecent dream
Tolerate my tyranny
When I say, *You're mine,* you are mine!

*in English in the original

Don't reproach me, beloved...
I even confess my eagerness to see
        A thousand waves of passion
        Drown you a thousand times.

    v.

When our heads touch
As if we were on a speeding train to the moon
The world falls back with a shriek.
The avalanche, Time, swirls madly
        then plunges to pieces.

When our eyes meet
Our souls are like a painting on a gallery wall:
Watery sunlight spreads in rings
        across our field,
Luring us deeper, deeper,
        into harmony, silence, and renewal.

    vi.

Just like this
We sit in the darkness, clasping hands
And let the voice of our love, ever old and new,
Pierce our hearts.
No need to stir, even though
An emperor is knocking at the door

Nevertheless...

VII.

Wait! What is that? What sound
Rouses the scarlet pulsing in my veins?
      Now I am dizzy with love
      On the ever-sober ocean
What is that? Whose will
Forces open the lids of my soul and body
      "You must carry the cross on your back
      Every day, and follow me."

VIII.

The dream, umbrella-shaped, takes off
And flies away, a dandelion gone to seed
In a cratered moonscape.

IX.

Wild plum branch: my passionate love,
You choose the precarious life
On a storm-swept slope
Not the elegant pose in a vase.

Wild swan: my temperament,
You vow to confront winter, unprotected
Even with a bullet wound
Rather than linger in the cage of Spring.

At any rate, my name and my belief
Are entered for the race,
A single runner, to represent my nation.
I have no right to rest.

In the marathon of life
Speed itself is the goal.

      x.

Toward heaven
Which will judge me in the end
I lift my head.

Wind may sweep me away
But for my heart I reserve the right
To refuse to be counted among the lucky.

      xi.

Raise your lamp, my love,
          and show the way
So that I and my poems may travel far.
Somewhere, beyond this morass, an ideal bell
Rings in the soft night.
Villages, towns, swarm into my arms:
          lights flicker and burn.

Let my poems travel with me,
But the tentacles of highways signal: do not pass!
Still I may walk through the fields
Guided by flowers.

      xii.

I walk to the square through the zigzag streets, back
To the pumpkin shack I guarded, the work in barley fields,
          deep in the desert (of exile).

Life never stops testing me.
On one side, the laurel wreath, the heavy yoke on the other.
But no one knows I am still that stupid girl
              bad at mathematics.
No matter how the great chorus seems to drown me,
You will hear my singular voice.

XIII.

Still I stand
Intrepid, proud, younger than ever!
The bitter storm deep in my heart
But sunshine on my forehead:
My bright, transparent yellow skin
My clean, luxuriant black hair!

Mother China
This daughter requires a new name,
She who comes at your call.

XIV.

So call me your birch sapling,
Your little blue star, Mother.
If the bullet comes
Let it strike me first.

I shall slide to the ground from your shoulder
Smiling, with clear eyes.
No tears. Red flowers in the grass.
Blood flaming on its crest.

XV.

My lover, when that time comes
Don't weep
Though there is no one
       who flings up her pastel skirts
       who comes through the narrow alley
       where cicadas sing like the rain
       to knock at your stained-glass window.
Then there will be no wicked hand
       to make the alarm clock ring
       saying angrily, "On your mark!
       Time to get back to work!"
But don't make a statue of me
On a jade pedestal
And never, to the sound of a lone guitar,
Turn back the calendar, page by page.

XVI.

Your post
Is beneath the banner.
The ideal makes pain bright.
This is the final word
I asked the olive tree
To pass to you.

To find me
Follow the pigeons.
Come in the morning.
I'll be in the hearts
Of women and men.
There you'll find
       your singing flower.

Bits of Reminiscence

A toppled wine-cup,
A stone path floating beneath the moon
Where the grass was trampled:
One azalea branch left lying there...

Eucalyptus trees begin to spin
In a collage of stars
As I sit on the rusted anchor,
The dizzy sky reflected in my eyes.

A book held up to shut out candlelight;
Fingers lightly in your mouth;
In the fragile cup of silence
A dream, half-illumined, half-obscure.

Unexpected Meeting

Suddenly the phoenix trees stop swaying,
The sound of bicycle bells is suspended
And the earth rolls back
To that night ten years ago.

Now the phoenix trees begin to sway again.
Flower petals are ground beneath the wheels
To fling their perfume through the pulsing streets.
The heaven-light of memory blends
With the sight of you.

Perhaps nothing happened. I didn't see you at all:
Hallucination caused by this familiar road.
But even if it did,
I'm not used to shedding tears.

Missing You

A multicolored chart without a boundary;
An equation chalked on the board, with no solution;
A one-stringed lyre that tells the beads of rain;
A pair of useless oars that never cross the water.

Waiting buds in suspended animation;
The setting sun is watching from a distance.
Though in my mind there may be an enormous ocean,
What emerges is the sum: a pair of tears.

Yes, from these vistas, from these depths,
Only this.

"?.!"

It's true, then,
That you will wait for me
Till I've sowed all the seeds in my morning basket,
Till I've chased home the errant bees of afternoon,
Till the oil lamps or torches of evening have been lit
In the windows of the junks, the shacks, the factories.
Till I have perused them all, both bright and dim,
   and communed with minds both bright and dim;
Till the highway becomes a song,
Till love emerges in the sunshine,
Till the silver river in the sky
   washes us apart,
You will still be waiting patiently,
Trying to tie up your trusty raft.

It's true, then,
That you will never change
When my soft hands are chapped
   and my cheeks have faded,
And my reed flute is stained with blood,
And the snow will never melt again?
Even if, whips on my back, I face the abyss,
Even if dark overtakes me before I reach dawn
   and the earth and I sink together
With no time to send you a message dove,
Will your patience, your loyalty
Be my only reward
For the sacrifices I have made?

Now let them fire on me
While I walk calmly toward you
          across open ground;
To you, to you,
As the wind blows through my long hair.
I am a lily in your storm.

To the Oak

If I love you
I won't imitate the morning glory
Borrowing your high branches to display myself;
If I love you
I won't imitate those infatuated birds
Who repeat their monotonous flattery to the foliage,
Nor the fountain
With its solace of cool waters;
I won't even be those background vistas
That serve to make you more majestic.
Not even sunshine,
Not even spring rain,
No, none of these!
I would like to be a kapok tree
Standing beside you as an equal,
Our roots touching underground,
Our leaves touching in the clouds;
And with every gust of wind
We would bow to each other.
But no one else
Understands our language;
You have your branches
Like daggers or swords
While my big red flowers
Are heavy sighs.
Though it seems we are separated forever
We are eternally together.

This is great love,
This is fidelity.
Love —
Not only for your splendid trunk
But also for the earth you stand on.

To _____

I pitied you
Beside the gunwale washed by moonlight
Along the rain-spotted way;
Back hunched, hands tucked in sleeves
As if afraid of the cold,
You carefully concealed your thoughts,
But failed to notice
My slow steps
As I walked beside you.
If you were a flame
I would have wished to be the charcoal
To nourish you
But I didn't dare.

Now I rejoice
In the light at your window at midnight,
At the sight of your back bent over your books.
Now you confide in me,
Saying the spring flood
Is brimming over your banks again.
But you neglect to ask
What is in my thoughts each night
When I walk beneath your windows.
If you are a tree
I am the soil.
I want so much to remind you
But I don't dare.

When You Come past My Window

When you come past my window
Bless me
For my light still burns

As the light was burning
In the night dense with darkness
Like the fisherman's light afloat.
You could say that my little shack
Was a canoe swept away in the storm
But it still hasn't overturned.
My light still burns.

My light still burns.
My silhouette against the curtain
Is the shape of an aging man
With no ardent gestures left,
With a back more bent than it was.
But you know my heart is not old
For my light still burns.

My light still burns
In response to greetings from every quarter,
With a love hot as an ember
My light still burns
Still fueled with an imperious pride
Contemptuous of coercion, open or disguised.
Oh, how long has it burned with this clear flame?
Since you began to understand me.
My light still burns.

My light still burns.
Bless me
When you come past my window.

Returning Home

Too many echoes
In the wind tonight!
Pine-soughs, fire-flies, lights

In the village power-plant,
All recalling a distant dream.
Memory: a rickety wooden bridge barely spanning

The river of time...
Is the moon still laughing down the stone steps?
My heart quivers with apprehension.

> Don't remember! Don't remember!
> The wandering feet grow weary.
> Rest your head on the mountain's shoulder.

Having walked far and far,
Yet you find yourself in the same place.
Pure eyes like rising stars
Shine on me as they did a decade ago
(When I was full of hope):
You had only to reach out your hand
And the golden apple would drop into it.
Once the turmoil of the blood
Fell like a brilliant revelation on the soul.
Now it's no longer true, no longer true:
Youth's image recedes through a forest of obligations,
Headed for oblivion.

Perhaps...

for the loneliness of an author

Perhaps these thoughts of ours
        will never find an audience
Perhaps the mistaken road
        will end in a mistake
Perhaps the lamps we light one at a time
        will be blown out, one at a time
Perhaps the candles of our lives will gutter out
        without lighting a fire to warm us

Perhaps when all the tears have been shed
        the earth will be more fertile
Perhaps when we sing praises to the sun
        the sun will praise us in return
Perhaps these heavy burdens
        will strengthen our philosophy
Perhaps when we weep for those in misery
        we must be silent about miseries of our own

Perhaps
Because of our irresistible sense of mission
We have no choice

Brother, I Am Here

Coolness, like the evening tide,
Covers, one by one, the steps of the twisting trail
And slips into your heart.
You sit on the threshold
Of the dismal shack that squats behind you.
Like birds, leaves drift from the locust trees
And little moon-coins float
On the ripple of waves.

You belonged to the sun, the prairie,
The dikes, the world of amorous jewel-black eyes.
Then you belonged to the hurricane,
To the route, the torches, the arms
Supporting each other.
Soldier, your life was plangent as a bell
Shaking the shadows from the human heart.

Now the wind steals away with alien steps;
It refuses to believe
That you are melancholy still.

But I am with you, Brother,
And the newsstand, the park benches, the apple-cores
Revive in your recollection
With smiles and lamps and delicate rhythms.

Then they glide away on the lines of the writing paper.

Only when the night wind
Shifts the direction of your thoughts,

Only when that trumpet of yours
Is suddenly silent, craving echoes,
I shall be back (with hope alive)
Calmly at your side, to say
Brother, I am here.

Notes

THE APOSTATE

The concluding section of Heine's poem "Frieden," in which he flagellates himself for becoming a convert to Christianity in order to obtain preferment, is omitted from various editions because, in the words of one critic, "it has all the horrible bad taste of a cold and reasoned sneer." The quotation, near the end of my poem, is from "Frieden."

CHINESE IMITATIONS

The epigraph, from the *Wên-Fu* of Lu Chi, is the translation of Achilles Fang.

A MONTH IN SUMMER

The final passage in *A Month in Summer*, in quotes, is from Bashō's prose poem on *The Unreal Dwelling* (*Genjūan no Fu*), as translated by Donald Keene. The earlier episode about Takamaru, the eleven-year-old priest, is taken from Issa's *The Year of My Life*, as translated by Nobuyuki Yuasa.

PRO FEMINA

I've often been asked to identify the women poets in Part III. They are composites to be sure, but the "married spinsters" I had in mind were Elinor Wylie and Sara Teasdale; the chief "barbiturate-drenched Camille" was Genevieve Taggard, another of my teachers at Sarah Lawrence. It was Amy Lowell who was "Swearing, sucking cigars and scorching the bedspread." And it was Sara Teasdale, again, who "draped her gauze over red flannels." The chief Quarterly priestess I had in mind was Mary McCarthy.

SEMELE RECYCLED

Because this poem has been misinterpreted by some critics and anthologists, here is an explanation: I was driving from Charlotte to Chapel Hill, North Carolina, after having minor surgery — a common procedure for women as they grow older. I said to myself that somewhere along the line the myth had had the roles of son and mother reversed: it was Semele, not Dionysus, who had been dismembered and then resurrected. Three years of study with Joseph Campbell at Sarah Lawrence had taught me how to *read through* the versions of myths as we know them to speculate on earlier accounts where the primary role of a female had devolved on a man. (One example: Athena, who in earlier versions sprang from the ground like a tree, in the story we know springs from the brow of Zeus. If one cares to examine Christian mythology in this light, it might be instructive to contemplate the story of Adam and Eve.) The next morning, I woke up and wrote the poem, with fewer changes than in anything I have written.

GERDA

The epigraph to this poem is from an old Swedish children's prayer, circa 1780, from which I've omitted the final couplet: "Lycken kommer, lycken gar. / Du förbliver Fader var." The whole prayer can be translated as:

> God, who loves little children,
> Take care of this small person.
> Wherever I wander in the world
> My fate lies in your hands.
> Fortune comes and goes,
> But You are our Father forever.

So much more comforting, I would say, than "If I should die before I wake..."

AN AMERICAN BEAUTY

The ERA, for those who are very young or who have short memories, stands for Equal Rights Amendment, for which Ms. London did the research and wrote the legislation.

TWELVE O'CLOCK

The inspiration for this poem came from an article in *The San Francisco Chronicle* about the widow of the late physicist, E.O. Lawrence, including a photograph of a very beautiful old lady. Mary Lawrence was trying to have her husband's name removed from the Lawrence-Livermore Lab, where some of the most horrendous experiments with "nuclear devices" are carried out. She felt this was a desecration of her husband's name and philosophy. I involved myself in this effort, to no avail. But Mrs. Lawrence had become a muse of mine. I, who had never taken anything other than a general science course in high school, began to study books on physics. I kept up this reading for about two years — not scientific tomes but popular accounts.

When I began to write the poem there were a number of things I wanted to accomplish. First, the dialectic of the poem: the belief of my mother and Einstein in an essentially orderly universe, versus Heisenberg's and my belief in a universe that is random and disorderly. Second, I wanted the poem to reflect Einstein's concept of simultaneity: everything happens at once! Third, I wanted the poem to be a piece of autobiography: to include everything — pathetically little — that I had ever thought or heard about atomic physics and physicists. Therefore nothing is invented; every quote is from memory. Though my memory is faulty in many respects, I have a clear recollection of what has been said to me.

IN HELL WITH VIRG AND DAN

Canto XVII was originally commissioned by Ecco Press for its excellent volume of translations of Dante by contemporary poets. My contribution was quite properly rejected for irreverence and "not fitting in." I just don't care for Dante's obsessions with shit and revenge. For me, he ranks up there with St. Paul as one of the most destructive literary geniuses of all time. Dante had a lot better sense of humor though.

MARRIAGE SONG

My friend, the distinguished Chinese scholar Jerome Seaton, pointed out to me two translations of a Chou Dynasty poem, one by Arthur Waley and one by Ezra Pound. The original song is anonymous, which suggests that it might well have been composed by a woman. The oddity of these translations is that one wouldn't know that they referred to the same poem — other than a reference to "tossing and turning" — and that the Pound version is three stanzas long while Waley's is five stanzas. Neither translation is an example of the best work of these great men, to put it politely. I was raised on the poems of both of them, and when they are criticized I hasten to remind all of us of the debt we owe them in their introduction of Asian poetry to Western readers and writers. Here is Waley's version:

> "Fair, fair," cry the ospreys
> On the island in the river.
> Lovely is this noble lady,
> Fit bride for our lord.
>
> In patches grows the water mallow;
> To left and right one must seek it.
> Shy was this noble lady;
> Day and night he sought her,
>
> Sought her and could not get her;
> Day and night he grieved.
> Long thoughts, oh, long unhappy thoughts,
> Now on his back, now tossing on to his side.

In patches grows the water mallow;
To left and right one must gather it.
Shy is this noble lady;
With great zithern and little we hearten her.

In patches grows the water mallow;
To left and right one must choose it.
Shy is this noble lady;
With gongs and drums we will gladden her.

And now Pound:

"Hid! Hid!" the fish-hawk saith.
by isle in Ho the fish-hawk saith:
       "Dark and clear,
       Dark and clear,
So shall be the prince's fere."

Clear as the stream her modesty;
As neath dark boughs her secrecy,
       reed against reed
       tall on slight
as the stream moves left and right,
       dark and clear,
       dark and clear.
To seek and not to find
as a dream in his mind,
       think how her robe should be,
       distantly, to toss and turn,
       to toss and turn.

High reed caught in ts'ai grass
       so deep her secrecy;
lute sound in lute sound is caught,
       touching, passing, left and right.
Bang the gong of her delight.

I thought it would be amusing to invent a genre: a poem which would incorporate pseudo-scholarly commentary on the work, from Confucius on down.

Most people will know most of the references, but here is a cast of characters: Part II: "Vasco" is the great Serbian poet, Vasco Popa (1922–1991), who was widely believed to be in line for the Nobel Prize when he died, which we thought untimely, but which saved him from the knowledge of the death of Yugoslavia. "Bogomil" is the poet and playwright Bogomil Gjuzel (B. 1939), of Macedonia, living in Skopje, whose friends have not heard from him recently.

"Then we have AIDS": Although I name real people, I prefer to have them stand for the friends and lovers everyone has lost.

Part III: "the man who reinvented the sonnet": John Berryman; "our great fat nature poet": Theodore Roethke; "two women" are, of course, Sylvia Plath and Anne Sexton. "Anne, Randall, Ted, Elizabeth, Delmore, John, and Cal": Anne Sexton again, Randall Jarrell; Ted Roethke again; "Elizabeth": Miss Bishop; "Delmore": Delmore Schwartz; "John": Berryman again; "Cal": Robert Lowell.

SECOND TIME AROUND

I said of this poem in *Best American Poetry 1998*, "Nearly every male poet of my generation has been married more than once, their first wives often women of considerable attainments.... Certain English poets may come to mind as well. I don't mean to be invidious. I have been married twice myself (the second being a vast improvement on the first....)"

THE ORATION

This poem, as was "Days of 1986" was written when my old friend Edmund Keeley, known as "Mike," wanted to create an anthology of poets who had been influenced by Constantine Cavafy (in Keeley's superb translations). I promptly provided these two poems. "Days of 1986" is written in close imitation of a famous Cavafy poem. "The

Oration" adopts the Cavafy-an device of writing about a great mythic or historic event from the perspective not of a king or hero but of an ordinary person. Thank you, Mike.

THE EROTIC PHILOSOPHERS

I was staying with the Very Reverend James Parks Morton and his wife, Pamela, at the deanery of the Cathedral of St. John the Divine, when I picked up Peter Brown's superb biography of Augustine, which prompted my renewed interest in the Saint. And one day I was in our Paris apartment when the phone rang and the caller asked if I was busy. I replied, "I'm just sitting her drinking kir and reading Kierkegaard." When I find myself talking pentameter — with rhymes — I know I am in the throes of a poem.

St. A. and S.K. were the favorites of my teacher at Sarah Lawrence, Charles Trinkaus. In the forties I worte a poem for him called, "I Dreamed I Was St. Augustine." (Later I thought briefly of suing Bob Dylan for swiping it from my college literary magazine, but gave up the idea.) I also wrote a poem about Kierkegaard, an undoubted masterpiece, which I lost. "The Erotic Philosophers" took one year to write, during which I wrote nothing else. It was published in *The Best American Poetry 1999*, on the day that Mr. Trinkaus died.

TIRADE FOR THE NEXT-TO-LAST ACT

A few teachers have been interested in one of my techniques for translation, both to avoid writing "translatese" and to loosen up: It consists of writing in what I've named "Antique Hipster." As you can see by my version of Dante, I stayed in that mode! But with the Cassian piece, I was able to convert to a straight poem. However, by popular request of at least three people, I include the hipster version that I trust Nina Cassian — that noble poet — will never see:

I'm splitting, so long, no way I'll get in touch.
Like, man, I've got nothing more to prove,
so why hang around for the drowning
of those molecules called, like, hands or eyes or mouth
in the dirt that doesn't hang around or want me.
That dirt knows it's got me, out to the zero rim.
I've spilled my guts, blabbed everything I know
and when I lie, it's 'cause I'm queer for piety:
I see that dumb lie come to life and get a body
like some dumb leaf, or some dumb bunny —
and I dig anything alive.
Also I'm splitting 'cause I'm fuckin' sick
of seeing this century sink into the one before
as if the milk the kid sucks from its mom's tit
flows right back into mom — or worse yet,
like, if the forehead of some heavy thinker
kept sloping back till it got to be, like, extinct,
some kinda throwback, all hairy, like, prehensile.

I figured out some stuff along the way:
not like that shit they shovel you in school,
a long way from that holy Great Books junk,
but the dope that you pick up from cold and heat,
birth, death, and all that jazz —
everything you get a shot at only once
so it's no use for whatever comes down next.
So here I am without any skin,
knowing the names for, like, a thousand things,
without a clue as to what they're really called.
And I don't know when they take off or how they change,
and I'm, like, floundering around
as if I swam in some damn pool of blood.
So I'm splitting; I won't ever get in touch.
You've said a bunch of times that you can't stand me
though I drew you a picture of me, super-careful,
just like you would have drawn it by yourself.
But, man, I'm no good at imitations,
I got no skill, no talent
to try to look like you, or even me.

Now when I give with a smile, nobody gets it:
they think it's, like, a leer.
And when I giggle, people turn their backs
as if I'd crawled out of a porno flick.
And I always bawl at the wrong times: like
it's some bogus patriotic holiday. I make a statue
and they scream some crap about graven images.
When I'm, like, shriveling up — like, terminal,
it's supposed to be some kind of a sick joke,
like my sad body's trying to start an epidemic.
So, man, I'm gone; I'm going, going, gone.

About the Author

Carolyn Kizer was educated at Sarah Lawrence College and was a fellow of the Chinese Government in Comparative Literature at Columbia University. In 1959 she cofounded *Poetry Northwest,* and served as its editor until 1965. She was the first director of the Literature Program at the National Endowment for the Arts, a member of the board of the Academy of American Poets, and has been a poet-in-residence at Columbia, Stanford and Princeton, among others. Kizer received the 1984 Pulitzer Prize in poetry for her collection of poems, *Yin,* and the 1988 Theodore Roethke Award. She currently lives in Sonoma, California.

Index of Titles

Index of First Lines

The Chinese character for poetry is made up of two parts:
"word" and "temple." It also serves as pressmark
for Copper Canyon Press.

Founded in 1972, Copper Canyon Press remains dedicated to publishing poetry
exclusively, from Nobel laureates to new and emerging authors. The Press
thrives with the generous patronage of readers, writers, booksellers,
librarians, teachers, and students — everyone who shares the conviction
that poetry clarifies and deepens social and spiritual awareness.
We invite you to join this community of supporters.

For information and catalogs:

COPPER CANYON PRESS
Post Office Box 271
Port Townsend, Washington 98368
360/385-4925 · poetry@coppercanyonpress.org
www.coppercanyonpress.org

The typeface used in this book is an instance of
Kepler, a Multiple Master font designed by Robert
Slimbach for digital composition in 1996. Kepler is
not a revival of a historic face or style, but is a new
face with elements of Renaissance and Modern type-
styles. The book was designed during the heat of late
June 2000 by Valerie Brewster, Scribe Typography.
Printed archival-quality 55# Book Cream by Trans-
continental Printing.